150

BLACK SEA

Constanta

Varna

BULGARIA

Plovdiv

★ SOFIA

GREECE

BUCHAREST ★

River

Danube

ROMANIA

Cluj

Arad

Szeged

Debrecen

★ BUDAPEST

HUNGARY

Pecs

YUGOSLAVIA

ADRIATIC SEA

D0053718

SOVIET EUROPE

HARPER & ROW, PUBLISHERS

NEW YORK, EVANSTON, SAN FRANCISCO, LONDON

Donald R. Shanor

SOVIET EUROPE

SOVIET EUROPE. Copyright © 1975 by Donald R. Shanor. All rights reserved. Printed in the United States of America. No part of this book may be used or reproduced in any manner whatsoever without written permission except in the case of brief quotations embodied in critical articles and reviews. For information address Harper & Row, Publishers, Inc., 10 East 53rd Street, New York, N.Y. 10022. Published simultaneously in Canada by Fitzhenry & Whiteside Limited, Toronto.

FIRST EDITION

Designed by C. Linda Dingler

Library of Congress Cataloging in Publication Data

Shanor, Donald R
  Soviet Europe

  Includes index.
  1. Europe, Eastern. I. Title.
DR10.S5 1975   947   74–15849
ISBN 0–06–013837–8

75 76 77 78 79 10 9 8 7 6 5 4 3 2 1

To Donnie

CONTENTS

ACKNOWLEDGMENTS

Writing about Soviet Europe or other closed societies presents difficulties when it comes time to deal with acknowledgments. The act of thanking many of those who helped me would really be no thanks at all to them, since it could result in loss of position or liberty.

But outside the area, there are many who can be given credit. My editors at the *Chicago Daily News,* Roy Fisher, Milt Freudenheim, Daryle Feldmeir, and Nick Shuman, provided the ideal conditions for a journalist: go anywhere in your area, write about what interests you. Columbia University and its journalism deans, Elie Abel and Frederick T. C. Yu, provided time to do some of the writing and the excellent libraries and institutes that helped in completing the research.

The analysts and translators at the American embassies in Eastern Europe and in Washington, and those of Radio Free Europe in Munich and New York, were sources of valuable background.

My wife, Constance, and my children, Rebecca, Donald, and Lisa, helped me in my reporting during our trips in Soviet Europe and bore with me during the writing. My secretary, Mrs. Frieda Schwartz, was swift and accurate with the typing.

The *Atlantic Monthly* and the *New Leader,* which published my reports from Eastern Europe, deserve credit for their encouragement.

Needless to say, none of the individuals or institutions that helped in preparation of the book can be held responsible for its imperfections, content, or findings, which remain my sole responsibility.

Demarest, New Jersey
October, 1974

INTRODUCTION

Soviet Europe is a ribbon of territory on the western borders of the Soviet Union, comprising six nations and reaching a thousand miles from the East German island of Rügen, in the Baltic, to the Bulgarian port of Varna on the Black Sea. On a map of the great Soviet land mass in Europe and Asia, the area occupied by East Germany, Poland, Czechoslovakia, Hungary, Romania, and Bulgaria looks inconsequential. At its widest, across Poland and East Germany, it is less than 600 miles. At its narrowest, between Austria and the territory the Soviet Union annexed from Czechoslovakia in 1945, it is only about 250 miles. But the six nations have an importance to the Soviet Union and the West far out of proportion to their modest impression on the map.

They form a buffer system between East and West that makes the Iron Curtain a more flexible dividing line. They are part of an alliance, political and ideological. They are important economically, both as producers and as markets. They have contributed ideas, from the astronomy of Copernicus and the theology of Hus to the discovery of radium in the last century and the soft contact lens in the last decade. Their most important contribution, however, is that they hold some of the keys to liberalization in the Soviet Union itself. By pushing for more freedom to write and speak out, a loosening of Party controls in the economy and the political process, and the right to travel, Soviet Europe's liberals think they can encourage similar trends in the Soviet Union, which in turn will reverberate to their advantage. Such an undertaking is difficult, since Russia does not want its allies to enjoy freedoms it does not permit at home. But Soviet Europe's dissidents hope their nations can serve as a testing ground for some cautious experimentation; if Warsaw's official daily *Trybuna Ludu* can be published without prior censorship, as it has since 1973, perhaps Moscow's *Pravda* can also be.

Soviet Europe's borders are defined by the limits of direct Soviet influence in the area. The U.S.S.R. is a great power and exerts influence on many of its neighbors, including Finland and Turkey, which are definitely not a part of Soviet Europe, as well as Yugoslavia and Albania, which, although Communist, do not belong in it either. The criterion is not fidelity to Lenin; both these nations contend they are purer in this respect than Russia. It is whether a nation is able to exercise its sovereignty independently of Soviet wishes. Albania and Yugoslavia can. The six nations in this book cannot.

More than 100 million people, who speak seven major languages, live in the area. They have made many contributions to the world's music, literature, art and science. Bach, Bartok, Liszt, Dvorak, Mahler, Smetana, Chopin, Enesco—all came from what is now Soviet Europe, as did Mickiewicz and Kafka, Bertolt Brecht, Conrad, and Ionesco, Peter Lorre, Bela Lugosi, and Hedy Lamarr. The contribution of the area to science is best illustrated by the fact that Hungary, with 10 million people, has produced six Nobel prize winners.

Except for periodic peaks of interest when revolution threatens, Soviet Europe's affairs go unnoticed in the West. The long preoccupation with Indochina is one reason; yet the six nations have two and one-half times the population of both Vietnams and twenty-two times the gross national product. In the old language of the cold war, these facts mean that Soviet Europe is a prize worth far more than Vietnam. Now both East and West are learning that prizes cannot be won outright by either side, but that does not diminish the importance of the six nations in international affairs. Their potential as a two-way bridge between East and West is greater than ever since bridge-building efforts have resumed between Washington and Moscow.

In this process of détente, Soviet Europe's links to both the United States and the Soviet Union are an important resource. About 25 million Americans have ethnic ties to the six countries, and despite a generation of hostile propaganda, Eastern Europeans maintain a great reservoir of good feeling for the United States and its people. The ties to the Soviet Union are often expressed in different sentiments, but they are there nevertheless.

The history of Eastern Europe is a history of domination from outside, and the people who live there have learned to expect little else. But they have not forgotten how to hope and dream.

HISTORY AND LEGEND

Eastern European history is full of the tales of its heroes and nation builders: Arpad, who led the Hungarians on the last stage of migration from Asia to the Danube basin; Samo, who united the Slavic tribes, fought back the Germans and Mongols, and extended Czech influence to the gates of Vienna; the Jagiellonian dynasty of Poland, which made its nation a great power in the fourteenth century. Some of the figures are historical; some come from the mists of legend and tradition. But all symbolize the yearning East Europeans have for a period of national greatness, perhaps in literature and the arts, perhaps territorial, but certainly a period in which their own affairs would be decided by their own people and leaders rather than external forces.

But just as the Greater Moravian Empire, as large and important as Italy in the ninth century; and the ancient empire of the Bulgarians, which extended into what is now Romania, Hungary, Yugoslavia, Greece, and Russia; and the Polish state that bordered both the Baltic and the Black seas, are all memories from the past, so is the time that the peoples of Eastern Europe had the right to decide their own affairs.

At best, they were able to snatch a few years or decades in between the crumbling of one empire and the establishment of another. East Germany is the exception; its history belongs to the rulers of empire rather than the ruled. But Slovakia spent a thousand years under the Hungarians (and they, in turn, nearly four hundred under the Austrians and two hundred under the Turks). Before World War I, the Slovak language, as a contemporary account put it, was "not merely banished from public life, but was not even tolerated in the post office, the railway station, or the cemetery."

All six peoples tried many times to change conditions by reform or revolution. Their histories are filled with tales of unsuccessful peasant revolts, which usually made things worse for the peasants and strengthened the rulers. There is a tendency in contemporary historical writing to make more of these revolts than they apparently deserved, with the aim being to show a continuum from early attempts at freedom to the present-day Communist bureaucracy.

But by the nineteenth century, the century of nationalism, there were real movements in each of the countries. The Bulgarian poet-guerrillas George Rakovski and Hristo Botev, who sought "absolute freedom" from the Turks for the entire Balkan peninsula, were defeated, but the more organized efforts of 1848 were harder to stop. Poets like Lajos Kossuth lost battles but won later concessions for Hungary. The German revolutionaries, Richard Wagner among them, gained parliamentary and social reform.

Poland, the most active, had to wait until World War I for success. Poland's 1848 rising failed, but it did train a cadre of revolutionary soldiers, some of them intellectuals, some generals, who served other nations. The Polish writer Adam Mickiewicz formed a Polish Legion to help the Italians fight the Austrians, then became editor of *La Tribune des Peuples,* published in Paris, with an editorial board made up of many nations, a sort of intellectual clearing house for revolution. The most famous traveling revolutionary was a solid bourgeois general, Jozef Bem, who helped organize revolutionary Vienna against the Austrian Kaiser's troops, and then moved on to Hungary to take part in the last great military operation of '48. Bem led the dissident forces in Transylvania and recaptured the province. He is commemorated today with a square and a statue in Budapest, and it is no accident that one of the key demonstrations that started the Hungarian revolution of 1956 was staged there. The other was at the statue of Hungary's own Kossuth.

The revolutions were defeated by the superior strength of the dominant nations, but they were also defeated by internal rivalries. When Hungarian patriots rallied to fight against Austria, their natural allies, the Czechs, sided with the Kaiser in the hope of better conditions in the Empire. And the Slovenes, Croats, and Slovaks ruled by the Hungarians knew that if Hungarian national aspirations succeeded, there would be no independence for them. Old hates and resentments die hard in Eastern Europe. Many of these quarrels continue to be a political factor today. The Soviet ambassadors and Party emissaries are no less adroit at exploiting them than were the Austrian bans and Turkish beys.

Most of the struggles for independence or democratic rule had to be won for Eastern Europe from the outside: by the great powers, as an incidental benefit to wars fought for other reasons. And the changing governments and shifting coalitions of the large nations meant that freedom was to be of short duration.

Germany's democracy was confined to the fifteen years of Weimar. Before that was the Kaiser; after that came Hitler, Ulbricht, and Honecker. Czechoslovakia had more time, from 1918 until the German invasions of 1938 and 1939. Romania and Bulgaria enjoyed the longest period of self-rule. The two principalities of Romania began to ease themselves out from under the Turkish and Russian empires in the 1850s, and became a modern nation in 1859, with the election of one ruler, Alexander Cuza, by both Moldavia and Wallachia. Bulgaria was liberated by the Russians, in the real sense, in 1878. It would be wrong to describe life in the two Balkan countries as idyllic, but until the final period of dictatorship in the thirties, there was a varying measure of internal freedom and external independence. The same was true of Poland, reassembled at Versailles, with a variety of democratic governments until the colonels took over in 1934. Hungary had enjoyed a measure of self-determination after the *Ausgleich* with Austria in 1867 but, when the dual monarchy crumbled in 1918, moved speedily from liberal democracy to Soviet Republic to military-feudal dictatorship.

Thus it is important in any discussion of democracy in Eastern Europe to keep in mind that it is an area where freedom, individual and national, has always had strong roots but has rarely been permitted to flourish.

On a sliding scale, for honest elections, fair representation, press freedom, rights of minorities, constitutional and legal guarantees, and cultural freedom, Weimar Germany must head the list, followed by Czecho-slovakia, where the main flaw in an otherwise fairly run country was the minority question, for both the Slovaks and the Germans, followed by Bulgaria, where under a monarchy there was a strong cooperative move-ment and real land reform, the heart of democracy in an agrarian so-ciety. After that, in no particular order, come Poland, Hungary, and Romania, where despite fine-sounding constitutions, one or more of the following kept the majority from ever knowing what democracy was: feudal land conditions, frequent suspensions of the constitution and rule by decree, suppression of political parties and manipulation of voting results, pursuit of irredentist claims to the detriment of real national needs.

The greatest test of the governments' responsiveness to the needs of the people, however, was in the economic sphere, and all six, as their succes-sors, the Communists, never tire of pointing out, failed. Mass unemploy-ment, famine on the land, emigration, all these specters from the twenties and thirties have an ever fresh role today in the propaganda of the area, with the aim of convincing the East European that however gray and shortage-plagued his or her life is at present, things were much worse in the recent past.

Much of the economic misery was beyond the capacity of even the wisest and most enlightened of governments to control: the inflation that followed World War I, the world depression, the fall in grain prices caused by the introduction of overseas wheat. But some of the economic problems could have been solved, particularly through land reform and a sensible policy of industrialization. Instead, the Polish and Hungarian nobles con-tinued to live off their county-sized estates, and the Romanian elite to import luxuries instead of machines. The tragedy of Eastern Europe is that everyone paid—the 100 million as well as the handful of ruling families.

CONFLICT AND UNITY

The cities, towns, and landscape of the six nations of Soviet Europe have provided rich and dramatic background for the events acted out there, for the poets who sacrificed their lives for patriotic causes, for the kings and khans who led their people on migrations of thousands of miles. Each city has its legend, each castle its tales of blood and im-prisonment, each province or county its monuments to battles and bravery in the recent or remote past.

The setting fits the deeds. There are the cliffs of the Danube at the Iron Gate, where Romania and Yugoslavia built a massive power project on the site of old Turkish camps; the brilliant blue of the Black Sea, where Romans, Greeks, Turks, and Slavs exchanged periods of supremacy over the centuries; Prague's hilltop castle, scene of the defenestration of the Hapsburg governors that started the Thirty Years' War; the magnificent Renaissance pillars of Krakow, thick as a house; the old oak of the Auerbachkeller in Leipzig, where Dr. Faustus drank; the marble walls and the fussy carving of the Hungaria Café in Budapest, where Hungary's literati gathered in the twenties.

But the dominant impression of Soviet Europe is one of contrasts—riches and poverty, rural and urban, developed and primitive, all within the space of a few miles or even a few feet. Kerchiefed peasant women graze cows at the entrance to Bucharest's airport, a prestressed concrete complex that handles jets of many nations. To get to a fashion show in Warsaw, where, thanks to the European television hookups, the Paris styles appear within days, one passes horsecarts on the avenue to Wilanow Castle on the city's edge.

Along with these physical contrasts go many political ones. The stationing of Soviet troops in Hungary, Poland, East Germany, and Czechoslovakia amid constant proclamations of fraternal friendship is one of the most obvious. The gap between the reality of today and the promises for tomorrow is another, particularly since Eastern Europeans have been watching the future recede for thirty years. An official vocabulary full of words and phrases about freedom, democracy, and worker control, where hardly any is practiced, is one more contradiction.

Finally there comes an issue that goes to the heart of the political process at a time when more and more nations, in Europe and Africa, Asia and Latin America, are finding ways to mesh economies and cooperate politically. This is the contrast between the unity proclaimed for Soviet Europe and the division practiced. The process can be observed when four of the Bloc's armies join the Soviet in invading the territory of a fifth, or when a Party leader in one capital appeals to his national minority in a neighboring country over the heads of the leaders in the neighboring capital. These actions are not the ideas of the individual regimes, of course. The Soviet Union, consistent advocate of Bloc unity, is, in reality, the greatest exponent of division. Nowhere is this more apparent than in the abortive plans of the six nations, from time to time, to form some kind of federation.

Russian ships sail the Danube with those of the seven other nations on the 1,770-mile course of the river: West Germany, Austria, Czechoslovakia, Hungary, Yugoslavia, Romania, and Bulgaria. Since World War I, a Danube Commission of these nations has tried to keep the river open to international traffic. The eight members have managed to cooperate most of the time, despite political differences, because all recognize the mutual benefits of the arrangement.

If it is possible to regulate shipping, why not politics? The idea of a Danubian confederation is as old as the empires along the river, but the flaw in its fulfillment historically has been the domination of one of the powers and the coercion applied to keep the others in. The Soviet Union contends that the necessary political union has already been achieved with the creation of the Socialist Commonwealth, but this does nothing to integrate Germany and Austria, and it ignores other differences, past and present, ideological and institutional.

When Tito and Bulgaria's Georgi Dimitrov tried to explore federation on their own in 1947, the Kremlin's disapproval was immediate, and was one of the main reasons for the break with Yugoslavia. Any other recent cooperation plans, including the revival of the Little Entente suggested by Czechoslovakia, Romania, and Yugoslavia in 1968, when such things were possible, have also been rejected by the Soviet Union, which wants all lines of authority to lead back to Moscow, not to cross between the capitals of the area.

There is a similar community of economic and political interests at the other end of the Bloc, the iron triangle or northern tier formed by East Germany, Poland, and Czechoslovakia, and the latter's dual position as a Danubian and a northern state could give it a key role in any future reorganization of the Bloc. Such a possibility was being actively discussed in 1968, when it appeared that Czechoslovakia was going to be the capital of dissent in the Bloc, the place which countries seeking to widen their independence could look to; now, as with so many other of those hopeful plans, it is heard of no more.

It may be said that in the current era of big-power politics, it is impossible for little nations to organize themselves in such a way as to benefit mutually and escape the domination of their big neighbors. But it was always so in Eastern Europe; no single small nation was ever able to prevail against the wishes of the large, whether it was Austria or Prussia, Russia or Turkey, and some of the few instances of success were the temporary alliances of the small against the large. Bulgaria joined successfully with Serbia, Greece, and Montenegro to defeat the Turkish empire in the first Balkan war, but the alliance fell apart in the next two years and led to the allies fighting among themselves in the second Balkan war. Yet such regional alliances must always be attempted.

THE RUSSIAN PROBLEM

From the inability to buy meat in the shops to the inability to form Balkan or other kinds of federations, the problem, East Europeans say, is the Russians. It is a problem that overshadows all others in their lives. That the problem is pervasive is unquestioned, but it is often used as an excuse, either to cover up the failures of the local Communist government or to conceal one's own individual failings. It is understandable if a Czech factory worker admits to drinking on the job because "the machines we make are only going to the Russians anyway," or if Romanian officials divert criticism of their lack of preparedness for disastrous floods by blaming the Soviet Union for not coming to their aid, but it is not altogether realistic.

The Russian problem, simply stated, is that the nations of Soviet Europe must consider the wishes of the Soviet Union before they make decisions about their economies, their internal politics, their cultural life, and their foreign relations.

Despite all the rhetoric in the constitutions and treaties of friendship that are supposed to govern relations in the Bloc, none of the nations has any sort of guarantee of independence, sovereignty, or self-determination. This is not to say that they are completely denied these rights. But every action of government, Party, or individual citizen in these nations must eventually be examined in regard to the universal touchstone: What will the Russians say, and how will they react? Those of us who thought the universal rule no longer applied learned a bitter lesson in Czechoslovakia in 1968. The fact that Romania seems to be flaunting the rule from time to time does not bear up under closer scrutiny. Every action there, even the individual decisions of student protesters, is taken with a figurative look over the shoulder, and in such circumstances, no matter how much independence and sovereignty is proclaimed, it can never be genuine. Throughout Soviet Europe, the era of direct "advice" from the Russian colonel or official is gone for the most part, but such advisers have been replaced just as effectively by the local leader who knows, or believes that he knows, what is acceptable up at the Soviet Embassy and what is not. It would be wrong to maintain that the limits of the acceptable have not been stretched, but equally wrong to imagine that they do not exist.

The effort of monitoring and directing decisions throughout Soviet Europe is a considerable one for Moscow. But the gains outweigh the trouble. The most important, from the Soviet view, is the creation of the buffer zone between the U.S.S.R. and the West.

With it, a set of captive allies has also been created, a group of nations ready to give automatic support to Soviet policy. Thus national leaders and intellectuals who might be expected to sympathize with Israel, a small country threatened, like theirs, by larger neighbors, join instead in a chorus of praise for the Arabs. Writers smother their own feelings of outrage against the mistakes and excesses of their regimes and line up to denounce the Soviet dissidents for giving vent to theirs. Those few exceptions are usually silenced.

The final advantage of the alliance to the Russians is economic. Despite the amount of aid and the number of experts Moscow has furnished the Bloc since 1945, the flow of economic benefits has been much fatter in the other direction, as the periodic exposés, written by exiles or experts soon to become exiles, show.

Soviet officials, of course, deny that they are exploiting anyone and patiently explain to Westerners that the six nations are eager, voluntary allies. The reason, they say, is that Soviet policies and goals are those shared by all of progressive mankind.

Soviet Europe, in this view, benefits from its often disadvantageous economic agreements with Moscow, just as it benefits from the foreign policy guidelines it must follow. This is so because all are serving the common goal of the building of socialism. If the Soviet Union seems to be the real beneficiary, then that is only because it was the first, the pioneer, and that it remains the motherland of socialism.

This historical factor looms large in official Soviet assessments of relations with Eastern Europe. The most valuable contribution from Moscow to the Bloc, therefore, is Marxism-Leninism, the invisible export that enables the six nations to chart their courses on the lines of scientific socialism. Thus they share, with very few of the nations of the world, the key to the future.

Most of the 100 million citizens of Soviet Europe, it is safe to say, dispute the value of this export. Communism has not won them over. Russia has been claiming creation of the new socialist man for half a century. Such men or women are hard to find in Soviet Europe. The general rule is acceptance of Leninism and Brezhnev as necessary annoyances, institutions perhaps suited to other people, not them—much as they once accepted Mohammedanism and the sultan. As long as they have to have Communism, they will work to modify it, soften the hard edges, find ways around it. And they will also dream of the hundred other systems they would like to see in its place. A few think a more radical communism ought to come. A few long for the monarchies. The majority want to be left alone, to work out a solution to the problems of East Germany or Poland in the way that the citizens of Belgium or Denmark are left alone to work out their problems.

This majority constitutes Soviet Europe's loyal opposition, although many of its members, including some in this book, would deny being oppositionists in any way. The loyalty of the majority is assured by the interlocking system of repression and reward. But the same closed system also makes inevitable some kind of opposition. If there are no elections, no guarantee of foreign or domestic policies in the national interest, no changes in leadership aside from shuffles decreed from the top, then opposition from below is inevitable. Its individual manifestations are weak compared to the strength of the regimes of Soviet Europe, but collectively it is a force of great magnitude.

The chapters that follow will trace the course of loyalty and of opposition in the nations of Soviet Europe.

II

POLAND

Karol Wojtyla

The best way to see Eastern Europe is by train, the romantic-sounding long-distance ones like the Balt-Orient Express, the Moscow Express, the Danubia and Hungaria and Vindobona and Chopin, and the little locals. The journey from Poland to Bulgaria, through the six capitals, takes three good days of travel, with overnight stops, although it is possible to do it a little faster or a great deal slower.

The journey begins on the Baltic. The train leaves Gdansk, the former Danzig, at 5:46 in the morning. Gdansk's long blocks of high ornate burgher houses are quiet, but the railway station is already busy with the start of the morning rush hour. East Europe gets up early, goes to work early, and goes home—or to a second job—early in the afternoon. In Poland in particular, the 3 P.M. luncheon date is a favorite with officials, because they are through for the day by then, having started at seven, and can stretch out the luncheon into early evening with iced vodka and good conversation.

In Gdansk, at a quarter to six, there is also drinking in progress. In the second-class or standup restaurant, dozens of workers are having their early morning mugs of beer. A few of the younger ones seem to have been up all night, but most are on their way back to work. In the ticket office, a serious young woman in a black satin smock calculates prices on an abacus and issues tickets for Warsaw. The platform is crowded with bureaucrats with briefcases, soldiers, students, peasant women with baskets, and when the dark green train comes in from Gdynia, the seats and then the aisles soon fill up. A five-hour trip through the sandy, flat Baltic countryside is uneventful, but for the ghostly borders that the train crosses.

Tczew, the first stop, was the last town in the Free Territory of Danzig, which the Allies set up after World War I. To the west was the Polish corridor, Poland's strip of land piercing German territory to get to the Baltic. The next town is Malbork, where the invisible border defines the "German territories under temporary Polish administration" pending a peace treaty ending World War II. This area of the Mazovian lake country used to be East Prussia. There was never any trace of a border marker; to the Poles, there was nothing temporary about its acquisition. Since the Polish—West German nonaggression treaty of 1972, the territory has become a little more securely Polish, although some Poles are not really convinced of this fact yet. At Dzialdowo, the last invisible line has been crossed, from temporary Poland to permanent, and the last few miles of the run to Warsaw follow the Vistula, the river that has been winding between Warsaw and Gdansk with less economy of design than the rail line.

Warsaw looks like other European cities: the upended boxes of new apartments strung out into the suburbs, and then, downtown, the old part, the monuments, parks, and palaces. And yet, there is a curious sense of the raw, the unfinished, the new, not only about the new housing developments, where trees have not had time to grow, but in the old town square, the gracefully bending nineteenth-century shopping street, called the Nowy Swiat or New World, and the elegant avenues of eighteenth-century nobles' palaces and gardens. The patina of age is somehow missing.

Warsaw gives this impression because it is true. The city, whether baroque or modern, is new. It dates from 1945. The Warsaw Ghetto uprising of 1943 and the Warsaw uprising of 1944 cost the city half its buildings. After the second defeat, the German occupation authorities ordered the rest of the town wiped out. For three months at the end of 1944, German destruction commandos went systematically through the city, blowing up houses, monuments, office buildings, even water and gas mains, felling trees in parks, and tearing up streetcar tracks and utility poles with tanks. The libraries and national archives were burned and the buildings blown up. When the Germans retreated, the city was dead: 90 percent of its offices and factories, 72 percent of its housing, all of its bridges, and 70 percent of its schools were destroyed.

The destruction was not only a reaction to the uprising; it was part of the German plan to wipe out the city as a tangible part of Polish history and culture, to eradicate all the monuments of the Polish untermenschen. Plans were in existence for a new, German Warsaw, with satellite housing areas for the Polish forced laborers.

For this reason, Warsovians faced the ruins with the determination to rebuild the historic part of the city exactly as it had been. Housing of any kind was needed, and the country was poor, but it became a matter of national pride to restore what the Germans had tried to annihilate.

Old plans were dug out. A series of eighteenth-century paintings by the Venetian artist Canaletto showed arrangements of streets and buildings of that day. There were also sketches of an architecture class assigned before the war to do all the historic buildings of the city. The sketches were hidden by the professors during the occupation. Rebuilding has already taken a generation and will take another to complete, not only in Warsaw but in

Poland's other cities, where the job of repairing damage of war and age takes priority over many projects that might seem more practical. But to Poles, there is nothing more practical than their links with the past.

Visiting hours are from eleven to one in the Krakow palace of Karol Cardinal Wojtyla. The first small groups begin to gather after ten in the upstairs foyer, where the black and white marble squares of the floor are worn by centuries of such traffic. Those summoned inside first wipe their feet carefully and unnecessarily on the thick floormat, then follow carpet runners into the cardinal's parqueted reception rooms, past gold-framed portraits, dark oak Renaissance chairs, and the deep blue, olive, and peach-colored walls. The portraits, many with dates before 1492, the year that defines remote history for an American, are of the cardinal's predecessors, the bishops and archbishops of Krakow, and the primates of Poland, who ruled the nation between the reigns of the Polish kings.

Priest secretaries open the tall white doors and move among the groups of visitors with the swift, silent steps of those whose sense of importance is derived from serving the powerful. There is handshaking and deep bowing as the priests, nuns, and lay visitors state their business. They are grave and seem impressed by the seriousness of the problems that have brought them this far. But from one of the side reception rooms comes laughter and loud talk. A dozen young priests, smoking, digging through briefcases, and arranging themselves around a table covered by green baize, are there to have a meeting with the cardinal.

The faces of the older visitors look like the portraits of the churchmen on the walls. Some of them add to the illusion through their dress or pose. A nun reads a prayerbook in a seat in front of a high, recessed window, and the light streams from behind on her square starched cap. In another corner, a monk in brown robe and hood writes in a note-book on an antique table. The effect is the opposite with the young priests. But for the cassocks showing beneath their nylon raincoats, they could be junior engineers from the Lenin Steelworks discussing the Five-Year Plan, or faculty assistants at the Jagiellonian University going over theses.

The talk stops and both groups rise when the cardinal enters. Wojtyla wears a plain black cassock, with a simple gold cross on his breast and another cross, also of gold but bent in the form of a ring, on his finger. He is bareheaded and wears neither jewels nor scarlet. It is a working day, and there is nothing in his dress to distinguish Wojtyla from the other priests in the room. But there is a marked difference between Wojtyla's stride and the busy little steps of his subordinates. He comes into the room with the purposeful walk of a man with business to attend to.

This business atmosphere is dominant in the cardinal's palace, from the little offices off the main gate downstairs where Krakow families come for help on personal, school, and housing problems to the regular meetings with the pastors and administrators of the archdiocese, which covers a mixed agricultural-industrial region of southern Poland.

The offices are there to advise parishioners, but in a real sense they are also the basic units of the Church's fight for influence in the nation. Cardinal Wojtyla is fond of quoting Christ's words: "Render therefore unto Caesar the things which be Caesar's, and unto God the things which be God's." But this division of government and church authority needs to be defined anew every day and in every individual case, with each side seeking to enlarge its area.

The Church fights for influence at every level, from village parish to national, and uses the services of everyone, from teaching nuns to Stefan Cardinal Wyszynski, the primate of Poland. The Krakow establishment seems low key indeed when compared to Wyszynski's Warsaw palace. The primate, Wojtyla's superior in the Church hierarchy, and nineteen years his senior, greets visitors in Hollywood splendor, in a setting of overbright chandeliers, thick carpeting, and shiny veneered furniture. The difference is in part personal; Wojtyla is unassuming to a degree unusual in such a high office, and Wyszynski is probably more assertive than other men might be in his place. But mostly the difference is the result of the different roles of the two cardinals. As primate, Wyszynski represents the Roman Catholic Church, not only to its members, who make up 80 to 95 percent of Poland's population of 33 million (depending on government or Church estimate), but to the regime. If his palace overemphasizes the elements of glitter and pomp, it is only as a counterweight to the conspicuous symbols of the Party in Warsaw: the skyscraper Palace of Science and Culture, with its Stalin-era masonry frills, and the massive stone Central Committee headquarters on a downtown intersection.

Wyszynski may find his stage setting a useful accessory, but he is a person impressive anywhere, whether talking to parishioners on the streets of the Old Town between his residence and cathedral or preaching in the austere brick Gothic church. He speaks and acts with confidence, in public and private, rarely avoiding religious or political issues, whether they concern his own old-fashioned views on Church reform or forthright criticism of the nation's leaders. Both Wyszynski and Wojtyla travel freely around the country and shuttle frequently to Rome. Visitors to their palaces in Warsaw and Krakow, in fact, find it hard to remember that the Church is an institution alternately repressed and tolerated by the regime. The feeling is one of independence, self-assurance, and confidence in the future.

These are not Christians operating out of catacombs, although that is the impression that the Church, Catholic or Protestant, sometimes gives in other countries of Eastern Europe, with the overcautious statements of its officials and its shabby offices and neglected churches. The postwar campaigns against the Church have been eminently successful in all the countries of the Soviet Bloc, with the notable exception of Poland. The Soviet Union itself has led the way in the campaigns to bring the Church to heel.

In the U.S.S.R., of the estimated 25,000 Orthodox churches in existence at the end of the war, only about 8,000 remain. Where once 30,000 to 35,000 Orthodox priests served, there are now about 15,000. Poland's church statistics show a curve in the other direction: 7,200 churches before the war, 13,200 now; 11,200 priests then, 18,000 now. There are many reasons for the differences. Poland has gained 10 million Catholics and thousands of empty German churches through postwar births and boundary changes; Poland's Church thrives under persecution; Poland confuses and identifies nationalism with Catholicism; Poland has had a Communist regime too much troubled with periodic worker uprisings, economic problems, and anti-Soviet feeling to dare to launch an anti-Church campaign on the Russian model.

Thus in Poland the Church is a going concern. The visiting period in Wojtyla's palace, in fact, resembles very much the business being conducted by the regime in Krakow's city hall down the block, and the priests are often as effective as the bureaucrats in getting things done for people. This competition for political power has been going on for more than a quarter of a century. The men in the Warsaw Central Committee building have strong allies. The Soviet Union considers Poland the key to Central Europe and has kept its troops in the country since they arrived in 1944 to help drive the Germans out. Even if there were no troops, Russian or Polish, and no security apparatus to support the regime, the Church would not be interested in a contest for direct rule. The days of the primate as interrex are gone, not only in Poland but everywhere else in the world, and no one in any responsible position in the Church would want it otherwise.

But this does not mean the Church seeks no political role. It is only a matter of definition. Let the Communists govern, the Church says, even though it is minority rule forced on the nation by its geographical position. But give us the right to speak for the majority, the people we represent, in the formation of government policy and the carrying out of decisions. It claims this right on two grounds: first, it fought with the rest of the nation during the long years of partition and occupation in the struggle to regain freedom and national identity. Second, it maintains that individual freedom is the state that God desires for man. This is where religion enters politics, and this is why the state has trouble fixing the limits of Church participation in public life. Wyszynski, Wojtyla, and the other bishops keep the issue alive. "Freedom is God's basic gift to man," the bishops told the regime after the 1968 student riots. In 1970 they responded to the workers' uprising on the Baltic with a more detailed demand for guaranteed rights.

The regime's reply has been that political freedom is impossible without economic freedom, and that before the Communist takeover the Church supported a semifeudal system that kept the majority of the nation so poor that political rights were meaningless. Now the Church's task should be the active support of the building of socialism—help, not passive acceptance, for government programs.

Catholicism's demand to speak for the majority is one a Communist regime cannot even acknowledge if it is to maintain the credibility of its own claim to represent the nation. But there are practical reasons for not rejecting the demand out of hand. The main one is that Poland's 2.3 million Communist Party members cannot make all the steel, organize all the harvests, and write all the books that the nation needs. In every Communist country, the Party members are a disciplined minority who direct the work of the majority and get its cooperation to a greater or lesser extent. But only in Poland is the majority as well organized as the minority, in the Roman Catholic Church.

This majority cannot hope to rule as long as the power relationships across Poland's borders stay as they are. But the majority can and does make its weight felt. It would be a great oversimplification to say that the Catholic Church has won Poles the right to read *Ulysses,* or keep 87 percent of their farms private, or have the first uncensored party newspaper in Eastern Europe. But it would be true to say that without the Church, without the political possibilities that the common religious identification of the majority offers, it is very unlikely that Poland would enjoy these and other freedoms.

The freedoms are limited, as one parish priest put it, because God is far away and the Russians are close. The saying is common in Eastern Europe, and is used to explain much. In Poland, it means that the state censors feel safe enough in clearing James Joyce for translation after fifty years, but not in permitting Jerzy Andrzejewski, author of *Ashes and Diamonds,* to be published after his condemnation of the invasion of Czechoslovakia. It means that the five independent parliamentary deputies of the liberal Catholic Znak group can criticize government policy but would always be outvoted in the Sejm, 485 to 5. The lifting of formal censorship for the Party paper *Trybuna Ludu* and weekly *Polityka* in 1973 was a step in the right direction, but so slight a one that many Poles did not know it had happened. In any case, the editors became their own censors.

But no one can censor the cardinals, and as a result, the Church takes on what in normal political circumstances would be the job of a critical but basically loyal opposition. This role gets the most attention when Wyszynski stands up in his cathedral and calls the regime to account, as he did in his Christmas sermon in 1970, eleven days after the rioting that killed forty-five persons: "We are capable of, and we can afford, true democracy in Poland, because it has been in the traditions of the Polish people since the times of the kings." Wojtyla's sermons are not political; both cardinals feel that there can be only one national spokesman, the primate. But there are many other elements in the Church's political activity.

Like any other well-run movement, it is based on careful grass-roots work. It takes advantage of the Church's historical ties with the nation. And it perpetuates itself through education.

Warsaw is the main place of political confrontation, but Krakow has an equally important contribution to make. It is both the intellectual center of Polish Catholicism and the link between the past and present that plays such a large part in the Polish citizen's attitude toward Church and regime. And Krakow, in common with every other diocese in Poland, is involved in the daily work with the people, in church and out of it, on religious problems and personal ones.

The group of young priests who had come to confer with Cardinal Wojtyla were youth chaplains. Their work is with the young steelworkers and university youth they resemble. In makeshift meeting rooms in the cellars of churches or in chapels, they lead discussion groups on the problems of modern society. "They deal with religious problems," a student who has attended many meetings said, "but not in the narrow meaning. They consider the whole picture, and talk about what we are talking about in the dormitories, or out at Nowa Huta in the workers' canteens." Attendance is often irregular; but the chaplains find their groups growing steadily. There are frequent projects that bring in new members, at least temporarily, such as modern morality plays and rock masses in Krakow's ancient churches. The authorities keep an eye on the groups but do not crack down. They accept their activity as part of the competition.

The groups are Church groups, but many, perhaps most, of their members go to church only to go to the meetings. This is the supreme advantage that both the Church and the individual dissenter enjoy in Poland. The Church can gather together the strands of criticism, resistance, and opposition that are present in every Communist country, and yet can remain officially sanctioned by the regime. No one can tell whether a student in Krakow goes to a discussion group to find his or her personal answers to religion or to talk about the shortcomings of Communist rule. No one knows whether families, including those of Party members, send their children to after-school religious instruction to learn about God or about their country.

Such a role is a difficult one for the Church to play. It is important not to go too far, but equally important to be firm. It requires the greatest understanding of the conditions of power in the nation, as well as of the needs and hopes of the workers and the intellectuals. In the division of labor in Poland, the first part is left to Wyszynski, the primate-politician; the second to Wojtyla. He is uniquely qualified for it: as a factory worker during the German occupation, as a teacher and theologian, and as a thinker and writer.

The window of Cardinal Wojtyla's office looks across the tile roofs of Renaissance Krakow to the spires of Wawel Cathedral, on the castle hill where the first Polish kings built their fortifications, and where they ruled until the capital moved to Warsaw late in the sixteenth century, for better administration of their enlarged dominions. (Krakovians still consider Warsaw the "new capital.") The Jagiellonian dynasty, uniting Poland and Lithuania by marriage, had stretched Poland's borders to within 100 miles of Moscow. It also brought Italian architects and artisans to Krakow, and their sixteenth-century work mixed in pleasantly with the earlier Gothic to give the city the shape and feeling it retains today. A thousand years of history in Poland means a thousand years of Christianity. The rulers were Catholic and the Catholics the rulers, except for the periods of partition and occupation, and the abrupt change of the last generation to Communist control. But in the scale of Polish history, these periods are not long.

The cardinal likes to point out the architectural features of his cathedral, linking its various periods with the reigns of the kings. In his early fifties, he has the gray hair that ought to go with his rank, but a youthful face and softness of speech that seem slightly out of place, as though he were only filling in the time until the real cardinal, a much older and more solemn man, could come. But as he talks, this feeling is quickly dispelled; here is a man acutely conscious of the position he holds, both historically, as the successor to all those prelates in the dark oils on the walls, and currently, as the protector and preserver of what has gone before—the latest, not the last, of the line. The cathedral, his cathedral, he explains, was begun in the fourteenth century, although there are the remains of two earlier buildings on the Wawel hill, one dating from the eleventh century. Beneath the hill flows the Vistula, Poland's river, which, unlike most major European rivers, crosses no frontiers on its 650-mile course from the Carpathians to the Bay of Gdansk in the Baltic. The river, called the Wisla by the Poles, links Krakow, the old capital, to Warsaw, the new, and connects the plains and lakes of the north to the mountains of the south.

Poland's kings were crowned by the primates in Wawel Cathedral and buried by the primates in the marble vaults beneath it. In Wawel's vaults lie Casimir the Great, who founded the university in 1364 and granted refuge to the Jews; Jan Sobieski, who defeated the Turks at Vienna, and

Stefan Batory, the warlike Transylvanian, whose tomb still gets decorated by Hungarian tourists. Queen Jadwiga, who for reasons of state gave up the man she loved in the fourteenth century, marrying the Duke of Lithuania, Jagiello, and combining the kingdoms, is commemorated in marble and remembered by thousands of schoolchildren, who leave their school badges on her tomb and scribble notes asking help in exams or expressing their love. Americans pause before the tomb of the soldier-patriot Tadeusz Kosciuszko, who built West Point and fought in the American Revolution, but lost his fight for Polish liberation.

"In Krakow," Cardinal Wojtyla said, "in these old buildings, you see the history of Poland, and the story of Poland." He speaks English slowly and carefully. His Polish, according to those who read his essays and listen to his sermons, is lean and precise, but in English he would rather use a clumsy phrase than risk being misunderstood. Poland's history, he stressed, cannot be separated from that of the Church.

The Christian missionaries brought Western culture to pagan Poland after 966. From 1572, the primate of Poland, first in Krakow, later in Warsaw, ruled the nation during the frequent stormy periods when there was no king and the nobles in the Sejm could not agree on a successor. The Church was a force of both reaction and progress, as the case of Krakow's most illustrious citizen, Mikolaj Kopernik or Nicolaus Copernicus, shows. Educated at Casimir's university by the Church, given a Church post by his uncle, an influential bishop, and permitted to continue his studies in Italy, Copernicus was able to work on the astronomical research that led to his 1543 discovery that the Earth was a moving planet. But it was also the Church that banned his *Concerning the Revolutions of the Celestial Spheres* nearly a century later.

During the three partitions of Poland in the eighteenth century by Russia, Prussia, and Austria, the Church was instrumental in preserving the language and culture of the nation against the efforts of the conquerors to Germanize or Russianize. When the Germans and Russians returned in 1939 with a much more brutal and efficient plan of obliterating the Polish nation, it was again the Church, working with lay resistance groups, that kept the idea of the nation alive and helped educate the postwar generation in underground schools. Cardinal Wojtyla, who was one of those students, believes that the sum of the Church's wartime effort, in the resistance and in educating tens of thousands of children, has relevance to its position today: "The Second World War claimed six million Poles' lives, among them thousands of priests and religious. Through those hecatombs, the nation and the Church were united anew, and that organic union constitutes today the singular source of resistance to programmed atheism, which the people, and especially the youth, face during this postwar period."

To Wojtyla, the best symbol of the Church in this period was Father

Maximilian Kolbe, the Polish priest who gave his life to save that of a fellow inmate at the Auschwitz concentration camp. Father Kolbe volunteered for the starvation cells in the place of a Polish resistance fighter who had a wife and children. He was beatified in 1971 in a Vatican ceremony attended not only by Wyszynski and Wojtyla but by an official delegation of the Polish government.

"In the life and death of Father Kolbe, love was triumphant to the end," Wojtyla said. "Only love can make human life truly human even in the most inhuman conditions, as was the case in the concentration camps. The beatification of Father Kolbe shows that man, basing himself on Christ, is capable of the greatest heroism. If one wishes to understand the Church in Poland and its link with the nation—as well as the relationship between religion and politics—it is necessary to think deeply on the event of the beatification."

The war left the Church stronger than ever. Its record was largely untainted by collaboration, in contrast to that of the Catholic hierarchy in Slovakia and Croatia. The tragic results of war and postwar policy—the annihilation of 3 million Polish Jews, the loss of territory in the East—changed a state that had been only two-thirds Roman Catholic to one that was almost entirely so.

But from the first months of the new regime installed by the advancing Red army, it was clear that the Church would oppose the Russians as it had opposed the Germans. Anti-Russian feeling had been as important an ingredient of Polish nationalism as anti-German, and if the latter had come to predominate during the occupation, the postwar years quickly evened things up. There was open warfare on both sides. The regime arrested and harassed priests, and the priests excommunicated Communists and those they considered their supporters. In the countryside, the Church helped the underground bands that fought the Communists in the first few years after the war, but it finally became clear to both priests and the remaining guerrillas that it was a losing fight. The imprisonment of Wyszynski in September 1953 marked the end of this period of resistance. But on the regime side, there were soon some second thoughts. The Pax movement of collaborating Catholics, handsomely subsidized by the government, was not attracting the support that had been hoped for it. The imprisoned cardinal was infinitely more powerful than the most favored of the peace priests.

The Church was the first to benefit from the Poznan riots of June 1956, which forced the regime to abandon the Stalinist extremism that had been directed against workers, intellectuals, and priests alike. Wladyslaw Gomulka, brought back to power after eight years of disgrace and imprisonment that October, behaved exactly as Edward Gierek would in 1970 when he replaced Gomulka. They both sought the broadest possible national support, and that meant a policy of conciliation toward the Church. Gomulka released the cardinal from prison and, in return for a loyalty pledge from the Church, permitted religion to be taught in the schools, as it had been before the Communist takeover. At the same time, the writers and journalists were largely freed from censorship, and farmers were allowed to leave the collectives.

Only the concessions to the farmers turned out to be permanent. After a brief flowering of Polish films, novels, and political writing, the censors returned. And Wyszynski's freedom to say what he wanted soon brought regime reprisals. The agreement with the Church could not last long because of the difficulty of identifying what was God's and what was Caesar's. The cardinal refused to accept the regime's definition, and it was not long before he was delivering protest speeches' instead of sermons. The state, in turn, shut down the schools' religious program and resumed its harassment of priests.

The tests of strength came with increasing frequency. In 1966, during the celebration of the millennium, Church and regime competed for crowds at rallies like Indiana politicians. The regime stressed the point that Poland was celebrating a thousand years of history. The Church said the millennium represented an anniversary for both Christianity and history. It was hardly a fair fight, and the Church won the crowds easily. In 1968, however, when students rioted in Warsaw and Krakow, it was the Church that lost. Although the bishops condemned police attacks on the students, there was no such forthright condemnation of the persecution of Polish Jews that followed. A large minority in the Church wanted it to speak out against the regime's blaming the rioting on the Jews and forcing the emigration of half the remaining Jewish population of 30,000. But the majority considered the plight of the Jews an internal Party matter, since most of those affected were Party members, and said the Church should stay out of it. By failing to take a strong stand in defense of another religious group, persecuted, as the Catholics had been, for reasons having nothing to do with religion, the Church lost support among the intellectuals, who accused it of having a double standard, or of siding with the regime on a platform of intolerant nationalism in the hope of benefits for itself.

Whatever the moral cost of 1968, the Baltic upheavals of December 1970 gave the Church a chance to redeem itself. Its action under the pressure of that national crisis is the best key to understanding the Church's own idea of its political role in the years ahead.

GDANSK

On a misty gray Monday morning eleven days before Christmas, the shipyard workers in Gdansk streamed out of the gates of the Lenin Yards and marched to Party headquarters downtown, shouting "We want bread" in a ghostly echo of the Poznan workers' demands of fourteen years before, singing the "Internationale," and protesting the increases of 10 to 30 percent that had been put on food prices the previous weekend. The spontaneous protest then took a course that has become classic in the brief history of dissent in the Soviet Bloc. First the march to the Party headquarters, where the explanations and excuses of the frightened official who appears before the crowd are shouted down, then the clashes with the police and the first shots, and finally the first day's retreat, the regrouping, and the search for allies. The Gdansk shipyard workers marched to the city Polytechnical College and shouted to the students to join them, and then appealed to Bishop Edmund Nowicki for help. They wanted him to arouse the populace and declare the Church on the side of the workers by ringing every churchbell in town, from the squat brick belfries of the Old City to his own cathedral on the outskirts in Oliwa, near a huge shipyard workers' housing project.

Both the students and the bishop refused. The protest flamed on without them, spreading all around the Bay of Gdansk and jumping to the port of Szczecin 180 miles away. At the end of a week of rioting, in addition to the 45 dead, there were 1,600 injured and 3,000 in jail, and Gomulka was finished. But without the students and the Church, the Baltic protests got no further.

Gdansk's students have ready explanations for their failure to join in. Most were apolitical, interested in getting jobs as engineers and earning money. They still felt the threat of the 1968 repressions. Most of all, they said, they were fearful of Soviet intervention; Kaliningrad, after all, is only 50 miles across the bay.

Bishop Nowicki died a few weeks after the riots, so his reasoning is not known. But it is clear from conversations with Church officials in Gdansk and elsewhere that the Church was as worried as the students about the Russians. It did not want a confrontation it knew it could not win, whether with the Polish or with the Soviet military. That is not the Church's style of battle. It opposed the price increases as an unbearable extra burden on the workers' families. But it did not believe that more blood should flow.

"The Church in Poland is very much bound up with the community," Wojtyla said in discussing the situation on the Baltic not long after calm had returned. "The bitter experiences of the last two centuries have brought it about, to a great extent. The events of the last few months, especially on the coastal cities, are proof of that organic bond The Church's foremost concern was internal peace in the nation, but it reminded everyone of the basic civil rights, especially of the rights of the employee and the laborer and the family."

It did this through Wyszynski's emotional Christmas sermon, then, as a less dramatic follow-up, but one with more weight, a list of demands.

The list was the joint work of the Polish bishops, with Wojtyla playing a prominent role in its formulation.

Wyszynski's sermon answered Gierek's appeal for cooperation. "Perhaps I have not cried enough, I have not admonished enough," he said in trying to explain the Baltic tragedy. "We bishops and priests . . . feel co-responsible, and we beg the families of those who were beaten to accept our confession and our plea for forgiveness."

This confession was more than an act of Christianity on the cardinal's part. It was a clear statement that the Church shared responsibility with the regime for what went on in the nation, whether good or bad. If the Church has a role in the education and the development of a moral sense in the majority of Polish citizens, then it must share the blame when things go wrong.

The bishops' demands were delivered a week later, in the same spirit of co-responsibility for the fate of the nation. In addition to demanding freedom for religion, the bishops called for social justice, freedom from persecution, adequate living standards, and "the right to truth in social life, to information in accord with the truth, and to free expression of one's views and demands."

The regime's response was a mixture of threats and concessions. Catholic groups were warned against stands that in the past had led them "down the road of negation and opposition to the state." But at the same time, Party secretaries across the country were calling in the local priests to talk encouragingly about applications for church construction and to offer better facilities for teaching religion. In Gdansk, surprised diocese officials were given permission on the day after Christmas to rebuild the stately brick shell of the fourteenth-century St. Birgitta's church in the Old City. For twenty-six years, their applications had been ignored.

The biggest concession was the government's decision to surrender title to the former German church properties in the Oder-Neisse and Baltic territories ceded to Poland after the war. The Church had been paying the government rent on the 4,700 churches and 2,200 other religious buildings, and got not only title to them but a refund of nearly $2.8 million.

The Church was glad to accept the concessions. Without buildings, it cannot function, and it is particularly interested in being able to build new churches in communities that have grown up because of the industrialization of recent years. There are often housing developments of tens of thousands near a new mill or refinery with no church, an overcrowded village chapel, or a makeshift building to serve the parishioners. Service, Wojtyla said, is basic to the Church's mission, because only in this way can people be helped to "realize their common good—which basically depends on the morality of the citizens, on the personal, family, and social morality." But in order to perform this service, the regime must grant "the elementary rights of the Church and the creation of such conditions which would enable the Church to fulfill its tasks."

Thus the Church does not want to be bought off with buildings, old or new, important as they are to its purposes. It insists on its right to be the people's advocate, to demand a certain standard of behavior by Party and government, without presuming to take over their rôle.

The cardinal believes that the early skirmishing over property and new construction permits is only the beginning of what will be a long struggle: "We received with real satisfaction the declaration of the new premier that the government is undertaking efforts toward full normalization of Church-state relations. The first step in that direction was the decision concerning the Church possessions in the north and western territories. We think there should be further action taken in that direction."

But full normalization, he stressed, "demands the settling of many matters, that is, the basic things necessary for the existence of the Church in Poland and for its mission." And this goes beyond buildings and classrooms. The Church does not consider its business to be the organization of the government, but it does have a strong claim to telling the people which government actions are right and which are wrong, since governments are run by individuals and individuals are subject to moral rules. It sees no contradiction between the moral code and national laws, if those laws are fair and are administered fairly.

The shock of the Baltic uprising forced the regime to consider these questions of moral rights and the position of the Church after years of neglect. The first indication of change was the decision of the new premier, Piotr Jaroszewicz, to meet with Wyszynski. The second was the opening of talks between the Vatican and the Polish government. Archbishop Agostino Casaroli, who, as secretary of the Vatican's Council of Public Affairs, was in effect Pope Paul's foreign minister, was chosen to conduct negotiations with the government.

The cardinal's talks with the premier were the first in eight years; the Vatican-regime negotiations the first since the war. Cardinal Wojtyla does not like to comment in any detail on either set of talks, but he expects them to continue over a long period, produce few spectacular results, and be of great advantage in the long run to the average Polish churchgoer.

"During the past twenty-five years," he said, "the Church in Poland verified anew its proper mission. For the sake of the good of the nation and the homeland, the Church is ready for dialogue with the State, which is founded on the assumptions of dialectical and historical materialism. It is without doubt a positive fact that the new ruling recognizes the right of the Church to ecclesiastical properties in the western and northern territories. We think that it constitutes an advantageous introduction to the dialogue begun by the government with the Apostolic See." Then, as an understated final argument to the impressive bargaining advantage the state might seem to have in the talks that lie ahead, he added, "One must remember that the majority of the Polish people are Catholic."

THE CARDINAL

In the dialogue to come, no one is better fitted to represent the Church and its members than Karol Wojtyla. The regime makes much of the fact that Gierek, a genuine worker, is its new leader. But Wojtyla, too, is able to discuss from firsthand experience the problems of a hard day of manual labor and what it means in family life, vodka consumption, and political attitudes.

Born May 18, 1920, in the village of Wadowice near Krakow, Wojtyla went to the village school and a neighboring high school. At eighteen, he enrolled in the Jagiellonian University in Krakow in the Faculty of Philosophy, intending to specialize in Polish language and literature. But the war soon broke out, and the university was closed in particularly brutal fashion by the German occupation, which set up its headquarters on the same Wawel hill of the cathedral and castle. In November 1939, a few weeks after the Polish defeat, the professors were called in for a meeting with the occupation authorities. They arrived punctually and in full strength, because they thought they would be told the new rulers' regulations for running the university. Instead, they were summarily arrested and taken to concentration camps. Only a few survived the war.

Wojtyla and the other students were sent home, and the fourteenth-century Collegium Maius, where Copernicus studied, and where his instruments are still displayed, was shut. But within a few weeks those professors still at large, other teachers, and priests organized an underground university, and Wojtyla was able to resume his studies. By 1942, other things seemed more important to him than literature, and he began studying for the priesthood, again using underground classes. He recalls that this phase of his education was particularly dangerous, because there were frequent and sudden roundups of young men for use as hostages against the Polish resistance. Whenever the resistance killed an occupation soldier or conducted a raid, hostages would be shot. Wojtyla recalled how his bishop would warn him and other seminarians to keep out of certain areas known to be targets for hostage raids.

He could not, however, escape forced labor. He was sent to the Solvay soda plant in Borek-Polecki, near Krakow, but managed to keep studying after his shifts. The work was hard but the experience valuable, he said: "I consider those four years especially important in my life. I believe that divine providence prepared me in that way for future tasks."

During this period, the underground seminarian helped found an underground theater, the Rhapsody. Wojtyla wrote plays for the theater and acted in them. Rhapsody's policy could best be summed up as patriotism. It was one more manifestation of the Church role in preserving the national idea against foreign attempts to crush it, in this case by acting out patriotic and historical plays in the vaulted cellars of Krakow while German soldiers patrolled above.

German occupation policy was harsh throughout Eastern Europe, but because of some murky Nazi theory on the relative worth of the various Slavs, Poland and the Soviet Union were singled out for the harshest treatment of all. Poland was not even permitted to have a puppet government; it was dismembered and ruled directly by the Germans. Wojtyla remembers those six years as a terrible time, but he is reluctant to consider his own role as anything unusual: "I must admit that, aside from the contempt of man which was most painful to all in my country, my physical work in the factory was a rather mild experience. It was nothing as devastating as that which my fellow countrymen had to endure." He refers frequently to Father Kolbe and the others who were killed at Auschwitz. Indeed, the death camps, the reprisal shootings, and the whole terrible history of the occupation often seem almost current news in conversations in Krakow. It is not hard to understand why: Oswiecim, the Polish name for Auschwitz, is a town an hour's drive away, and elsewhere in the area there are little monuments to the lesser-known places where Poles lost their lives in the holocaust.

The occupation taught Wojtyla two lessons that were to serve him well by the time he was ordained a priest in 1946. One was how to get along with the working people among his parishioners, and the other how to operate in a hostile state. Two years of travel followed, for study in Rome and for work among Polish miners in France and Belgium. He lived in the emigrant communities in the West, saying Mass and helping the miners with their problems, which ranged from personal difficulties to bad working conditions. Gierek, as a Communist party official, was engaged in the same work among the émigrés at the same time, although there is no record of their having met. It was in those years that Wojtyla learned of the effectiveness of the Christian youth organizations in France. In 1948 he had his chance to apply his knowledge in Poland, when he was given the post of junior priest in the village parish of Niegowic, near Krakow.

He returned to Poland in a period when the fragile postwar coalition had collapsed, the popular Peasant party leader, Stanislaw Mikolajczyk, had been forced to flee, and the Church had begun to feel the weight of the regime's policies of repression. Priests were called in to take loyalty oaths to the regime, and many of them would disappear suddenly, only to emerge later as confessed spies and saboteurs. No one bothered the country priest in Niegowic, however, and by 1949, Wojtyla had a new assignment in St. Florian's in Krakow. The thirteenth-century church is one of the oldest in the city, in a neighborhood near the brick city walls that has changed as little as possible since that time. But Wojtyla's two-year term in St. Florian's coincided with sweeping changes in Krakow. On the outskirts of the city, the government was building Nowa Huta, the great steel mill, and bringing tens of thousands of peasants to Krakow. They sought the familiar, and the familiar in this case was the counsel and help of men like Father Wojtyla, the village priest who had also come to the city.

Wojtyla continued his studies during this period, becoming a doctor of theology in 1951. From 1954 to 1958 he taught at the Catholic University in Lublin, and also served as a youth chaplain, with duties like those of the young priests who now meet him to consult on their work in Krakow. He was very popular with the students, and no wonder: their thirty-four-year-old chaplain was as active as they were, organizing weekend hikes, cross-country skiing, and camping and canoeing trips on the Vistula. In 1958 Wojtyla was camping with his students in the Polish lake country when he received word that he had been appointed auxiliary bishop of Krakow. It was an important promotion for a young professor. But Wojtyla did not want to have the camping trip spoiled. The students, comfortable with their chaplain, would have been uneasy tenting with a bishop. He withheld the news of the promotion until their return to school.

There are many other Wojtyla anecdotes from this period. Once, while skiing in the Tatra, the mountains that Poland and Czechoslovakia share, he got too close to the border and was stopped by a guard. He produced his bishop's identity card and for some time was under suspicion of having stolen the real bishop's credentials. No one would believe that such a young man could be a bishop. On another occasion, he spent some time at a Church vacation home, dressed, as usual, in his plain black suit. An older priest took advantage of his seniority, ordering him around, and by the end of his stay, Wojtyla, too unassuming to reveal his identity, was running errands for the priest.

The cardinal is still popular with the young. With dozens of churches to choose from, and strong regime encouragement not to go to church at all, Krakow's young people climb the castle hill and crowd into Wawel Cathedral to hear him preach. Their reasons, they say, are many and various: he seems to understand youthful aspirations, he is in tune with the liberal trends in the Church, although a long way from the Western Catholic radicals, but most of all, he can express, in his plain but eloquent sermons, their own conflicts of conscience, and can offer them some guidance on the day-to-day problems of dual loyalty to the Church and the Politburo.

Wojtyla became acting head of the archdiocese when the archbishop of Krakow died in 1962, and was confirmed to the post two years later. Pope Paul made him a cardinal in 1967. At the time, he was forty-seven, the second-youngest member of the College of Cardinals.

More important, however, was the fact that Poland had a second member of the College for the first time since the war.

Wojtyla's elevation to cardinal was the logical result of two parallel Vatican policies begun under Pope John XXIII. First, the Vatican gradually abandoned the cold-war stance of the forties and fifties and began to recognize the permanence of Communist rule in Eastern Europe. This permitted negotiations for improvement of the Church's position in the countries of the Bloc; it was making do within the existing system rather than trying to continue the all-or-nothing policy of liberation. But it took more than the new pope to make the change possible. As long as the Communists kept cardinals and priests in prison, negotiation was impossible. In Poland in particular, it would have been destructive to the morale of every priest. But after 1956, and despite many setbacks, both sides found their moves toward liberalization complementing each other.

The second policy represented by Wojtyla's selection was the Church's decision to come to terms with the problems of the modern world. The Vatican Council of 1963–1965 had drawn guidelines for a new Church role in an urban, industrial society. Wojtyla was an active participant in the council. Since 1967, he has made frequent trips to Rome as a member of the Vatican Council for the Laity, which deals with relations between the hierarchy and the lay members of the Church, particularly the role of lay men and women in helping make policy.

"The Church of our time," he said, "is deeply concerned with peace and justice in the world, as there is a great lack of justice, and peace is always being threatened. At the same time, however, the post-Conciliar Church expends every effort to form itself, commensurate to its mission from Christ, in the contemporary world. In that sense, it is the main task not only of our generation but also, I think, of the future generations to realize in full the teaching of the Second Vatican Council."

The Council's decisions were particularly valuable for the work of the church in situations like Krakow's. Even if Communism did not exist, the Church would have been in trouble there, because it was being jarred out of its comfortable old relationship with its members. In the sixties and seventies, Krakow's priests found it was no longer possible to behave in fatherly fashion to a largely unsophisticated and uneducated rural population. The peasant believers had become urban skeptics, or were still trying to sort out the effect of their move from country to city and the bewildering array of new influences they had to contend with, from the frequent apartment block meetings led by Party activists to the films depicting Soviet labor heroism.

When Wojtyla was ordained at the end of the war, Poland was 25 percent urban and 75 percent rural. By the time he was created a cardinal, the rural-urban division had changed to half and half. At no other time in Poland's history has there been such a rapid change, and the cardinal believes that the sudden alteration of centuries of societal patterns is as great a problem as any the Church faces. But he finds the teachings of the Vatican Council a great help in dealing with it. He is also glad now that he had the experience of living many of the problems of the new, and perhaps not altogether willing, industrial worker and urban dweller: "My job in the factory at the beginning of my vocation gave me an opportunity to prove to myself and to my fellow workers how right and timely the Church's social doctrine was."

Despite the efforts of the Church to modernize itself, is there not an inevitable falling away of membership when people change old habits and jobs? "In every country," Wojtyla said, "the percentage of believers, or of those who attend church, is smaller in the cities than in the country. We, too, have this problem. But through the work of very active priests, such as the one at Nowa Huta, we are coping with it."

NOWA HUTA

Nowa Huta is set in what used to be farmland on the edge of Krakow. Both the mill and the villages surrounding the city are necessary stops on any exploration of the area, whether its purpose is sightseeing or trying to understand Polish society. On one side of the city, there is the steel plant and dormitory city, begun in 1950 and still under construction and expansion. On the other, not much has changed since the Austrian Kaiser Franz Josef ruled. Cobblestone roads bisect loghouse villages. The logs are chinked with mud and painted a bright, flat blue. Yellow thatched roofs are common, their brightness depending on their age. They are not chosen for quaintness, as in English villages, but because they are cheaper than tile. Everything is neat and tended, especially the roadside shrines, with fresh flowers, green boughs, and flickering candles. Horsecarts plod the main highway, their drivers as little concerned for the cars on the E-22 that connects Berlin and Odessa as for the pigs on the local rutted paths. At night, the carts are a particular hazard. Often their only warning lights are lanterns as dim as a candle, and the collisions between the three-mile-per-hour carts and sixty-mile-per-hour Polski Fiats are frequent.

On a Sunday morning, the pedestrians predominate. They are the churchgoers, walking from villages that have no church to the next larger one. In the winter, the women's costumes are hidden beneath plaid shawls that look like car blankets, but in warmer weather they are splendid: red-embroidered white blouses, layers of petticoats and skirts, babushkas and aprons in yellow and deep-red prints, high black boots. Most of the men are in their well-brushed blue or black Sunday suits.

What is notable about the scene is that the whole village seems to be out on the road, or if not everyone, at least a good cross section of the population; teenagers, young couples, children, old women, old men: enough to contradict with visible evidence the regime's claim that yes, the churches are full, but only with old women. (The city churches from Warsaw to Gdansk supply the same kind of evidence. On weekdays, they are busy; on Sundays, crowded; on religious holidays, packed.)

The smokestacks of Nowa Huta appear suddenly over the rolling hills, and soon the huge Lenin works covers the horizon for more than a mile. Nowa Huta, which means new mill, was started at the height of Stalin's heavy industrialization drive in the Soviet Bloc. The Lenin works was built to make steel, and that it does: three times the production of all of Poland's prewar mills combined, 4.5 million tons annually, 40 percent of the current national total, which in turn is the tenth-largest in the world and the seventh in Europe.

But it was also built to create a new Socialist man out of the backward peasant who moved to Krakow to work in it. The peasants came partly because they were being forced off their farms while the collectivization drives were still on, and partly because they wanted to enjoy the promised benefits of high wages and low-rent apartments with indoor plumbing. The Party contended that if Marxism teaches that the material base determines the superstructure of society, then it also shapes the individual. The Party was not reaching the individual in the villages because of a combination of his own accumulation of centuries of prejudice and the reactionary influence of the village priest. Since it would be difficult to eliminate these influences on the spot, the answer was to transplant the villager to the city.

"Most of the working force of the steel mill came from the peasantry," a local Party official explained in a conversation in one of the cheerless self-service restaurants on the Plac Centralny, where the blue streetcars from Krakow screech and rumble as they swing around the loop at the end of the line. The square's arcaded buildings are downtown for the 170,000 residents of Nowa Huta, who live in similar apartment blocks on the grids of streets that lead from it.

"They were peasants when they moved here," the official continued, "but most were glad to get away from the village.

"In exchange for a good apartment, baths, and a movie house down the block, they gave up their dependence on the village priest. The Krakow area was a center of conservative thinking before Nowa Huta. We have made it attractive to work and live here. With the new conditions come new ways of thinking."

If the regime was going to such efforts to promote new ways of thinking, there was obviously no place for a church in Nowa Huta, and the pleas of priests in adjoining villages, whose churches are soon overcrowded with the new arrivals, were ignored. The works grew, and Nowa Huta, the residential town, grew with it. Soon there was a bronze bust ot Lenin and stainless steel letters as high as a man to spell his name in front of the main gate. Red banners blossomed on the Plac Centralny on every Party anniversary.

But that other familiar part of the Polish scene, the church spire, was missing. Nowa Huta was known throughout the nation (for good or ill, depending on one's viewpoint) as the city without a church. The description was not entirely accurate, as it turned out; for one thing, the area was soon incorporated into Krakow, a five- or six-mile streetcar ride away, and Krakow is richly endowed with churches. For another, a makeshift barracks for the Nowa Huta worshipers soon appeared. The barracks was permitted in 1953, after long arguments between the arch-diocese and the Party in Krakow. But another thirteen years were to go by before the Catholics of Nowa Huta could begin construction of a real church. In the meantime, their parish had grown so much that it be-came the largest in Europe.

The barracks building soon developed extensions and then spawned outbuildings. The main aim was to provide classrooms for religious in-struction. School came before worship on the priority list of the Nowa Huta priests. The worshipers stood outside the church, kept in order by painted lines on the asphalt courtyard, and waited to go inside for com-munion, which one-fifth of the parish took every Sunday. The barracks was the size of an American storefront church, about 60 by 90 feet, with cubicles in back for priests' offices. But the congregation was huge—in the neighborhood of 100,000. Priests worked in shifts to handle them, saying ten or more Masses a day. Every Sunday, the courtyard would be full of churchgoers, waiting patiently in line and shuffling forward as others left the little building to make them a place. When it rained or snowed, thousands of umbrellas appeared to roof over the area. On holy days the lines stretched back into the street.

Was this stubborn insistence on churchgoing a victory for village super-stition and a defeat for the Party? Many of the Party leaders thought so, and thought they could win out in the end by refusing to let the Church establish a permanent base in Nowa Huta. But there was also a minority that thought it senseless to resist.

"It was foolish to oppose the church for so long," a loyal but pragmatic member of the Krakow Communist establishment said. "It is an inte-grative factor. The people who come to Nowa Huta are disoriented for many months, perhaps years. The Houses of Culture are as strange to them as the mills, and the message of the People's Theater Group does not reach them because they have never seen a play before.

"But the Church is familiar, and the priest has a familiar role. There are good priests and bad priests, but those at the barracks are a far cry from the village priests who controlled every facet of life from bap-tism to funerals, who read the letters from the bureaucracy in Warsaw, because the peasant couldn't read, and answered them, because he couldn't write, who ruled on family quarrels, and in general were in charge of everything. These new priests know the stresses of an industrial society. They are a help to us, not our natural enemies."

Cardinal Wojtyla, the leader of the drive to get a permanent church built at Nowa Huta, found allies in the Party. Some agreed with the official who found the Church a help in integrating the newcomers. Others realized that standing in the rain to worship was doing little to shake the faith of the Nowa Hutans. But there seemed to be no graceful way for the regime to back down from its original stand of opposition. In 1966, however, the millennium provided the opportunity; the regime was able to approve the construction of a new church as its contribution to the celebration of a thousand years of Christianity.

Wojtyla dedicated the cornerstone of the church in 1969, with the fullest use of symbols to make up for the years of having been disadvantaged by the Lenin display. There was a blessing from Pope Paul, and the cornerstone itself was a fragment of masonry from St. Peter's Basilica in the Vatican. The poured-concrete church was designed for 10,000 worshipers, with two auditoriums for conducting Masses simultaneously, offices for nine priests, and classrooms. Until it is finished, the barracks church and the five barracks classrooms continue their work.

"They've got twenty-five state schools in Nowa Huta," one of the barracks priests said. "That's two schools for every priest we have here. But the teachers are from the country. They're all Catholic. They've also got three Houses of Culture, with beat music, films, and dancing. But half the town's five thousand teenagers still come to my classes, and a lot more of the younger ones."

The priest stood before an Italian-language wall map of the Holy Land, a gift of the Vatican, and explained how crowding and shifts manage to get the children of Nowa Huta into the barracks. Religious instruction must be given after school, and the first children come directly from class, followed by other groups late into the evening. They sit on backless Formica-covered benches and learn about dogma, the life of Jesus, and other religious subjects. Do politics get brought up? Of course, the priest replies, particularly by a group of university students he works with. "My answer is to offer them the fare to Warsaw to talk the matter over with the Party or government. They are in charge of politics in this country, and we are in charge of religion."

In the generation since World War II, millions of students have gone through these religion classes. One church estimate is 6 to 10 million, a fifth to a third of all Poles, young and old. The grade school students of the early days have long since finished college and gone on to teaching posts, the government, the state-run industry: places where they can influence others. To Wojtyla, this is one of the most important developments of the last generation. No matter what they have accepted or rejected from their religious training, these millions of Poles have a broader education than the average state school graduate, in Poland or elsewhere in Eastern Europe. And their numbers are growing. Despite intermittent regime campaigns to eliminate or restrict it, the religious education program has continued, expanded, and flourished.

After the teaching of religion in public schools was abandoned in 1957, the government agreed to let the church teach in so-called catechistic points outside the schools. Every afternoon, in every Polish city, the children in black satin smocks and the older students in blue jeans and maxicoats can be seen on their way from government to church school. Statistics on the percentage of attendance are not made public, but the proportion that applies to Nowa Huta is a good working figure for the nation—about 60 percent. Parents who are not churchgoers themselves make sure their children have religious training, and not only to learn about the Bible. They feel it gives the children another viewpoint to help balance what they learn in the state schools, read in the regime press, and hear on the government radio.

The regime's harassment takes various forms. There are frequent editorial charges that the church classes are interfering with regular school activities. Actually, it is usually the other way around. There is constant pressure on priests to supply the local authorities with lists of children taking the instruction. The Church simply ignores the demands in most cases, realizing that the lists would be used against parents, particularly those in the Party. Other forms of harassment include demands for frequent inspection of the catechistic facilities and the refusal to let monks and nuns who are members of religious orders teach. The grounds for the first are concern for the students' health and safety, and for the second the prevention of "religious fanaticism."

THE NEW INTELLIGENTSIA

But despite the difficulties, Poland today has a large and ever increasing intelligentsia with a dual education. It is possible to go all the way through university under Catholic educational auspices; the Catholic University in Lublin, where Wojtyla used to teach, is, it need not be added, a unique institution in the Soviet Bloc. The majority of the Catholic intellectuals choose the more stimulating secular atmosphere of the Krakow or Warsaw universities, but they maintain their contacts with the movement through their local church discussion groups and the officially sanctioned Catholic press.

The Church is limited in many ways. A civic pressure group of Catholics organized for the overt purpose of bringing about political change would be illegal, and its members would risk arrest for subversion. There can be no lay movements or clubs of Catholics, Wojtyla stresses. Any organization has to be based on religious instruction or the solution of personal, not local or national, problems. But since such limits are very hard to define, much can be done in the youth discussion groups run by the young chaplains, the family counseling sessions, and, most importantly, the religion classes.

"Don't think that the parish priest is going to refer a questioner in his religion class to the Party secretary if it touches on politics," a young Catholic intellectual said in response to the claim of the Nowa Huta priest. "He's going to answer it, and on his own terms, and that is a difficulty the regime cannot solve. Taking the religious instruction out of the schools did nothing. In every Polish village, they just go over to the church or parish house after school. These priests don't send anybody out to ask the Party secretary for answers. They do the lecturing and the answering themselves, on everything—family life, modern life, economics."

On the national scale, however, the Church works at considerable disadvantage in its competition with the regime in shaping public opinion. It has a weekly newspaper; the pro-regime Pax group has a daily. The Church has no access to radio or television; a Pax editor does a regular TV commentary. Part of Pax's wealth and favored position, however, aids the church: it enables books by Catholics and about Catholicism 'to be translated and published in Poland, and there are enough by Western Catholic thinkers to satisfy some of the needs of the intelligentsia. Regime support for Pax has brought Communist Poland to the curious situation of having more Catholic books and periodicals in print than Catholic Poland had before the war. This new intelligentsia, increasingly better educated, less involved in the daily struggle for living standards, and secure in the knowledge that the regime needs its skills, is beginning to ask more and more questions about Communist society. This is true throughout Soviet Europe. But only in Poland can this group turn to the Church for answers.

Poland's intellectuals watch the same television programs, read the same newspapers, live under much the same conditions with size of flat, waiting time for car, promotion, Party, government, or academic duties depending on the same combination of regulations, luck, and influence. In all of this, they find something lacking, and are particularly disappointed when the acquisition of a refrigerator does not have the effect of improving life that they expected it to have. The feeling is growing among them that there must be some better medicine for the soul than vodka.

Some of this group had always been loosely connected to the Church; others are joining, with various shadings of commitment. Gierek's appeal for the help of the whole nation, "believers and nonbelievers," has made it easier. So has the modernization of the Church, since its liberal leaders, at least, now seek answers to the same problems the intellectuals do: above all, the emptiness of modern life. Now more and more Poles can feel they can belong to the community of believers and still maintain their loyalty to the state. They want their children to be educated, but neither within the limits of the Party ideology nor in the old agrarian national ideas of the Church. We are Catholic, they say, not because we believe in God, not because we're Poles, but because we are seeking some of the answers to our modern dilemma.

The Catholic Church in Poland today is a mixture of the modern member of this type and the old, rural kind of devout believer. But time and education are on the side of the first group. Poland graduated only 85,000 university students in all the twenty years between the world wars. By the seventies there were half a million college-level students.

This adds up to the beginnings of political pluralism in Poland, in the opinion of leaders of the Znak group, the Church's parliamentary voice. Their view has been sharply attacked by the Party, a monopoly that wants no partners. Because of regime sensitivity to the issue of pluralism, Wojtyla is reluctant to discuss its potential, but he does welcome the growth of the non-Party intelligentsia: "I consider this to be very important. After World War II, Poland became the meeting place of two opposing ideologies. A particular ideology is not only a system; it is the essence of the spiritual life of man. The struggles between the two ideologies penetrate the souls of contemporary Poles. Decision in this is a matter of conscience and a matter of greatest import. It is easy to understand how important the formation of Catholics, by choice and conviction, is, especially among today's and even tomorrow's intelligentsia. It is necessary to note that more and more Polish youth are getting into the ranks of today's intelligentsia."

THE WORKERS

But the workers, not the intellectuals, have brought about the most dramatic events in Poland's postwar history. Twice they went on strike, demonstrated, and finally rioted, and twice they brought down governments and Party leaderships. The experience of Poznan in 1956 and Gdansk in 1970 thus suggests that while other oppositional forces in Poland may be powerful, the real power lies, as it should in a workers' state, in the hands of the working class, which needs only to be goaded enough to wield it and bring about needed changes.

The intellectuals have benefited from the protests, but the workers have not needed them as leaders. In Gdansk the workers behaved exactly as the Party histories of the struggles under capitalism say they should: they elected their own leadership, took decisions without asking permission from the top, and brought pressure to bear on their rulers.

It was possible for Westerners to watch the process in action in Gdansk in the weeks after the first upheaval. Its most spectacular result was the removal of Gomulka, but that was brought about by the rawest forms of expression of public opinion: the strike, the protest march, and eventually the riot. The workings of participatory democracy could be observed in more refined form after the violence had subsided, when the

18,000 workers of the Lenin shipyard were holding daily meetings and taking the actions that, at least for a time, transformed the Polish system of government into something more responsive to the people.

The authorities kept Westerners out of the yards during this period, but other strikes and discussions were impossible to conceal. On one dark morning before seven, the Polish rush hour, the cream and red streetcars and buses had disappeared from the main square in front of Gdansk's whimsically Victorian railway station. The motormen, conductors, and bus drivers were in their garages, choosing committee members, leaders, and spokesmen, and working out demands in a rough and ready exchange of shouted questions and answers. In this process, most of the regular Party and union officials were ignored, since there would have been no need for the strike if they had been doing their jobs in the first place.

The new ad hoc transport workers' committees next made the rounds of all the garages, collecting demands. Pay figured large; at $70 a month they were getting a third less than the shipyard workers. Then came complaints about working conditions. One driver wanted to know why the buses were always so dirty. Why were there no toilets at the end of long runs? Why were tickets not on sale early enough in the morning at the state newsstands? Political demands followed. The workers' response in this area was uncomplicated. They simply demanded the removal of everyone responsible for the conditions they were condemning.

Party and government officials reacted to the demands with a mixture of concern and annoyance. They joked about the toilet situation, but promised it would be remedied. They could not explain why it took a strike to accomplish this after twenty-five years of Communism. The Gdansk idea soon caught on in other parts of the country, and for more than a year the grievances that had been pent up for so long continued to pour into Warsaw. "The importance of social problems and working conditions has considerably increased in our public life over the past few days," the daily Zycie Warszawy noted at the time, with a certain amount of understatement. Gdansk's Lenin Yards presented more than 2,000 resolutions to visiting Party leaders. After first ignoring the strike committees, Warsaw was forced to grant them concessions, and then to negotiate with them for more. The delegations shuttled between the Baltic and the capital on the overnight trains or little LOT commuter airliners. They got results: a thorough overhaul of provincial and district leaderships, a rollback of the price increases, $2 billion in subsidies for low-income workers.

GOMULKA AND GIEREK

In all those many months of discussions, demands, and meetings, the workers were dealing with someone who spoke their language, just as Cardinal Wojtyla does. Gierek had been a miner for seventeen years, from the age of thirteen, in Poland, France, and Belgium. A Communist Party member in all three countries, he had joined the Party at eighteen in the coal fields of France. Three years later, he was deported for helping the Communist union organize a strike among the Polish emigrant workers. In 1937 he returned to Belgium for an eleven-year stay. He fought in the resistance during the war, and then organized a Polish branch Communist Party in Belgium. Returning to Poland in 1948, Gierek became a Party functionary in grimy Katowice. At a time when Wojtyla was studying theology part-time, Gierek was busy getting his degree as a mining engineer. Gierek ran his domain with such independence from Warsaw that it came to be called the Polish Katanga.

After his promotion to the national Party leadership in 1970, there were many attempts to sketch in a liberal background in Gierek's record. It was simply not there. The ex-coal miner was fair, open to modern ideas, and zealous in the protection of his miners and steelworkers. As a result, Silesia enjoyed the highest living standards in Poland, with above-average pay and, what is equally important in a Communist economy, well-organized consumer goods and food supply systems. The lines were always a little shorter in Katowice and the shop windows a little more appealing. But it was benevolence from the top, designed to keep the workers and miners happily producing. No one in Katowice's Party headquarters ever talked seriously about freedom of the press or the rights of its small intellectual community. And the trade unions and workers' councils in Silesia had no more power to object to Party decisions than they did anywhere else in Poland.

After his move to Warsaw, Gierek nevertheless was talked about as a liberal and, although he is only seven years Gomulka's junior, was classified with the able, younger group of technocrats that is always supposed to be coming forward to save the Polish economy. One of the tragedies of Gomulka's career is that, at sixty-five, when he was removed, and indeed at sixty, he had all the inflexibility of a man much older, and it is not surprising that Gierek looked like part of the youth revolution by comparison. In his final years, Gomulka shut himself off from advice, even from the inner circle of the Politburo, and played favorite with his lieutenants with all the misguided cunning of a Hindenburg or Stalin. It was as easy in the weeks after his fall to collect Gomulka stories from Party officials and journalists as it was difficult to get most of them to say anything even mildly critical in the weeks before. But it required no special inside information to see how isolated Gomulka had become. Anyone who could order drastic price increases two weeks before Christmas and then express surprise when the workers rioted had indeed lost contact with ordinary people.

But the real tragedy of Gomulka was a national, not a personal, one. That was in the mistaken belief of the Polish people that in October 1956, when under pressure of the workers of Poznan and in defiance of the

Soviet Union he was brought back to power, they had chosen a liberal. The concessions granted then were not the work of Gomulka the liberal but the reply of Gomulka the tactician to the pressures for all these liberties. He knew he had to give way or face far worse. But if Gomulka's first year or eighteen months were devoted to setting up this liberal framework, the last dozen years were devoted to dismantling it.

Gierek showed great contrast in his style of leadership from the first. He was a regular fixture on Polish television screens, an impressive figure of more than six feet, in the hard hat of the shipyards, speaking to workers, citing figures on the economy, arguing, appealing. He asked for frank questions and got them, and he gave equally frank answers (sometimes too frank for Polish TV; some of Gierek's shipyard confrontations were screened without the sound). He spent nine hours one wintry day in a discussion with shipyard workers in Szczecin. "We're all in the same boat," he told them at the end. "If you help us, I think that together we'll succeed. So—will you help us?"

COUNCILS, CHURCH, AND STATE

Gierek's ability to convince and persuade in these worker-to-worker talks is certain to play a role in the distribution of power in Poland in the years to come. Will it mean a rearrangement of the traditional political balance between Church and state? If Gierek can speak *to* the workers so effectively, will he not be speaking *for* them in the years to come? It seems reasonable to assume that if the government is truly responsive to the wishes of the people, then their need for the Church as protector will be diminished.

The flaw in the argument is that it assumes the continued existence of genuinely democratic workers' representation. Two conditions must be met if the workers are to have a voice: truly representative organs and a climate that encourages people to speak out.

Both the history of worker democracy in Poland and the trends discernible as early as the summer of 1971, only half a year after everything was supposed to have changed, are discouraging. As the tension on the Baltic ebbed, the Party press resumed its stern warnings that socialist democracy did not, after all, mean that the leading role of the Party was to be given up. There were frequent references to the chaos that worker self-management was supposed to be causing in Yugoslavia. The strike committees, renamed workers' councils, continued to function, to argue, to needle the bureaucrats. But there were disturbing reports, which never appeared in the press, that leaders of wildcat strikes in Katowice and other areas were being jailed instead of put in touch with Gierek.

Poland's earlier experiment with worker democracy offers little ground for optimism. The councils spawned in the 1956 reform wave did not survive long. The regime soon began to cut them down. A 1957 law that was supposed to guarantee their rights was actually a means of limiting their scope to economic and social issues. Political activity and any kind of national organization were forbidden. The following year, a rule required each council to have a majority of Party and Party-run union members. Even this was not enough, in the eyes of the Party, to deal with the threat of grass-roots democracy. Further new rules restricted the councils to approval of decisions already taken from the top. Some met only three times a year. Often they were called on to pass judgment on complicated plans and documents handed to members only on their way to the meeting hall.

The reason for the death of the councils in the 1950s is the same as that for their illness and probable death in the 1970s: it is dangerous for the Party to have such a popular competitor for power. If workers' councils can set price and wage levels, veto appointments to local Party and government posts, and even take aim, as they did with success, at Politburo members of the rank of former security chief Mieczyslaw Moczar, who ordered the use of troops in Gdansk, they constitute a challenge to the leadership that cannot be tolerated. And even if the regime would agree to sharing power in this way, the neighboring leaderships, the Soviet in particular, could not. Thus the workers' councils may be useful in times of crisis, when the Party is under fire and needs the direct and immediate views of the man in the shipyard and factory, without any bureaucratic filtering. But the councils are a threat in the long run.

The Church is not the same kind of threat. Its reaction to the Baltic upheavals was described most succinctly by Wojtyla: "There arose prayers for Poland in all the churches throughout the land."

Can prayers do much against armor and troops? The Church uses many weapons. As guardian of its members' well-being, it must act when that is threatened, whether the threat is fighting in the streets or the economic conditions that led to the fighting. It has a legitimate right to seek better conditions, not by strikes or ringing churchbells in times of upheaval, but by a whole range of alternate means, including prayer, but also including education, discussion, persuasion, and pressure, the kind of work that Wojtyla does in his community and the kind of diplomacy that Wyszynski practices in Warsaw.

This kind of advocacy is less dramatic than the periodic uprisings of the workers, but more lasting. The workers have demonstrated how a great deal can be accomplished in a short time. But these bursts of progress are temporary. The workers win important short-term concessions for themselves and the nation, but then lose most of them. The Church has never toppled a Party leader. Its role instead has been in posing long-term challenges, in working for gradual but lasting change.

The Church can do this because everyone in Poland knows that it will survive (although strike committees will not) and that it cannot be bought or overpowered (although workers' councils can). If the Church has anything, it has its thousand years of history behind it, its record of survival, and its capacity for taking long views and slow steps.

"The Church in Poland," Wojtyla said, "as we have said before, is very closely bound up with the entire people. The Church is deeply concerned with peace and justice."

But this does not solve the problem of how to obtain justice in a society with so many built-in injustices. The Party and government in Warsaw control the police, control the courts, and control the five-year plans that put shipyard expansion ahead of housing construction. They also control the right to object about these conditions, whether through press, parliament, or attempting to organize an opposition.

The Church circumvents this monopoly by seeking the broadest possible limits of legitimate religious activity, and trying to influence the individual rather than clashing with the institutions.

The Vatican Council provided guidelines for these tactics, although it merely confirmed what the Polish Church had been practicing for decades. To Wojtyla, a key Vatican definition is of the Church as "at once a sign and a safeguard of the transcendence of the human person." But the Church cannot expect the first secretary of the Party to tailor his policy to Vatican pronouncements, despite his early record, never mentioned officially, as a devout Catholic. To make matters more difficult, if the Church is to safeguard the individual, it must do some trespassing on what the regime considers to be its territory.

It manages both its concern for the individual and its trespassing by carefully defining its religious prerogatives, and then stretching them. To Wojtyla, it is in the state's as well as the Church's interest to grant religious freedom, since it provides stability: "The life of the political community has as its subject the same people who exercise their religion. A profound respect for their religious freedom is one of the fundamental conditions for an orderly functioning of a state as a political community. One of the fundamental conditions for the proper development of the life of the people is the full recognition of the rights of the Church."

The stretching begins here. Its basis is the Church role as the interpreter to what is right and wrong. If Church rights are guaranteed, and the present Polish regime says they are, then priests and bishops have full freedom to speak out on the morality or immorality of government actions affecting individual Church members—which means almost every Pole. If pay cuts or price increases or the censorship of news is wrong from an individual point of view, then the Church's objection is religious, not political, and no trespassing is involved, even though the results might be the same.

This is why it is so difficult to decide what is God's and what is Caesar's. "You ask whether the Church in Poland, or anywhere else, for that matter, should have a political role, and what should its limits be," the cardinal said. "Certainly, within its proper mission. Christ commanded his disciples to go also 'ante reges et praesides.'

"The mission of the Church does not call for carrying on politics, for that would be encroaching upon the competency of the state. However, the Church has the right and the duty to participate in political matters from a moral aspect, to speak out even if it should cause her suffering and difficulty. Christians cannot be mere onlookers."

III

EAST GERMANY

Heinz and Gisela Kramer

From Poland, the train heads west. The Moscow Express crossed the border at Brest-Litovsk early that morning, and now, at 10:02, is ready to leave for East Berlin. Shades are still drawn in most windows along the long line of sleeping cars, but in one, a group of young Mongolians stare out at the activity on the siding. They seem to be athletes or a youth delegation—official travelers, like most of the other Soviet citizens on the train. Only a few Poles seem to be en route to Berlin as tourists.

In view of their memories from the past generation, it is not surprising that the Poles speak of their "border of peace" with East Germany with a certain ironical inflection. The Moscow Express reaches it at five in the afternoon, having crossed another ghostly border, the old western frontier of Poland near Poznan, in the interim. The border searches and other formalities also seem a little out of place for a frontier between fraternal members of the Socialist Commonwealth, although they are less stringent since 1971, when Poles and East Germans were given permission to travel to each other's countries without passports. Nevertheless, border guards and customs officers of both countries paw through luggage, look under seats, and even climb up to peer into the ceiling space of the railway cars, using short ladders which they then carry off the train.

Moving the Polish border westward put Berlin within 50 miles of People's Poland, and soon the Express is clattering over the switches on the outskirts of East Berlin.

If Warsaw's first impression is of a mixture of the old and new, East Berlin's is pure nineteenth century, the era of the railroad and the factory. Two rings of rail, on brick trestles or earthen embankments, have surrounded the city for nearly a hundred years. On their sidings are the red brick factories and warehouses that made prewar Berlin one of Europe's industrial centers and contribute today to make East Germany the leading producer of Soviet Europe. The faded lettering on some of the factories gives rise to images of the mustachioed entrepreneurs of the days of the Kaisers, whose machines and patents are the basis for much of East Germany's contributions to Comecon today.

The factories now carry red banners and slogans denouncing the United States or West Germany, but the aura of what West German visitors call "Opa's Deutschland" is still strong. The East Germans, of course, are doing more than simply running the old factories they inherited from their grandfathers; automated textile plants, the new steel mill at Schwarze Pumpe, and the nuclear power plants are modern and wholly the work of the postwar engineers and planners. But the basis was Opa's industrialization, his rail net, his training and apprentice systems that produced the skilled workers—this, not any supposed conversion to worker control, was the secret of East Germany's rise to the top of the Comecon production index.

The train stops at the East Station, connected, like the rest of Berlin, by a sensible network of elevated and subway trains to the rest of the city and its airports. The sensible system was disrupted in August 1961, when Communist authorities, to stop the fatal drain of refugees, put up 29.6 miles of ugly cinderblock wall through the center of the city, and the wall overshadows the East Berlin landscape, showing up unexpectedly but inevitably down the end of streets and around corners, even though there have been efforts of late to replace parts of it with chain-link fencing in the more public areas and give tourists the impression of a factory fence. It is a factory fence, however, patrolled by soldiers who have orders to shoot to kill fleeing citizens, and who do kill an average of six a year.

The Wall spoils the effect of the modernization that has replaced the rubble in the center of East Berlin. But even if the Wall didn't exist, there would be a forlorn quality about street life in East Berlin. People stay off the sidewalks. There are few good restaurants—no good restaurants, in fact. There are excellent theater and opera, good ballet, some marvelous museums—all, except those dealing with Party history, dating from the Kaisers—but there is a sense of joylessness in the city that strikes most visitors, whether on gray November days or bright summer ones. It used to seem that the ruins caused it; East Berlin was saturated with bombs during World War II.

It took until the sixties to recover, and there are still gaping vacant lots next to windowless buildings, the remnants of apartment blocks. But the planners of the new city have somehow managed to build the joylessness in, with their wide squares, handy for orchestrated demonstrations and parades, and the faceless architecture that surrounds them. Pedestrians in East Berlin never seem to be strolling for the sake of strolling, as in Bucharest or Budapest. They seem to be scurrying somewhere, to the store or home, anxious to get off the streets.

When dusk comes to East Berlin and the blue-gray squares of the television sets light up in regular patterns in the windows of the monotonous new apartment blocks, no one can tell from the street whether the figures on the screens are heroes of Socialist labor, Humphrey Bogart, or Helmut Schmidt. East Berlin viewers can choose two Communist and two Western television channels, and although there is no way to determine audience ratings, most take advantage of their ability to see both sides, either occasionally or regularly.

Heinz Kramer, a thirty-eight-year-old economist who lives near the Lenin Allee, and his thirty-six-year-old wife Gisela are among the regulars, although Heinz is a member of the Socialist Unity Party of Germany, the East German Communist Party. The fact that the Party condemns the Western stations as "an arm of NATO's ideological subversion" does not bother Heinz. He watches them because he wants to be better informed and entertained than he can be from his own network. It is an option that the other people of Soviet Europe do not have, since there is no West Hungary or West Bulgaria. Even the Western radio broadcasts in the Eastern European languages do not have the same impact as the regular TV fare from the other half of a divided nation.

This electronic window to the West creates many problems for the Party and government of the German Democratic Republic, as do all the other contacts its 17 million citizens manage to have with the West German state. Each such contact is an act against the policy of isolation that successive GDR regimes have pursued, building border fences and a wall, jamming broadcasts, and censoring mail, books, and newspapers. But there are also problems for the individual citizen. Knowing what the outside is like sometimes makes it harder to live on the inside, particularly if there are children to bring up, as is the case with Heinz Kramer and his wife.

Two simple mechanical operations are all that are needed to switch from East to West, as Heinz cheerfully shows visitors. He moves his rabbit-ear antenna from the left to the right side of his set and clicks the channel selector. There is no need to search for remote wavebands or try to get around the harsh buzzing of the jamming. If the Communists tried jamming Western TV, their own product would suffer. As it is, the TV picture from either side of the Wall comes in in perfect technical quality. Its other qualities are a different story.

A typical evening's problem on GDR television gave viewers the choice of "The Golden Stream," a Soviet documentary on oil production in the U.S.S.R., and "Harbor Story," an East German drama of life in the dockworkers' collective in which the Communist brigade members come to the aid of the heroine by teaching her erring fiancé to observe Socialist morals. That morning's schedule had offered English and Russian lessons, a look at the state of collective farming, a documentary on the

East German customs guards, the story of the Soviet airline Aeroflot, and a visit to a factory by a group that sang revolutionary songs. In the afternoon, there was more collective farming, a political commentary by Karl-Eduard von Schnitzler, sports, and an old East German film, *The Blum Affair,* a detective story of the twenties in which the crime turns out to have been perpetrated by the Fascists, a common device to make propaganda palatable. This was followed by the Free German Youth program, reporting on the progress of preparations for the next Party Congress, and the news, again with von Schnitzler, the son of an I. G. Farben director, who worked for the BBC after being taken a prisoner of war and with this unlikely background became a Party member and chief commentator after leaving West Germany for East in 1947.

On the Western side, where there is no morning TV, the afternoon had brought children's cartoons and traffic safety films, news, and *Laramie,* an American import series, but synchronized so everyone speaks German, Indians as well as cowboys; *Lassie,* and a German adventure series on diamond detectives in Africa. Nothing very stimulating, Heinz commented, but no propaganda, either.

The evening's schedule looked better, and in any case was much to be preferred to Soviet oil wells and East German docks. Heinz moved the antenna and turned the channel selector. This time, the first few clicks produced an old Bogart movie. Heinz clicked further and found the second West German channel, with a spirited discussion on youth problems, including statements by New Left panelists that would get them jailed in East Germany. He had no particular interest in either program, but suggested waiting for an interview show in which Schmidt, the West German chancellor, would discuss East-West negotiations.

Schmidt, it turned out, went into some detail on an offer to continue the negotiations in the hope of gaining some improvement in the daily lives of the East Germans and the contacts between the two halves of the country. The Party newspaper *Neues Deutschland,* which the Kramers get every morning, reported the interview two days later in one paragraph saying that Schmidt had not said anything new, but not disclosing what he had said. The East German regime, of course, could not agree with Schmidt that its citizens' lives are in need of improvement, and insists that they do not want anything to do with the West. But Heinz and Gisela Kramer and the other viewers in the GDR who can click the channels do not have to depend on the Party press and broadcasts for all their information, and need no Party permission to keep this kind of contact with the West. Or, as Heinz Kramer puts it, with the world: the West German stations bring them not only the parliamentary debates from Bonn, but the demonstrations in the United States, the fighting in Indochina, the crises in the Middle East. It is not a fully objective picture of the world, since objectivity is hard to attain, but when juxtaposed with the picture they get from the other side, it does provide a sort of rough balance.

It is impossible to say with any degree of accuracy how widespread the Western TV watching habit is on the other side of the Berlin Wall. Countless conversations with East Germans over the years in many parts of the country show that most are familiar with the variety stars, quizmasters, and news commentators from Hamburg or Mainz. Few are afraid to admit they watch the West German programs, although they are cautious in discussing what they see with other GDR citizens unless they are close friends. With Westerners, however, some even hum the advertising jingles they have memorized to show they are regular viewers.

The Kramers and the 1.1 million other East Berliners have the best viewing conditions, because the Western transmitters are in West Berlin, a few miles from them, and they need only the indoor antenna to receive them. East Germans who live close to the West German border have similar conditions. Farther inland, it is more difficult, and often rooftop antennas, their branches pointing in the telltale direction, have to be used to bring in the weak Western signals. It is not against the law to watch Western TV, but many pressures are used to discourage the practice.

The state encourages teachers to question children on their favorite programs in order to find out which families watch the Western stations. Those in the lower grades unhesitatingly answer *"Flipper"* and *"Bonanza"* unless they are coached by their parents to say that they have been tuned to the Communist Youth show. The Kramer children, Erich, eight, and Brigitta, seven, do not have to lie to the teacher because they do not know there is such a thing as Western TV. Their parents switch Westward only when the children are out playing or in bed. Often they come home and demand to be allowed to watch a popular cartoon program or the Saturday night quiz from West Germany, because all their friends are doing so. Heinz and Gisela have to tell them that their set does not get these programs, and prove it by switching to the two local channels, where the chances are good there will be factory scenes or von Schnitzler. But soon the children will be old enough to work the knobs for themselves, although still too young to understand political subtleties.

The regime has launched campaigns from time to time to enforce orthodox viewing practices. Teams of activists from the Free German Youth used to go around from building to building ripping down the so-called oxhead antennas, which were capable of bringing in the West German telecasts. But since this cut off all television reception for the residents of the buildings singled out, citizen protests stopped the campaign. There have also been recurrent warnings that although individual viewing is not a crime, inviting others over to watch the Western programs, or discussing them with others later, constitutes "spreading antistate propaganda" and is illegal.

THE PROBLEM OF ISOLATION

Television makes it difficult for the GDR to maintain a complete policy of isolation, but there are also other factors that the East German regime finds hard to control. The crowning act of isolationism was the construction of the Berlin Wall in 1961. It returned international relations to the state of development of the Middle Ages, when walled city-states and xenophobia were accepted as normal reactions of governments. But the Wall was not wholly successful. Its success in keeping East Germans inside their country, the primary purpose for which it was built, has been considerable: it cut the number of escapes from 4,000 a week in 1961 to about 1,200 a year in recent years. But its secondary purpose was to keep Westerners and Western influence out, and in that it failed.

West German radio broadcasts are widely heard in East Germany, despite energetic jamming efforts. Western businessmen were admitted into East Germany in increasing numbers in the decade of isolation after the construction of the Wall. But the greatest change of all was the 1972 treaty between the two German states and the four-power agreement the same year regulating the status of Berlin. The treaty, which set out the conditions for the two states to "develop normal good neighborly relations with one another on the basis of equality," provided for the exchange of missions, cooperation in trade, science, and technology, renunciation of force, and a readiness, "in the course of normalizing their relations, to regulate practical and humanitarian questions." The Berlin agreement eased access to the Western sectors of the city by eliminating the East German border checks for travelers and, for the first time since the Wall went up, gave West Berliners the right to visit relatives in East Berlin.

The effect of the two agreements was dramatic. In 1972 the visits quadrupled: nearly 7 million West Germans and West Berliners visited East Germany, the highest total by far in two decades. The annual totals for Westward travel are still only about 220,000—200,000 business and official visitors, more than half of them truck drivers and barge and train crews, 10,000 tourists, most of them pensioners allowed to travel because their defection would represent a gain for the GDR's finances, and about 10,000 refugees, most of whom escape by less dramatic means than climbing the Wall or border fences.

The figures show that while the GDR regime has been quite successful in shutting its citizens inside its fortified borders, it is impossible for a modern state in the middle of Europe to return completely to the Middle

Ages, no matter how much its authorities might want to. For with the Wall, the regime had hoped to be able to create a contented population through a combination of increasing the standard of living and decreasing the contacts with the West.

As long as East Germans compared their lives only with those of the other East Europeans, it was easy to convince them. As living standards rose, travel—restricted, of course, to the Soviet Bloc—increased, and families like the Kramers have had ample opportunity to look at life in Czechoslovakia, Hungary, Bulgaria, and Romania, those being the routes to the resorts on the Black Sea. They discover that their salaries are usually about double what people in those countries earn, that their apartments are roomier and more modern, and that prices are not much higher in the GDR, and indeed lower for many manufactured goods.

After two weeks of having to boil milk, eat what to them seems greasy and unpalatable food, and line up for bathroom and toilet facilities that fall far below German standards of cleanliness, the GDR tourists are glad to see their own borders and the signs of welcome to the "German Socialist Fatherland."

But, as the Kramers discovered after their last trip to the "Friendship" holiday camp in Bulgaria, this mood of contentment can easily be shattered back in the Fatherland. The TV ads from West Germany show families who seem no different from the Kramers buying boats and power lawn mowers, the interview programs show West Germans complaining about their government, letters arrive from Gisela's aunt in Dortmund announcing plans to travel to Italy again, and an occasional visitor arrives in East Berlin to gossip—and then leave.

"We realize then," Heinz says, "that we don't have it so good. We come back from Bulgaria laughing about the pigs in the highways, and proud to drive on our good German autobahns, but when you think about it, we belong to the side of the world with the Bulgarians."

So many other East Germans came to realize this that the policy of happiness in isolation could not be made to work. It has not been abandoned; the Party continues to make pronouncements on how one world, the imperialist, ends at the GDR borders, where another, the Socialist, begins, and that the two German states have nothing in common.

But with the rush of contacts that resulted from the 1972 treaty, a new policy had to be grafted on to the old. It acknowledges the rivalry of the West and takes for granted that East Germans are exposed to Western influences, but tries to convince them that their life is not only different but better. It does this through an elaborately constructed rationalization of the difference in living standards, and through proclaiming the creation of a Socialist New Man in the GDR.

East German living standards, the regime says in countless articles, Party meetings, and broadcasts, are far higher than those in the neighboring Communist countries (and here, since they are entering dangerous ground, particularly in regard to the Soviet Union, the point is made by inference). But that is not all. They are equal, or superior, to those in West Germany. It is true that wages in the West seem to be higher; average pay for industrial and construction workers, for example, is 40 percent more in West Germany. There are hidden benefits, however, in the GDR that more than make up the difference. The GDR worker is not threatened with being fired, since there is full employment; yet in the Ruhr there are strikes, plant shutdowns, and layoffs. Strikes in the GDR are illegal, since it is impossible to strike against yourself, the citizen-owner of the means of production. The argument is weakened somewhat by the stable conditions in West Germany.

But it is strengthened by a list of the benefits of East German subsidy policies, from nickel streetcar fares to low rents that cost an average family 3.5 percent of its income, compared to 12 percent in the West. The list also contains free medical care, kindergartens and day nurseries, cheap opera tickets, cheap or free vacation homes and camps. The cost of all these concessions is then totaled up to make the monthly incomes in East and West nearly equal. The fact that the streetcars are old and usually crowded, the housing is often overpriced even at such low rents, and the kindergartens too few to take more than half the children eligible does not go into this argument, nor does the fact that the East Germans have no control over how their pay supplements are being spent.

The final part of the argument deals with political representation. The freedom of speech that GDR viewers think they see on programs coming from the West, they are told—all the political parties, the debates, the criticism—really is part of an elaborate charade, because under capitalism the actual controls are pulled by the monopolists and militarists.

In the GDR this is not supposed to be the case: true democracy is possible because of heightened socialist consciousness. There is not only prosperity in the GDR, there is a new society, and a new man. In films, novels, and plays, the lesson is repeated—that "we" must replace the "I." When the government congratulates people for getting to be one hundred years old, the standard text runs: "Best wishes for health, good luck, and for further lovely years in our socialist community." "Our socialist property" is the favorite label for the tools and products of the state enterprises, a term usually used to protest their being wasted, destroyed, or stolen; "Our New Music" the name of a record series. Nowhere in the West outside the kindergartens is there so much teaching of the community spirit and the rules of togetherness, and indeed, much of the East German effort seems at the kindergarten level. To protect "our socialist health," a short film instructs movie patrons not to go outside unless they are warmly dressed, and thinly clad actors go through the motions of catching cold to prove the point. Front-page cartoons in *Neues Deutschland* instruct workers not to leave messy workbenches;

those with colds are told not to shake hands with those without. Through it all, there is a streak of genuine idealism, particularly as expressed by the youth who go out and cut grass, plant flowers, and dig ditches in their spare time, convinced that they are thus free from the contradictions of capitalist selfishness.

But one great contradiction occurs in the two aims of the policy: in order to live the good life materially in East Germany, the citizen must keep, or acquire, all the acquisitive qualities of petit-bourgeois thinking. He or she must be more of a hustler than a utopian socialist who is ready to share and work together. Thus the two sides of the main social policy in East Germany are mutually destructive. Keeping up with the West Germans requires not only adopting their material-oriented mentality but surpassing it.

A DAY IN THE LIFE

A day in the life of Heinz and Gisela Kramer shows the disproportionate part the pursuit of material things plays in GDR society. Heinz, slight, dark blond, with steel-rimmed glasses of the unfashionable kind, does not look the part of a wheeler-dealer. But he frequently engages in illegal private speculation, as the law would term it if he were caught, and almost every day he and Gisela (and, lately, their children) cheerfully lie and cheat in the course of normal retail transactions or civic business.

Once or twice a month, Heinz loads up the trunk of the black Volga sedan he uses on company business and leaves East Berlin for meetings in the industrial centers of the GDR. As a senior economist for a chemical combine, he works most of the time at a desk in downtown Berlin, but there is often a need for on-site consultations, particularly if plan fulfillment is not going well or if there are bottlenecks in supply or distribution. Heinz puts enterprise records, plan figures, and other working material in the trunk of the Soviet-made sedan, but he also loads in his own contribution to the alleviation of supply bottlenecks. It varies with the pattern of shortages in the GDR, but on this particular morning it was four family-size packages of Spree, the new East German detergent. It can be bought in limited quantities in Berlin, but in the provinces it cannot be had. In Karl-Marx-Stadt, on the other hand, Heinz can get Dega, the deodorant spray, for the state-set price of $1.50 a can, if he buys some hard-to-sell items as a kind of premium. Another scarce item in Berlin is impregnated kindling for the coal stoves that heat many homes. It is particularly desirable because of the chronic coal shortage and the need to stretch out supplies. Heinz sells one product and buys the other. By nightfall, the Volga trunk will have both Dega and kindling.

An interesting sidelight on the transaction is the fact that both the detergent and the deodorant spray were produced by GDR factories in unacknowledged response to the products offered in the commercials on West German television. East German women, of course, have always had some sort of soap, and of late, deodorant. But the exaggerated claims of the Western admen made them discontented with what they had. If a popular West German detergent sweeps through your washing machine like a white whirlwind, or if another makes the Hausfrau's wash glow like fresh snow, then the East German women want their own stores to stock similar wonder products. The same goes for the cosmetics that the ads show making the women of Frankfurt and Stuttgart so desirable for slim, wealthy-looking young men. The irony of the situation is that the East German women apparently tend to take the Western TV claims at face value, and no matter how much the GDR's chemists improve the local detergents or blend sexier scents into the cosmetics, their customers are bound to be disappointed. But at least the Western competition does put some new products on East German shelves. It takes high skills, however, to get them from there into the home.

Gisela Kramer, a petite brunette, is a worthy partner for Heinz in the daily acquisition game. Like any professional, she prepares well ahead of time. The private communications network that exists in all East German plants and offices had tipped her the previous afternoon on what was available. Gisela works as a secretary for an electronics company, and there had been a lively discussion in the office about the mysterious unlabeled cans of Schmalzfleisch, a kind of fatty boiled pork that Germans in East and West like to spread on their breakfast bread. The Schmalzfleisch had suddenly appeared in the butcher shops, under the counters, of course, but the word spread quickly through the network.

Gisela had been shopping in the same state store since her marriage nearly ten years before, and thus was privileged to ask for two cans of Schmalzfleisch. Then she sent little Brigitta for a third can. She had been careful not to have the clerks at the store connect her daughter with her. The Kramers enjoyed the Schmalzfleisch, but its identity remained a mystery. The secretaries' network had three theories: It was an import from West Germany, with the label removed for political reasons; it was an import from Communist China, with the label removed for a different set of political reasons; or finally, it was surplus from the East German National Volksarmee, which Gisela believes gets much better food than civilians do and has plenty to spare.

Her next step was to establish relations at another state store in the next neighborhood because of the Kramers' plans to move. The process consists of being pleasant, buying a certain number of unwanted goods (this time it was a cheap scrub brush from a bin of thousands of them), and in general becoming known as a regular. The family move had been planned for eight years, ever since Heinz and Gisela got on the waiting list of a cooperative. At that time, the new neighborhood did not exist. It was a wasteland of bombed buildings, vacant lots, and piles of rubble.

Now the cream stucco boxes of apartment buildings have replaced the bombscape. But somehow, the desolation remains. New empty spaces replace the old ones: overdimensional squares, pompous broad boulevards, and dreary, treeless little parks.

But the Kramers have dreamed and talked for years about becoming part of this new neighborhood. The apartment they moved into after their marriage is in one of the massive gray stone turn-of-the-century buildings that survived the bombing intact, even to the carved stone plaque beside the front door that expresses in old German lettering a sentiment akin to "A man's home is his castle." After the war, however, this was hardly applicable, as the double and triple nameplates next to every apartment door show. The Kramers first had a single room, then became entitled to three after the children were born. But for five years they shared both kitchen and bath with the couple in the other half of the apartment, and even though the other couple has now financed its own little hotplate kitchen, they still share the bath.

The doubling up and the long wait for the new apartment both result from the low priority that the GDR government gives housing construction. It is neglect compounded: the housing plan figures are set low to permit a maximum use of resources in building factories and office buildings, and then the plans are frequently not fulfilled. Nearly half the apartments in West Germany were built after the war; in East Germany, fewer than 20 percent. For a decade, instead of trying to make up the difference, GDR planners built a decreasing number of apartments and an increasing number of factories. There were 92,000 dwelling units built in 1961, 76,000 in 1963, and only 60,000 in the 1970 plan, which was not fulfilled by an undisclosed number of units. As a result, state housing became almost impossible to find, and even a crash program to build half a million units in the current five-year plan will not solve the problem. The only hope for most couples is to join a cooperative, usually connected with one of the big enterprises, put up capital, and wait.

The Kramers invested $1,500 in the cooperative for their new three rooms plus kitchen and bath, and will pay $35 monthly rent, both easily within their budget and low compared to West Germany. But, as Gisela notes, so are the standards of the new apartments. She reported after visiting a friend in one of the raw new blocks that their conversation was interrupted by the crashing of water through the plastic drain pipes that go through the living room and come to life every time anyone in the five stories above flushes a toilet. There is one swivel showerhead fixture that serves both bathtub and washbasin, and, as in most East German homes, there are only little islands of heat: the slow-burning tile stove in the living room, with a side sticking through the wall to the children's room, a tiny gas heater in the bathroom that is turned on when the room is in use, and only feather puffs to keep the icy master bedroom warm.

But it is an improvement over the old place, which despite its carved oak doors and much-waxed parquet floors has facilities that are more primitive and besides do not work much of the time. The most important thing to the Kramers is the removal of the double nameplate next to their doorbell, which has stood for hundreds of hours of waiting outside the bathroom, or awkward scenes in the kitchen over broken dishes and cleanliness.

In leaving community life for privacy, the Kramers must conform to one last rule of socialist togetherness. They are required to perform a certain number of hours of "socialist reconstruction work," which means self-help in their building or another one, planting lawns, carrying bricks, or, if they are qualified, electrician's or carpenter's work. Their total was seven hundred hours. But Heinz was able to plead a bad back and get permission to buy his way out at the rate of about a dollar an hour, thus providing some moonlighting workmen with extra income and himself with some more petit-bourgeois mentality.

Heinz sees no contradiction between his membership in the Socialist Unity Party and his and his wife's bootlegging activities. His rationalizations are these: he does not make money from his private supply system, and he actually strengthens the state distribution network by getting Spree to the provinces and provincial products to Berlin. The fact that he bought more than his share of Spree was perhaps wrong, but he did not keep it. As far as the socialist community goes, Heinz is of the opinion that he does more than his share of attending meetings on the Lenin or Engels anniversaries, contributing to buy an ambulance for North Vietnam, or doing economic ghostwriting for his plant Party chairman.

"To provide for my family, that's the private sphere," he says. "I suppose we are acquisitive here in the GDR, even more than the Germans in the West are. But they have so much; they don't need to be always on the lookout for a line to stand in or to have to pass the word along when there's something in the stores."

Heinz has further rationalizations. One is that the system of consumer alerting is a form of community sharing, as is helping someone get hold of scarce goods. When he or Gisela gets into a line—which they usually do without bothering to see what is being offered—they try to get two or more of whatever it is. Then, if they need only one, they can share with friends or relatives. In this way, Heinz helped his brother build a weekend house on the outskirts of Potsdam, with precast concrete sections diverted from the state housing program through bribery, cement bought by the bag in villages by having several different people—including a stranger—stand in line, and doors and windows bought from workers in a lumber plant. "They probably stole them," Heinz admits. "But that's not our business."

He also admits that his help in the weekend house was not entirely altruistic. (He even paid half the $250 fine that his brother had to pay for building on nature preserve land. It is cheaper to pay the fine and be able to get a long lease on the land at 25¢ a square yard than to buy real building land.) Heinz, Gisela, and the children will begin sharing the little house on alternate weekends as soon as it is finished.

The case of the Trabant is also not entirely above board. The Trabant is the Volkswagen of East Germany, but it is a sorry little car, with a plastic body that shatters when nudged slightly in traffic and is rumored —Heinz denies this—to be very tasty for rats, so much so that Trabant fenders are said to be under constant attack in the port city of Rostock, where the rat problem is particularly severe. It is powered by a 23-horsepower motorcycle engine, which, when wound up, will propel it at 60 miles an hour, but the pace cannot be continued for long, or the motor will burn out. While it is going at this rate, it consumes gas at the rate of 24 miles to the gallon, an unheard-of luxury in Eastern Europe.

The one thing one can say about the Trabant, however, is that practically everybody in East Germany wants one, and the export market, too, will absorb all it can get—in Hungary and Bulgaria, of course, not in the West. East Germans get a Trabant by signing up on a waiting list. After three or four years—the time depends on supply and demand—they pay half the $2,000 price. After another three years or so, with regular payments in between, the Trabant is delivered, and the proud owner, having paid more than the West German does for his better-built Volkswagen, puts it under its canvas cover and saves it for Sunday drives and vacation trips to the neighboring Socialist states. Heinz never drives his to work; the cost of gas works out to much more than the subsidized streetcar fares.

The Kramer Trabant, however, doesn't belong to them, but to a friend of Heinz's in the enterprise, a man who has never ridden in it. This came about in the following way. Jurgen, the friend, put his name on the list. Heinz felt he could afford to sign up only after Gisela had gone back to work after the children were born. At that rate, there would have been no Trabant for a decade under waiting list times then current. Jurgen was called in to pay his thousand dollars, but could not raise the money. There was no way he could sell his share to Heinz, or assign Heinz his place in line, and it was illegal to get the car and then turn around and sell it. This would be private speculation for profit. Any car paid for but not claimed must be sold back to the state.

Jurgen and Heinz made a private written agreement that the Kramers would put up the money, Jurgen would take possession of the car, but the Kramers would drive it as their own. The agreement has no legal status, although thousands of them have been made. The Kramers do not worry that Jurgen would ever claim the car as his own. But there is one clause in their agreement that does bother them some. This is the lotto provision. Jurgen regularly puts his five marks on the government's weekly lotto, and hopes, with the optimism of those with no other chance for riches in their lives, to hit some week and take the prize of $5,000. If he does, the agreement gives him the right to buy his car back at a weekend's notice.

The last chapter in the Trabant story was Gisela's decision to put her own name down for the next Trabant. (Heinz cannot risk putting his own name down; there might be questions about the car he drives.) If she does that in 1977, as planned, and the family makes its half-payment in 1979, then by 1982 it may have a car of its own. In the meantime, the current Trabant will serve the Kramers, unless Jurgen wins in the lotto.

Heinz's final justifications for the hustler's life have the soundest basis. They come from the wide reading he has done in the Party press and in books on history and economics.

"Germany lost the war," Heinz says. "The Russians made terrible sacrifices, lost millions of people, civilians, soldiers, and children. Whole cities were wiped out, whole industrial areas. When the Russians arrived in Germany, it was natural that they should want to be repaid for this. But the West Germans mostly got out of this repayment. They did give up a few reparations for a while, but then the West stopped it.

"Yet this debt belongs to West Germany as well as to us. The trouble is that it fell on our shoulders. But why should we pay it all? I was a child when the war ended. My father was a good Social Democrat. So if I do my work, and in my own time attend to the comfort of my family, that's not unreasonable."

Heinz draws a distinction between those who use their positions and neglect their work in the pursuit of the necessities or luxuries of life and those who devote their own time to it. He refers often to the great scandals of plan failure or mismanagement, and considers much of the trouble to be the sum of all the neglect of everyone involved in socialist construction, from the hodcarriers to the chief engineers, because they are so busy plotting ways to get ahead as individuals—whether to the head of a line for Schmalzfleisch or to a new title and position.

THE CHILDREN

Gisela Kramer, whose $100 monthly secretarial pay contributes a third of the family income, after deductions for the day care for the children, is not as certain as her husband about the justification for the double standards she feels they maintain. Unlike Heinz, she is not a Party member, since she did not need membership to get ahead in her job as he did, and has successfully resisted even the German-Soviet friendship society. But it is not the issue of opportunism that divides them. The word has no real meaning in East German society as far as joining or agreeing to something that one does not believe in. Heinz does not have any second thoughts about his Party membership or the resolutions he signs, although he would do neither of free choice. But in a country where he feels everyone has acted on opportunistic grounds, from Party chief Erich Honecker on down, he does not feel he should single himself out for any particular blame.

The difference in outlook, Gisela explains, comes from her role in raising the children. She must bring them up to tell the truth, be good citizens, obey the authorities, observe a moral code, and yet send them out to stand in line at the bakery on a Sunday morning for fresh rolls when she has already bought the family's quota, because extra rolls are needed for a visitor, and what is worse, as had happened a few weeks earlier, to have Erich caught in the deception, identified as a member of the family, ejected from the bakery in full view of the others in line, and then come home tearfully to demand that she explain it.

There is a great body of law and opinion in the GDR to guide Gisela in the task of raising her children, and frequent meetings with teachers and discussion groups to talk about it, but in none of this are any answers offered to these everyday problems of socialist morality. In East Germany, Gisela is often reminded, raising children is not a private matter, but part of the building of socialism. GDR family law says, in fact, that there are countless and close connections between the two.

"The family," the law says, "is the smallest cell of society. . . . New and characteristic for our society is the fact that the family basically has the same wishes, goals, and interests as society, and vice versa. . . . The family has its firm place inside society; it is not something counter to society." Family ideology comes straight from Marx, who taught that the ownership of the means of production was reflected in family as in other human relationships; in other words, those living under capitalism would have sexual and parental behavioral patterns ordained by capitalism, and when capitalism was swept away by socialism, the patterns would change.

But now Socialism is supposed to have arrived, and Marx has nothing relevant to say about Heinz and Gisela's problem with the two children: how to reconcile the realities of everyday life with their own private thoughts and feelings about the system in which they live.

Erich came home one afternoon with a small collection of cards of soccer players, which European children collect as Americans do baseball cards. He was particularly pleased with some cards he said were "Western." Since all the soccer stars on the cards were international, men like the Brazilian Pele, there was no East or West identification on them.

But Erich knew the Western ones were the prizes of his collection. Why? Because they were better printed, had brighter colors. But how did he know that that was from the West? And why not North and South, instead of East and West? Did he have any Northern cards? His answer was firm. They were from the West because they were better, just like the felt-tipped pens one of his schoolmates got in the mail from his grandmother in West Germany.

It is relatively easy to explain away the soccer cards or pens. The Party offers guidelines in its own excuses for economic failures—we are using our resources for more important things; someday ours will be better than theirs. But when the children's questions move from economics to politics, the answers are harder.

Gisela spent every weekend one spring helping her children gather waste paper and old bottles for the Lenin Year. That summer, she helped them make wooden letter openers to sell at the bazaar for the children of Vietnam, and in the fall she clipped pictures of Angela Davis from newspapers and magazines for a school exhibit.

Her behavior was exactly that of an American matron helping out with Girl Scout projects, even to using the family car to haul the bales of newspapers. But there is one important difference. Neither Gisela nor Heinz believes what they read about Vietnam, the importance of Lenin in present-day life, or the persecution of Miss Davis and other political opponents of the United States. Part of their skepticism is the natural resistance of intelligent people to the barrages of propaganda they live under, part is doubtless a result of their exposure to Western news media, and part is what the regime would call the remnants of petit-bourgeois mentality.

Gisela's solution to the problem has been to adopt the portions of the official line that she can accept as her own and stress that in discussing the issues with the children. Like many Girl Scout mothers, she does oppose the fighting in Southeast Asia and any other war, and thus, when the children bring up the subject she can talk with complete sincerity about the desirability of peace everywhere. She does not believe *Neues Deutschland's* contention that the Americans are many times worse than the Nazis, but the children have only vague ideas of who the Americans or the Nazis are, so this requires no explanation. Lenin was a great man; this takes care of the Lenin Year. No one should be persecuted for the color of his or her skin or what he or she believes; this takes care of political prisoners and racism.

The Kramers' real problem will come when the children are old enough to ask more penetrating questions, yet too young to understand all of the reasoning behind the answers or lack of them. It is a problem that every family in a totalitarian society must face, and Party agitprop booklets are no help. Heinz's older brother in Dresden has teenage sons who had often visited Prague—a day trip for them—during the 1968 liberalization and have been uncomfortable questioners since then. The Kramers will face the issue when it comes up, hoping in the meantime that a decade of progress in the GDR will make the answers easier. "We want to pass our values down to them," Gisela says, "and yet we don't want them to grow up to be rebels, or skeptics about the system. They will have to live in it."

The conflict here is that the system is socialist, and the Kramers' values, despite the gold Party pin in Heinz's lapel, are bourgeois. If the Kramers were suddenly transplanted to Munich or Düsseldorf, there would be no perceptible change in their attitudes toward making and spending money, toward their family, their government, or their world. Heinz would only be relieved of his long evening Party meetings and anti-Fascist petition signing. But they would probably be replaced by sales conventions and churchgoing.

THE NEW SOCIALIST MAN

If the Kramers are not much different from their counterparts in West Germany, they are also quite typical for the GDR. The fact that the regime proclaims the existence of a new type of Socialist citizen, or family, or society, does not mean that it exists. This makes it easier to solve the conflict between practiced and professed beliefs in the GDR. The Kramers know that they are not alone in their attitudes.

This is not to say that the whole twenty-five-year effort of propaganda, education, and persuasion has been wasted. Conversations with East Germans, particularly those of the generation which grew up under Communism, show a strong awareness of the ideology, and in particular its humanist aspects. It is hardly surprising that this should be so, since East German children are exposed to what is called socialist upbringing at an early age—25 percent are in nurseries before the age of three, and nearly half of the first to fourth graders spend all day in school and day care centers. The figures would be higher if more facilities were available, because the GDR has the highest percentage of working women in the developed world—48.7 percent of its work force. This state of affairs brings the regime three-way benefits. It increases family incomes (like the Kramers' by a third); it provides the production force to keep a country as small as the GDR in the ranks of the ten top industrial nations, and it permits what the GDR family law describes as "education toward socialistic attitudes toward work, to observance of the rules of socialist cooperative living, to solidarity, and to socialist patriotism and internationalism."

But as the young GDR citizens grow older, their socialism seems to weaken. Part of the reason is the need, already discussed, for sharp acquisitive instincts to survive in the shortage society, and the television window and other Western contact. A further reason is the general suspicion that no one else in East Germany is living the prescribed life of egalitarianism. Gisela, informed by her network of the arrival of children's ski jackets in the Lenin Allee clothing store, hurried to the scene, but she was too late—there were none even under the counter or in the back room. In the next few days, she noted that the daughters of the neighborhood Party secretary, the restaurant manager, and one of the clerks at the local shoe store were wearing the bright new jackets at the playground. It was obvious that there had been a higher-level exchange of favors than she had been privy to. The Party official's inventory of favors is practically unlimited, from housing to recommendations for jobs, prizes, and promotions. She suspects that the restaurant manager exchanged Saturday night or even New Year's Eve reservations for his daughter's jacket. The shoe store man, she guesses, traded a pair or so of his scarce imports from Czechoslovakia—perhaps even from Italy.

If such privileged positions are known for a fact to exist on the neighborhood level, it can be imagined what the rumor network says about the men at the top. The days of the fenced-off and guarded villa area in the Pankow section of East Berlin are over, and the *payoks,* the Soviet-distributed packages of hard-to-get food and drink for Communist officials, are no longer necessary. If the East Germans were able to compare their leaders' style of life with that of other dictators, those in Latin America, for example, they would find it quite modest. But they do not have the opportunity; they see only the curtained Chaika limousines sweeping by, or occasionally watch arrivals for diplomatic receptions, not realizing that the fare inside is on the level of a middle-class country club in the United States.

The private lives of the officials are related mostly through rumors—little appears in the official press, although there are, from time to time, homey little articles about Erich and Margot Honecker, who are depicted as hard-working and simple-living. This, according to former aides who have fled to the West, is an accurate account. The rumors, of course, will have nothing of such modesty. Honecker, for example, is said to have well-developed bourgeois tastes, including a hunting lodge that could stand comparison to Hermann Göring's. TV commentator von Schnitzler, it is said, demanded a weekend house on short notice and, by paying construction workers an unheard-of $6 an hour, had it built in a week.

Whether these stories are true or not is not important; they are repeated so often in East Germany that they are accepted as truth. And this, in turn, affects the attitude of the new Socialist men or women when they are deciding whether or not to divert something from the Socialist property stockpile to their own personal use. If the new Socialist man does not exist at the top, where he has all the advantages the Party can offer, from ideological training at the Lenin Institute in Moscow to the example of the Soviet comrades he associates with, why should he exist at the bottom?

The new man—or woman—emerging in East Germany is, in fact, cut on a completely different pattern. The rewards are pay and privilege, not equality. When the Kramers go to the Black Sea, for example, they are allowed to take $15 a day out of the country in East German marks. The workers who make the same trip are allowed only $3. All of the discussions about production and plan fulfillment in the Party press feature the pictures and rewritten opinions of the blue-collar workers. But it is clear that the real payoffs are directed toward those in the background in the white collars.

East Germany is in the front rank with the development of this new kind of citizen because it is in the front rank of Bloc industrial countries. But the new kind of citizen is being equipped with tastes, habits, and ambitions that are exactly the opposite of those the regime wants him to develop. It cannot take away his pay and privileges, his Trabant and his summer cottage, without putting the brakes on technological progress. Honecker's speeches praise both the development of socialist consciousness and the industrial achievements of the nation, but the emphasis is on the latter. And every time there is a new industrial success, a new combine opens, or a new class of engineers graduates from Humboldt University in East Berlin or Karl Marx in Leipzig, more hundreds of members join the bourgeoisie.

Marx did not foresee a difference in Communist Party members as wide as those between the East German driving to the Black Sea with his new white house trailer and the North Vietnamese working in his rice paddy. When the representatives of these two kinds of Communism get together at international meetings, it is not surprising that they disagree. But states like East Germany do not concern themselves with the fate of the revolution in the rice paddies, except to take up collections and look for West Germans in the American armies.

THE ECONOMIC BASE

As the country grows more prosperous, it is able to reward those responsible, and this in turn is a spur to greater efforts. The results thus far seem impressive. They are emblazoned on banners, spit out of computers for the public to read at exhibitions, and repeated in the schoolmasterly tones of the GDR media: with only half of 1 percent of the world's population, the East Germans produce 2.2 percent of the total industrial production. Incomes have trebled since 1950; industrial output more than quadrupled. The East German mark can still be bought for black-market rates at half the official rate in West Berlin, but it is black-marketed the other way in the Bloc. Poles who live near the border pay double for East marks to spend in the well-stocked stores of Frankfurt on the Oder for goods they must smuggle back into Poland because of a short circuit in Socialist good neighborliness.

What is more, the GDR has managed to work its way to prosperity without the help of its occupying power, unlike the West Germans, and indeed often against it, as Heinz Kramer noted: "When Frankfurt's factories were being rebuilt by the Americans under the Marshall Plan, Chemnitz's were being dismantled and carried off by the Russians under the Potsdam agreement. They didn't even leave us the name." (Chemnitz is now called Karl-Marx-Stadt.)

More eloquent than all the statistics was an East Berlin exhibit on the nation's postwar reconstruction, from the bombed factories of the forties to the automation of the seventies. Workmen had to truck in several cubic yards of rubble and rusty, twisted girders to show the 1945 conditions. A few years ago, their efforts would have been concentrated on hiding real rubble with billboards and banners. As East German parents tugged their children past the rubble display, they pointed with pride to the slogan of the early occupation years: "First work harder, then live better." It is one of the few promises made by their government that has come true.

The pride can also be seen in the parades and demonstrations on the Unter den Linden and Marx-Engels Platz, as tens of thousands of blue- and red-jacketed Free German Youth march by, their faces shiny with sweat and happiness. Older people along the curbs frequently note that they have seen the same expressions and much the same uniforms a long time ago, in the thirties. There are other disturbing parallels to the Hitler Youth: the mass swearing of oaths, the torchlight ceremonies, the para- military training. It is easy to imagine that the regime has succeeded too well in restoring the old German virtues. The officially nurtured pa- triotism does indeed go far beyond what one encounters in Hungary, Czechoslovakia, or other Bloc states. The difference is the result of a deliberate policy.

"At the end of the war, to be frank, none of us thought the East Germans would make it," a Soviet official with long experience in the GDR remarked one evening in the late stages of a cocktail party. "They had an enormous inferiority complex, based on two factors. First, they took on themselves the guilt for all the terrible war crimes. And then, they were so small and weak compared to the West Germans."

To cure the inferiority complex, the Soviets began building up the East German state, psychologically and physically, after an early period of unparalleled exploitation that ended at about the time of Stalin's death. The new leaders in Moscow were realistic enough to realize that a strong and confident GDR would be a counterweight to West Germany and a valuable business partner as well. East Germans were not sur- prised to find their hard work being rewarded, but many were a little puzzled over being praised again for the nationalism for which they had only recently been punished. The insertion of the word "socialist" before fatherland seemed to solve the contradiction for the Soviets, if not the East Germans.

The policy worked. As the GDR economy grew, so did trade with the Soviet Union, and for more than a decade East Germany has been the U.S.S.R.'s biggest trading partner. It has also become a reasonably sturdy rival to the Bonn government, even though the old inferiority feelings have never been overcome; a sign that greets visitors at the border crossing from Bavaria proclaims: "Millions respect us."

The Soviets have no illusions about the thinness of the veneer of Communism that they have applied on the surface of East German society. The same Soviet official who was reminiscing about the GDR inferiority complex considers the greatest problem for the future the rooting out of bourgeois tendencies. In this view, the Soviets made a basic mistake in their evaluation of the attraction of Socialism and the staying power of the old way of thinking.

"We thought that we had smashed the bourgeoisie by removing the key men from public life and the economy," he said. "They were hopelessly compromised as a class. In none of the countries were they free from the taint of collaboration; in Germany, in particular, they were completely identified with the Fascists."

The purges and trials of the forties, which reached even into the ranks of the Party leaderships, were aimed at rooting out these remnants of the wrong class mentality. But in the process, the ordinary people were neglected.

"It was planned so that these examples would show them how discredited the bourgeoisie was and our own example would point the way for them," the official continued. "But we underestimated the attraction that middle-class ways of thinking and living have for great numbers of people in this part of Europe, above all in Germany. Even if the parents formally espouse the new ideas of class, we find the old ideas cropping up in their children, which shows that there has been no change in what goes on in the home."

BEHIND THE WALL

Since even good East German Communists can be suspected of being middle class under the skin, the Soviet Union needs a large standing army on hand to protect Socialism. From Stralsund in the north to Dresden in the south, the quarter-million men of the Red army are a familiar part of the scenery. Convoys travel the autobahns, tanks tear up fields, and balalaika music goes out on the airwaves for the occupation troops. In the cities and towns, the purple-trousered Soviet officers take their families shopping or attend gravely polite meetings of the local friendship societies. Military buses haul selected troops to town for dances, but otherwise contact is minimal.

In addition to this force, there is the East German army of 125,000 men, and behind it stands another army of security agents, police, and informers to sniff out the beginnings of dissent in the Party, factories, or universities.

The Berlin Wall is the best symbol of how little the GDR and Soviet leaders trust the East German citizen. The East German, of course, earned this distrust by disappearing over the border at a rate that puts all previous refugee movements in the shadow—more than 3 million between the end of the war and the construction of the Wall. The official explanation when the Wall went up was that it was necessary to prevent "open attack on the GDR, civil war, and open military provocation."

But in private conversations, East German officials now feel confident enough to discuss the Wall in realistic terms: as a necessary sacrifice, even including the 150 persons killed since 1961 trying to flee to West Berlin or West Germany. In their view, the loss of prestige and lives is more than balanced by the end of the refugee drain.

"Building socialism is no picnic," a Party veteran in the foreign office said. "Not everyone can understand and accept the sacrifices. Yet we could not let them go, could not permit the economy to be bled to death. The Wall had to be built to keep these people from leaving the country, and will be necessary until this time of transition is over."

No one in official East Berlin is willing to say how long this transition period will be. Nor can anyone place a time limit on the "temporary" stationing of Soviet troops in the GDR, or predict when the threat of Western spies and saboteurs will be considered to have subsided to the point at which the huge security apparatus can be reduced in strength and influence. Until the transition is over, however, GDR citizens will have to put up with the burdens of the system, from the arrogance of the traffic cops who know they have the apparatus of a police state behind them to the real and constant dangers to those who speak their minds.

The greatest restriction of all for the average citizen is the refusal of the right to travel. Like other people who live in places dominated by industry and ugliness, the East Germans long for faraway places. A cabaret program of the Leipzig Worker and Amateur Theater reflected this longing. Conceived as a series of sharp commentaries on the foibles of the West, it turned out to be a travelogue, with nearly every song or skit set in the Alps, the Riviera, or the other distant places the East Germans have only read about or seen on calendars.

It used to be that travel to the Communist countries, at least, was easy, but of late that, too, has fallen victim to political considerations and the shortage economy. Politics cut off Czechoslovakia as a vacationland for East Germans during the more dangerous phases of the Prague Spring, but after the GDR Volksarmee helped root out the dangers, tourist traffic was permitted to resume. Yugoslavia, however, continues its heretical ways, and no ordinary East German can visit its beaches and mountains.

The shortages put restrictions even on ideologically safe Bulgaria, as well as the other members of the Soviet Bloc. Every spring, little notices in the Party press inform citizens that the limited number of tour vacations will be passed out. By the time the Kramers arrive at the state travel bureau, all the places are usually gone; some people wait in line sixteen hours to be at the head of the list. The Kramers are able to make their own way to the Black Sea in three days of Trabant driving, but those without their own means of getting there are limited to East Germany's own chilly Baltic coast or the hilly area misnamed "the Saxon Switzerland."

Asked why there is such a shortage of vacation opportunities in the Soviet Bloc, an unusually frank tourist official replied: "They don't like us." It turned out that he wasn't referring to anti-German feeling on the part of the Eastern Europeans, many of whom still harbor resentments dating from the war, but to their preference for West Germans over East. Bulgaria and Romania may proclaim their iron friendship for the GDR during state visits, but when it comes to allotting hotel rooms or reserving restaurant tables, they look Westward, for the big charter jets and their passengers bearing hard currency. There are no known examples of "Socialists Not Wanted" signs, but the quotas granted the East Germans mean the same thing.

In this connection, Heinz Kramer likes to read from the official party biographies that rest on his bookshelf between *Buddenbrooks* and a volume of translated Hemingway short stories. Almost all the books on the Kramers' three shelves reflect the same sublimation of the travel urge that the songs in the Leipzig cabaret did. Only a few are by post-war GDR authors, but even these are set in exotic places.

One tells about the Wanderjahre of the late President Ulbricht, visiting the Doges' Palace in Venice, the Pinakothek art museum in Munich, the mountains above Lucerne, the Rembrandt exhibitions in Amsterdam, the Cologne Cathedral. In the biography of Honecker, who grew up in what is now West Germany, even depression era descriptions of the Saarland fascinate Heinz. These are places the Kramers would like to go.

"If the Wall were torn down tomorrow," Heinz says, using a phrase that appears and reappears in conversations with East Germans, "of course we'd go to the West as soon as we could. But we'd also come back. We both have good jobs, an apartment, a car. We have friends and relatives, neighbors and the routine of our life. How long would it take to get settled, to start anew, over there?

"Then, another thing, they have their troubles, too. Life isn't ideal here, but they have demonstrations, student riots, and that sort of thing. We don't—of course, we know why: if a student would stick his head up here, it would be clubbed. But here, at least, we know the way things are going to go. There, we would have the uncertainty. A lot of our younger people would leave, and perhaps not come back. But some of them would spend a half year or so, seeing what the other side is like, and then probably come back home, too."

Heinz concedes that the record to date does not give the authorities much grounds for confidence in the rate of return. But in his view, there is a difference in officially permitted travel and in the old open border era. Permission to leave would show a new confidence on the part of the regime, and this, he thinks, would have psychological effects on those leaving, improving their chances of coming back. Heinz and Gisela had thought Ulbricht's death and Honecker's taking power might change things. They were wrong, but they still hope.

ERICH HONECKER

Erich Honecker became first secretary of the Party in 1971, replacing the seventy-nine-year-old Ulbricht two years before his death. A new man was needed for the new turn in East-West relations. The initiative had not come from the East Germans, of course; the opposite was true. The GDR had long resisted West Germany's approaches, particularly after the shock of seeing GDR citizens cheering Willy Brandt, then West German chancellor, during his 1969 visit to the East German city of Erfurt. But in this policy, as in so many others since the war, the East Germans had no real say if their wishes clashed with those of the Russians.

Erich Honecker is no more an apostle of East-West contacts than Ulbricht was. His speeches over the years show even more insistence on *abgrenzung,* the doctrine of separation between East and West Germany. But when the Soviet leaders finally became convinced of the need for Western technology and equipment to develop their economy, and the West Germans led the way in 1970 with a $400 million deal for a gas pipeline in exchange for shipments of Soviet natural gas, one phase of *abgrenzung* was finished, and the East Germans had to fall back to a new position to defend their isolated bastion from the Western inroads.

There were consolations, of course: not only the Soviets but the East Germans benefit from the increase in Western trade. East Germany, over the years, has allocated a steady 10 percent of its business to what Bonn calls "inner German trade," and has benefited far beyond any of its Bloc neighbors dealing with West Germany, both in the import of advanced equipment and in the export of hard currency-earning goods. Bonn is often called the GDR's secret pipeline to the Common Market. The new East-West trends make it seem likely this percentage will rise, and the secret pipeline enlarge.

Honecker also has received diplomatic benefits that Ulbricht tried for years to attain. With the conclusion of the German treaty, the number of nations recognizing East Germany rose rapidly, from a scant dozen Bloc and Third World countries to more than seventy. United Nations membership for both German states followed in 1973. Whether these gains were enough to balance the additional risks the East Germans were taking is of no importance; Honecker had no choice. But he did have considerable latitude in internal measures against the contacts.

It was not possible for East Germany to limit the number of West Germans seeking visits, but it did prove possible to dictate the terms of these family reunions and, in some cases, discourage them entirely. The means were registration forms and pledges of secrecy issued to all government employees and other citizens in what are considered sensitive posts. It is estimated that the category covers 2 million of the 17 million East Germans.* Government employees, from high officials down to janitors, were issued three forms. One required them to list all relatives in West Germany, another to promise "absolute silence about all facts, issues, and news that must be kept secret in the political and economic interest and for the security of the GDR"; a third to report what they had talked about with Westerners and how contact was made. The intent of the measures was to discourage East Germans from extending invitations to relatives, and it seemed likely that in addition to the pledges and other forms, there was a rather wide-ranging list of people forbidden contacts of any kind with their Western relatives, although such a ban was never made public. Diplomats who manned the few lonely missions in East Berlin before the widespread recognition of the GDR used to complain about being entirely cut off from the people around them, which was not surprising, since GDR regulations made it a crime for a citizen to visit one of the missions, even to pick up a tourist pamphlet, without getting permission from the Foreign Ministry first.

Honecker also took a series of steps to tighten Party control. The Workers' and Peasants' Inspectorate has been given increased power. A link between Party and government, with channels to both, it has become the most important means of enforcing Party decisions in the economy, government, and society. The Inspectorate supplements, but does not replace, the Party; Honecker made it clear shortly after coming to power that new demands would be made on the Party, "on its theoretical political-ideological, and organizational work, because to the degree that socialist construction progresses, so much more complex becomes the role and responsibility of the Party." This was a rejection of tendencies in Hungary to make government and economy run more smoothly by subordinating the Party role. But it was also characteristic of Honecker, the supreme product of the organization, to stress the virtues of neat organizing.

Born in 1912 in the Saarland to a coàl mining and Communist family, Honecker got into the organization at the age of ten, when he became a member of the Communist children's movement. Organization after organization followed: The Spartakusbund, the Red Young Pioneers, the Communist Youth Union, and finally, at seventeen, the Communist Party. When the Party was banned after Hitler came to power, Honecker, by then youth leader in the Saar, went underground. Arrested in 1935, he was sentenced to ten years in prison in 1937, and liberated from the Brandenburg-Goerden prison in 1945 by the Soviet army.

Communist Organization Man. Honecker used the same route to Party

* David Binder in *The New York Times*.

leadership in the forties and fifties that Ulbricht had in the twenties and thirties. Neither was a good speaker or writer; the description charismatic is as far from Honecker's flat and somewhat self-conscious behavior on the public platform as it was from Ulbricht's squeaky and much-parodied Saxon accent and fussy mannerisms.

One of the ironies of contemporary Communism is that these leaders, familiar with their tables of organization and lines of control and completely lost in the world of the barricades and the guerrilla warrior, must nevertheless use the rhetoric of the revolutionary when the occasion demands, and the demand is frequent. One typical example was the 1970 "International Scientific Conference on the Growing Role of the Communist and Workers' Parties in the Revolutionary Process of Building Socialism and Communism" in East Berlin, where Honecker gave the keynote address.

"Our Party," he said, "directed its efforts in the anti-Fascist, democratic revolution toward a deep change in ideology and cultural life. What did the main content of the anti-Fascist democratic revolution consist of? It consisted of the complete destruction of the political and economic power of the monopolists and large landowners, and the erection of a force of the type of the revolutionary-democratic dictatorship of the workers and peasants, in which the working class has the decisive position."

Does this represent reality in the GDR? No one in the hall thinks so. But Honecker plunges ahead into the unreal. Some say that the regime in East Germany owes its existence to the Red army rather than any revolution, he admits. But this is wrong: "The anti-Fascist democratic order was the work of the working class under leadership of its revolutionary proletariat and in alliance with all the working people. The anti-Communist slander of the imperialist class enemy about the alleged 'development forced from the outside under the power of Soviet bayonets' crumbles before this fact."

Over Honecker's head is a ten-foot sketch of Lenin in classic pose, leaning into the crowd, gesturing with outstretched hand, carried away by his oratory. But the man in the East German equivalent of a gray flannel suit beneath him makes no gestures as he reads about revolution and struggle in flat tones. When it is finished he folds up the text and walks stiffly back to his place as the ritual applause is produced.

In Party meetings, however, aides who have come to the West say, he is very much in control of the situation, criticizing reports, dressing down subordinates, and running the group as he would like to run the country: as a well-lubricated, precision East German machine. Honecker found a place in the organization the year after the war ended, and since then has belonged to the Party executive or central committee without break. In the crucial years from 1946 to 1955, which include the workers' uprising in 1953 and the first Party struggle to get rid of

Ulbricht, he was head of the Free German Youth, even though he was forty-three when he finally gave up the job.

If caution, orthodoxy, and discipline have been the hallmarks of Honecker's career, then he seems no more likely than Ulbricht was in his quarter-century of rule to open the way to reform. Indeed, Honecker's prescription is the same as Ulbricht's: affluent Stalinism, a program of filling the bellies, the garages, and the TV sets of the East Germans so that they do not think about their political hunger.

REFORM

But no one expected reforms from Honecker; the East Germans had known for a decade before Ulbricht's retirement that more of the same was in store for them no matter who among his lieutenants would inherit the Party leadership. A few of the lieutenants had been involved in the reform efforts over the years, along with an assortment of intellectuals ranging from the philosopher Wolfgang Harich to the professor of physical chemistry Robert Havemann to the ballad singer Wolf Biermann. All failed, and all were punished with loss of position or liberty or both.

The most courageous was Havemann, who had been a fellow inmate of Erich Honecker's in the Brandenburg-Goerden prison under the Nazis and, as a prominent scientist and prewar Communist, had risen to a high position in the intellectual life of the GDR: professor, director of Humboldt University's Physical Chemistry Institute, member of the Academy of Science, chairman of many scientific committees and peace groups. He had first demanded reform in 1956, calling for a freeing of science from the restrictions of ideology. In the academic year of 1963–1964, he repeated and expanded his demands in a series of lectures at the university. As is the usual practice, the lectures were duplicated and distributed to the students. But no one had expected the weekly demand for 1,500 copies, and no one had expected that the lectures eventually would be reproduced and circulated in clandestine ways to all parts of the nation. The lectures hit hardest at the authoritarian aspects of GDR society, the idea that the people cannot be trusted, but must be led, controlled, and then watched suspiciously. "The idea of spontaneity," Havemann said, "is denigrated in dogmatic fashion, as though it meant aimless, selfless, chaotic action . . . it really means the courage to go forward. . . ."

The regime found Havemann's thoughts too dangerous. Professor Kurt Hager, the Party ideological guardian, said Havemann wanted "freedom for every human being, obviously for reactionary enemies too, an aim which abolishes socialism and can be described only as anarchistic."

Havemann was, of course, dismissed from his university and scientific posts and expelled from the Party. He was not sent to prison, however;

whether because of his record in the Communist underground or because at least some reforms have succeeded in the GDR was not clear. Havemann continued to analyze and to write; his later interviews and his book *Questions, Answers, Questions,* published in West Germany, made his earlier criticisms seem mild indeed. The Party and government apparat, he wrote, are designed in a series of layers in which each is dominated by the one above it and in turn dominates the one below it. This means that "formation of democratic opinion from below is absolutely ruled out," at least any effective opinion.

"Of course, public opinion does exist, for every important question, and in many variations," Havemann said. "But these opinions of the man on the street are almost always against the official opinion, which is decreed from above. . . . Inside the apparatus of power, too, the thinking of the state and Party functionaries is completely schizophrenic. They know what they have to think. But still they think otherwise. One can only learn the real views of these people in private, and then only when they are not worried that a secret listening device is present."

If Honecker's hope is to smother ideas like Havemann's with affluent Stalinism, there are some signs of success. One great asset of the regime is the inertia of many GDR citizens, men like Heinz Kramer. Those who want to get up and complain or read uncensored books are still outnumbered by those in line for a Trabant, and probably will always be. The promise of a promotion or a better job makes them more content with the system; the attainment of advancement makes them part of it. During the rioting in Prague in August 1969, on the first anniversary of the Soviet invasion, as Czech students chanted their defiance of the Russians and police armored cars bore down on them, firing tear gas shells, two East German students who scrambled for cover with me expressed their shock: "We'd never dare try anything like this. In our society, we've got too much to lose."

It is symptomatic of the current course of the GDR regime that those spoken of as reformers are all in the economic sphere, men like Dr. Guenter Mittag, the Politburo member, and his team of young university graduates with plans for computerizing, containerizing, and all the other kinds of izing designed to make the economy work more efficiently. The results are already noticeable. Wages, adjusted to allow for inflation, have been going up as much as 11 percent per year, an achievement unequalled in the Bloc. There are promises of more of everything, from housing and cars to suede jackets.

Will it work? Heinz Kramer does not think so, and there are many factors besides that very important one of the skepticism of the East German consumer that point to the same conclusion.

Affluence, as history in the Bloc and elsewhere shows, stimulates the appetite for freedom instead of stilling it. It is not only a question of more time and energy to devote to politics; part of the economic process itself leads to political frustration. Honecker can put more Trabants on the roads, as he has promised, but the GDR and the neighboring countries considered safe for tourism are small, and the more cars there are, the more the demand will rise to be permitted to drive them to the West, to visit relatives in return for the visiting now permitted in the East. In the factories and planning offices, as Heinz has noted, as the economic reforms delegate more authority to the individual enterprises, there is a growing feeling that Berlin should also be delegating more power to Leipzig and Rostock, and the Party and government to its members and voters. In short, the label of economic giant, political dwarf that used to be applied to West Germany now is beginning to fit the individual East German, if he or she is a manager, engineer, or specialist.

To Heinz Kramer and the men he works with, their lack of political power is a sign of the regime's lack of trust in them. They resent this, because they are constantly being told that the future of East Germany is being built around them. Without the scientific-technical revolution, as *Neues Deutschland* frequently stresses, the GDR could not maintain its position on world markets, which is to say its position at the head of the Soviet Bloc economy. Yet these important men are refused the opportunity to choose their political representatives, or to attend a scientific meeting in the West, and when they want to meet their relatives from West Germany they must fill out three official forms and incur official suspicion.

The treaty with West Germany is another flaw in Honecker's plan to buy off discontent. For years, the Western world, as revealed on television, has been a powerful argument against the regime's claims of how good the East Germans have it. Now that world is appearing more and more frequently in the GDR in person. It is natural for East Germans to be dazzled by the Mercedeses and fur jackets of their Western cousins, but the deeper threat to their feeling of contentment is what they talk about: a son studying in Scotland, the latest Italian film, the exposés of government corruption in *Spiegel* or *Stern,* and a host of other topics from the day-to-day business of living in the West that show the Easterners how much they are forbidden.

It used to be relatively easy for the regime to counter this attraction of the West by waving the swastika, pointing fingers at the war criminals, and equating West German with Nazi German, or by insisting that for every well-to-do visitor, there were hundreds of unemployed huddling in the Ruhr. This is difficult to do in an era of few employment problems in West Germany, with a Social Democratic government.

But the second part of the classic formula is still in use: look to the future, and the future belongs to Socialism. As Honecker said at the 1971 Party Congress while Leonid Brezhnev looked on with approval, "Our cause is the cause of the future . . . above all, through the constant growth of the power of the Soviet Union through the strengthening of

the international position of the socialist community, the power relationship is changing further, changing to the benefit of socialism and the
anti-imperialist movement."

We don't belong to the West. We belong to the Russians. That is how
East Germans interpret this policy, which, of course, is neither new nor
surprising to them, given the facts of the Red army defeat of the Wehrmacht in 1945. But this knowledge constitutes the one final element
that spoils the regime's program for contentment through material goods.

Gisela Kramer described the feeling with considerable vehemence one
day after returning from a visit to Wuensdorf, a town south of Berlin
where her sister lives. Since Soviet troops withdrew from East Berlin,
it has been a major headquarters of the Soviet occupation army.

She had been shown the apartments of the Russian army families, and
it ruffled her Hausfrau feelings: "They have been there as long as the
regular, the German, residents of the new blocks. But they use newspapers
for window curtains—these are the modest ones. The others used none.
They all had bare light bulbs, dirty halls." She looked, as though for
comfort, at the depth of the red wax polish on her own floors.

Heinz spoke of a factory visit by Russian technicians. "We were surprised—some of them were very civilized and well trained. But they
were also overbearing; they acted as though the entire development of
the past decade in petrochemicals had been originated in the Soviet Union.
We were polite in discussing our own achievements; we had to be. But
we are Germans, and we have been an industrial and inventing nation
for more than a century, and ever since the war, this small economy has
been giving theirs enormous help, at our own personal cost."

Gisela continued: "We are told to cast off our petit-bourgeois attitudes
and be like *those* people? This is socialism. This is what we are working
for. And worst of all, these people are supposed to be our models. This
is our future."

IV

CZECHOSLOVAKIA

Zdenek Hejzlar

The early train for Prague leaves Berlin at 5:43, and by 6 A.M. is rattling past Schoenefeld airport, skirting the Wall, and heading for Dresden, capital of the Saxon kings, city of magnificent Baroque churches and palaces, art museums and concert halls, almost completely destroyed by Allied raids that cost 100,000 lives in 1945, and now rebuilt, partly true to the original, partly in the GDR modern so reminiscent of American hospitals.

From Dresden to the Czech border is less than an hour, with about as much time spent in changing engines and getting searched and inspected. A steam locomotive replaces the GDR diesel at the border. On one trip, this switch was the cause of a long discussion of the virtues of Germanness on the part of four officers of the East German army in my compartment. It went along the lines of this: well, we've left the developed, efficient world, and now anything can happen. Look at that engine! And feel these tracks! These Czechs don't understand technology. Or politics.

Despite the engine and the tracks, the train reaches Prague at noon, and the smells of grilled sausages reach the platform from the wrought-iron and glass Central Station. Prague is Dresden and Warsaw unbombed. Its Gothic cathedral of St. Vitus tops the castle hill, and all around, on little alleyways, off small squares, down long flights of stone steps, tucked under the stone bridges across the Vltava, are the riches of architecture, Gothic, Renaissance, Baroque, the National Revival of the late 1800s, even the faded modern of the twenties and thirties. On one square is a peeling Baroque church with the music of an organ spilling out into the street. A few streets over, and there is the church again—but no, it is replastered in bright cream, and the music is from a cello. The confusion is understandable: Prague has 113 churches.

Someday the Old City and Lesser Town will be closed to automobile traffic. For the present, Czechs, like other East Europeans, are too attached to the cars they have only recently acquired to want to give them up. But the best way to see the city is still to walk, over the worn paving stones, through the downtown arcades, across the bridges. Such a walk is the best way to learn history, from August 21, 1968, back through the era of National Revival, to the Hapsburgs, Jan Hus, and good King Charles, less celebrated in song than Wenceslas but much more of a benefactor.

The walk could start at the National Museum, at the head of the Vaclavske Namesti, the famous Wenceslas Square where the events of 1968 were fought: first the demonstrations of Czech against Czech, pressing for more liberalization, then the stones against the Soviet tanks, and finally the flowers, the candles, and the students' speeches for the martyrs. The museum, dating from the ambitious architectural period of the nineteenth-century nationalism, is the backdrop of it all, and there was no more eloquent testimony to the armed force that finally decided the issue than the pattern of Red army bullet marks across its facade, fresh tan stone color where the soot-darkened stone had been chipped away.

Old Prague begins just past the foot of the Square, where little streets lead into the Old Town Square, and other little streets branch off into a dozen delightful neighborhoods around the Gothic Tyn Church, begun in 1365 and built in a style in which large spires sprout smaller ones. Stone streets lead across the Charles Bridge, past houses still bearing the names and symbols that identified them before the use of numbers: the Black Stag, the Green Frog, the Jug.

There also are spires on the town hall, with its marvelous fifteenth-century clock showing the phases of the moon and a parade of Christ, the Apostles, and the Grim Reaper. But the dominant figure in the square is the statue of Jan Hus, and the dominant feeling of the history there is one of long struggles against foreign rule. The old Town Hall was a center of Hussite activity; Hussite leaders were tortured and hanged in the square. The movement grew up at a time of Prague's greatest glory. Charles IV had founded the university in 1348, and in this center of culture and learning, Hus became the forerunner of the Reformation, preaching individual conscience and the Bible against the authority of the Church and Rome, and finally perishing by fire after Church trial for heresy in Constance in 1415. But the Hussite movement outlived Hus by two centuries, until Austria's final defeat of the Czechs at the White Mountain outside Prague in 1620.

Charles University is his best monument, but the bridge he built across the Vltava the most striking. The path to the bridge leads past the Old-New synagogue, oldest in Europe, and the Jewish cemetery, where the graves lie in layers ten deep, and Franz Kafka is buried. The bridge spans the river between spired towers, and thirty statues of saints guard its length. On the other side is the Lesser Town, but the name does no justice to the wealth of riverside gardens, hidden squares and perfect little palaces, wine cellars and restaurants, and finally, the network of streets, alleys, and steps leading up to the Hradcany, the castle complex that includes the cathedral, battlements, and the large-scale counterparts of the little palaces below.

This perfectly preserved city—the Baroque can be scraped away to reveal Renaissance, and that to reveal Gothic, and that to show the traces of Romanesque—is the way it is because the Czechs knew the techniques of survival, whether under the Hapsburgs or Hitler. That is certainly the opinion heard in neighboring countries, where the monuments are less perfect but the pride of resistance, particularly in World War II, is greater. "We lost forty percent of our nation and made ten war films," a Polish director once re-marked. "The Czechs lost nothing and made a dozen films last year alone about their resistance record." Who is right, the proud guardians of the rub-ble or the shoulder-shrugging victims of Soviet occupation, their third change of foreign ruler in the past half-century?

In August 1968, in the days following the Soviet invasion of Czecho-slovakia, the gaunt, gray stucco headquarters of the Czechoslovak Radio was surrounded by the wreckage of vehicles and buildings, the aftermath of the street fighting for its control between Czech civilians and Soviet troops and armor. It was clear who had won the battle. The olive-drab Russian tanks, striped with white for visibility during their nighttime movement into the city, controlled the Vinohradska, the broad avenue between the station and Prague's main square. Soviet soldiers, most of them frightened-looking teenagers, with close-cropped hair and uniforms stained with sweat, stood guard in the doorway of the radio building. They kept anyone from entering or leaving, and they seized passers-by if they took pictures of the damage too openly, confiscating their film and sometimes their cameras.

Across the street, someone had put up a small red, white, and blue Czechoslovak flag on the blackened shell of an apartment building. Its purpose must have been to honor those killed there, but it also served as a symbol of the end of the Prague Spring, the failure of the attempt to run a Communist society on the principles of participation and per-suasion.

The eight months of the experiment conducted under Alexander Dubcek had brought renewal and hope to the people of Czechoslovakia, but had also caused a crisis in the leaderships of the Communist states on the Czechoslovak borders and beyond. These men were convinced that it could not be contained—neither within those borders nor within political limits that would preserve what they understood to be the essen-tials of Communist rule. By this, they meant the leading role of the Communist Party in every facet of public life, from the direction of the national government to the manufacture of razor blades; the maintenance of Soviet control through dozens of lines of communication, including the secret ones in the security apparatus; control of the journalists and writers through precensorship of all newspapers, books, films, and broadcasts; subordination of the national defense and foreign policies to the needs of the Soviets; and finally, an ideological dependence on the Moscow model that would rule out all but the most timid experiments in the economy, education, and culture.

And thus, the five Warsaw Pact states—the U.S.S.R., Poland, East Germany, Bulgaria, and Hungary—acting in the way the ruling Communist parties have always acted, used force to overcome an opposition that could not be overcome by the power of their ideas. They labeled the Prague reforms counterrevolution and invaded the country with half a million troops to put it back on the approved path.

The Russian soldiers at the radio station were guarding what their superiors considered one of the main centers of counterrevolution. For the same reason, other troops and tanks were stationed at the Writers' Union, the television studios, and the newspaper offices in other parts of Prague. In a certain simplistic way, the Soviets were right; freeing the writers and journalists from censorship was an act that distinguished Dubcek's program from all previous attempts to modernize Communism. In Czechoslovakia, free expression quickly became as powerful a factor in the political situation as the Party itself. This, in the orthodox definition, is indeed counterrevolutionary. The function of the press is to praise the regime, propagate its ideas, and spur the populace on to greater efforts. The function of public opinion is to evince solidarity and approval for the acts of the regime. But if Czechoslovakia's press was thus departing from its approved role, the guardians of orthodoxy were wrong in thinking they could overcome the threat by sealing the doors and occupying the offices from whence it had come. The elusive spirit of free expression could not be captured so easily.

Although their country was occupied, Czechoslovakia's journalists kept working, moving from one clandestine site to another, often vacating a studio or editorial office by the back door as the soldiers entered by the front. "We are still fighting with our only weapons, with words, although this may be our last fight," the Writers' Union weekly *Literarni Listy* said in its first occupation issue, which was produced in a makeshift office on Vaclavske Namesti, the St. Wenceslaus Square, literally behind the backs of the Soviet troops stationed there. "We believe, however, that the need which evoked these words will not come to an end, even if their sound is muted: the will to live in freedom and decency, in an age of reason."

Zdenek Hejzlar arrived at the radio station late in the day of the twenty-first of August, while the fighting was still going on in the street in front of the building. Hejzlar had been the director of the Czechoslovak radio for only a month. He was one of the scores of liberals moved into key posts in the Party, government, and communications media that spring and summer. At that time forty-seven, Hejzlar had been putting in ten- and twelve-hour days, not only in directing the affairs of the radio, but in preparing for the Fourteenth Communist Party Congress planned for the following month. His associates of those days say he had the energy and enthusiasm of a thirty-year-old, which is not surprising, since Hejzlar's public career had been interrupted by arrest and forced labor at about thirty and had been permitted to resume only the previous spring. Hejzlar was particularly active in working for a slate of committed liberals for the Congress, so that a Central Committee and Presidium fully backing Dubcek would be elected. This would have been an important institutional guarantee for the permanence of the Prague Spring. All the conservative holdovers on the leading Party bodies who had been resisting the reforms would have been turned out. The Soviets, of course, were as aware of this as the liberals, and thus timed their invasion to prevent the Congress' being held.

THE EMERGENCY GOVERNMENT

Under the occupation, Hejzlar found his energies needed for a much more difficult fight: to save as much as could be saved of the reform leadership and program. The radio, press, and television were the only instruments left to the nation for this task. Dubcek, National Assembly President Josef Smrkovsky, Prime Minister Oldrich Cernik, and all the other members of the liberal leadership were prisoners of the Soviets. President Ludwik Svoboda was preparing to go to Moscow to negotiate for their release and for as favorable a set of terms for his defeated nation as he could get. It was not certain in the first days of the occupation, with the example of Hungary's Imre Nagy before everyone, whether any of them would even return.

In these conditions, the journalists took on the function of an emergency government, acting for the arrested leaders, transmitting their messages and speeches, and, when no speeches could be made, deciding on their own policy and broadcasting it to the nation.

Their first task was to reassure their countrymen that although they had been betrayed by their neighbors and allies, there was no treason from within, that the entire leadership opposed the occupation and wanted to continue its reform course. The Soviets sought to counter this impression through the broadcasts of Radio Vltava, a transmitter near Dresden in East Germany that tried to create the impression that a large body of collaborators had been found. Thus it was important for authoritative voices to go on the air to explain the real situation. Hejzlar was broadcasting soon after he reached the station and entered its still-unoccupied studios by a side door.

"Dear friends," he began, "our history is a history of unhappiness. This is one of the saddest days of all. . . . Friends, our weapon is our dignity. Outside, it's getting dark, but the tragic day isn't over yet. We cannot answer all questions and messages, but do trust us: we stand firmly behind Dubcek and Svoboda. We will be on the air all night long, and if they silence us, we'll broadcast from elsewhere. Beware of provocateurs and adventurers trying to spread poison and panic. Be careful and be watchful. We are with you; be with us." *

Hejzlar takes no personal credit for the radio's performance in the first two weeks of the occupation. "It was a spontaneous effort by responsible people," he said. "They were probably better prepared for such a role than any other group in the world at that time, since they had been making politics on the highest level all through the Prague Spring, and even before; they were thoroughly committed to the reforms and had had a major role in bringing them about, and they were not only highly motivated but highly skilled." When the invasion began, he had been in Bratislava, the Slovak capital, for a meeting with the Slovak radio director, and had hurried back to Prague. He found that broadcasts were going out despite the fighting out front, and that preparations were already well along for the evacuation the staff knew it would have to make when the Russians finally burst inside.

Most of the announcers, writers, commentators, and technicians had made their way to the station during the night and had organized their work well: the first broadcast about the invasion was made at 10 minutes to 1 A.M. on the twenty-first, only three hours and twenty minutes after the first secret landing of the Soviet transport planes. Prague went off the air for an hour later that morning, but from then on, with only a few short breaks, from studios in factories and apartments, from makeshift army transmitters, and from regular studios that the occupation soldiers could not find, broadcasters kept the nation informed and played a major role in keeping it united.

"The journalists saved the situation in August," Hejzlar said, "and in a real sense, saved the nation. There is no other way of putting it." The radio, he believes, played the most important role, because it was able to reach more people than the television and clandestine newspapers. "Many young people were very courageous in distributing the newspapers, of course," he added, "but the radio reached quickly into every corner of the Republic. In those August days, everyone in Czechoslovakia carried a transistor, and our people, many of them at great personal risk, worked hard to keep them informed."

The first service of the radio, Hejzlar believes, was to spare Czechoslovakia the tragedy of a futile uprising against the invaders. It was a fight that the Czechs and Slovaks could not have won, and its only result would have been thousands of casualties, a Soviet military government, martial law, and the executions of prominent liberals, whose counterrevolutionary plans would have been considered proved. Others equally

* As monitored and translated by Joseph Wechsberg in *The Voices.*

committed to the Dubcek program disagree with this view. Jiri Pelikan, the director of television during the invasion, thinks it would have been better if the Russians had been met with guerrilla warfare instead of passive resistance. It is an argument that can never be resolved.

Both sides agree, however, on the second achievement of the journalists: "They forced the Soviets to change their plans," as Hejzlar put it. "They told the invaders and the world of the national support for the legal leadership of Dubcek, Cernik, and Svoboda. The Russians expected no trouble in forming a collaborating government, and were truly surprised by the resistance that greeted them, particularly by the response of the radio. The broadcasts created a climate in which it was psychologically impossible for any traitor to step forward and collaborate. Even those who had been actively working on the planning with the Soviets denied it, were afraid to offer their services as ministers, and used our own radio facilities to protest their patriotism."

The journalists also saved the progressive leaders from prison or worse, Hejzlar believes. If there had been a radio network backed by the legal government in Hungary in 1956, as there was in Czechoslovakia in 1968, it might not have been possible for the Soviets to kidnap Nagy for trial and execution. In any case, it proved impossible in the case of Dubcek and his lieutenants. "It's true that they have all been removed from power since then," Hejzlar said, "but it would have been far worse for us if this had been accomplished from the start."

With Dubcek's dismissal and the realities of occupation and satellite status that have been imposed on the Czechoslovak people, the united front of the first months also has vanished. For a time, it was maintained at what seemed an impossible level of solidarity. When the broadcasts of August and early September told people not to give the Russian soldiers even a drink of water or a piece of bread, they complied. Not until the third week of the occupation were there breaks in the front. It was months before the Soviets achieved the later stage of official thanks for the invasion.

But what is important for the future, Hejzlar believes, is that people will remember that such national unity of purpose did exist at one time and might be brought back into being at another time. Both Party and people realized that a genuine bond existed, that Dubcek and his team had achieved popularity unique in Eastern Europe, and that if it had been possible to hold elections either before or after the invasion in 1968, the 90 percent plus margins that East European regimes extract from their electorate might have been the real result. Such consciousness is particularly valuable for a defeated nation, because it must be the source of the new ideas and political solutions for the future, just as it has been so many times before, from the Hussite revolution of the fifteenth century to the national cultural revival in the fading days of Austro-Hungarian rule.

Hejzlar is certain that the process of liberalization will resume, that the episode of the tanks, the purges, and the direction of policy from outside the country will be but a brief one in the long chronicle of Czech and Slovak history. He bases this belief not on the eternal hopes of the exiles—since his expulsion from the Party in 1969, he has lived in Sweden—but on his understanding of the political processes of a modern society governed by an antiquated system.

"There will be an inevitable repetition of the political development that took place behind the back of the regime in the late 1950s and 1960s," Hejzlar said. "This time there will be different people and different grievances. But the result will be the same; such deep differences between the levels of society and its rulers cannot exist forever." He feels that he understands this development well because of his own role in the political processes that led to the Prague Spring.

ZDENEK HEJZLAR

Hejzlar is tall, with a high forehead, an angular face, and deep-set eyes. His slightly curling gray hair is left slightly long, in the manner of the Central European intellectual rather than the new style of the West. He has a deep voice and the ability to organize his thoughts quickly on complex political matters, then talk clearly and simply, whether in a discussion or on the speaker's platform. It is an attribute that must have made him particularly effective when, as a twenty-five-year-old, he became head of the nation's youth organization and was assigned a key role in preparing the way for the Communist takeover.

When he was twenty-seven, he took the oath of office as a deputy in the National Assembly, and he could reflect that only five years earlier, he had been an inmate of the Buchenwald concentration camp in what is now East Germany. But before five more years had passed, he was a prisoner again, this time of the Communists, in what he once described in a newspaper interview as the "hard but profitable university of forced labor in a mine." What happened between the two terms was the liberation of Czechoslovakia, the Communist takeover, and the purges and show trials of 1952.

Hejzlar's career is, in fact, a fever chart of his nation's political health and sickness, with highs and lows that register the despair of the German occupation, the euphoria of the liberation, the hysteria of the Stalinist purges, the long, slow climb through the sixties to the sudden liberalization of 1968, and finally the plunge: invasion, occupation, new purges, and exile. The rises and falls in Hejzlar's and the nation's fortunes show that life is never simple in a small country surrounded by great powers intent on dominating it. But the fact that there are peaks as well as valleys means that it is realistic for the 14 million Czechs and Slovaks to think, as Hejzlar does, that new peaks will be possible, no matter how unjustified this kind of thinking might seem to be in current conditions. Austro-Hungary's rule was still absolute when Thomas G. Masaryk, in exile in the United States during World War I, began completing plans for independence. By war's end, the Empire had collapsed, and Masaryk was able to win President Wilson's immediate endorsement of independence in October 1918. Zdenek Hejzlar does not have any realistic expectations of leaving exile to help lead another free Czechoslovakia. But, as his career shows, there were times when he did not dare hope at all.

Born in 1921, the same year as Dubcek, in the East Bohemian village of Dobrany, population 200, Hejzlar became a Communist while in teachers' college, at the age of eighteen. "We saw that the society of relative democracy on the Masaryk pattern wasn't doing anything for us," he said of his decision. "We students knew that it couldn't provide jobs for us after graduation; we had been told as much during our studies. After Munich, in 1938, we knew that the democracies, our own or the Western, would not defend us against Fascism. The Communists were the only ones consequently fighting on both fronts: to change the economy, so there would be jobs, and to oppose the Germans, so we would remain independent. Of course we looked to the Soviet Union for our salvation."

Hejzlar's parents were conservative and religious, and he saw their beliefs as no answer to the problems of the nation, although he says he did not join the Party as a protest against them. "Youth tends to respond to its times," he said. After graduation, he did manage to get a job teaching in Dobrany, which by this time was part of the Nazi Protectorate of Bohemia and Moravia, but he soon came under the suspicion of the Gestapo, and in 1943 was arrested and deported to Buchenwald.

Liberated in 1945, he returned to a nation trying to find itself in the excitement of its own liberation. Czechs and Slovaks had been united against the German occupation as they were to be against the Soviet occupation thirty years later. But they soon found how many things divided them once the one great issue of freedom from the Germans had been resolved. Returning members of the Western armies, the London exiles, the Moscow exiles, the Slovak partisans, the Czech resistance, those tainted with collaboration, the passive majority—all wanted a place in the new order. The Communists, Hejzlar recalled, were never in doubt that their hour had come. "We had the enthusiasm, we knew where we were going. We worked hard, and we gained support steadily. In the open conditions of postwar politics, it was genuine support." In the last free and fair elections Czechoslovakia has had, in 1946, the Communists got more than 38 percent of the vote. In the Czech lands, without conservative Slovakia, it was 41 percent—slightly less than Richard Nixon polled to win the 1968 election.

THE YOUTH

Young people were important for the regime in that period, and Hejzlar was important for them. As head of the national youth union, he controlled the non-Communist as well as Communist youth organizations. Almost every young man and woman in Czechoslovakia was automatically a member, through either his or her school or an apprentice or young worker program. Hejzlar's task was to mold this force of 3 million youths into an avant-garde for the Party. There seemed to be no limits to the zeal of Hejzlar and his friends in those days—working volunteer night shifts at the Kladno mines near Prague on their weekends, organizing Proletkult street theaters, agitating, polemicizing, writing poems in praise of the Soviet Union and breathless reports about visits to Moscow, editorializing, organizing. Czechoslovakia was in the midst of a genuine revolutionary situation. Communism had been brought to the rest of Eastern Europe as a more or less completed package of the Red army. In Czechoslovakia, with its democratic traditions, and its position as an ally, not a defeated nation, things were to be different. Persuasion, not coercion, was to bring about the revolutionary transformation in society. The Red army was in the background, but after a few months in 1945 it had been withdrawn from the country.

The youth was one of the Party's main hopes in swinging the weight of the nation over to the side of the Communists, and Hejzlar, as the personal appointee of Party chief Klement Gottwald, bore heavy responsibilities. As one member of that generation, now in his forties, described the situation: "Everything seemed to be on their side. They were convinced they could bring about the classless society a few weeks after being handed power. They said the proof of the superiority of Communism was the fact that the Soviet army had liberated us; that Red army tanks proved Marx was right. Many of them believed that private property would be wiped out in a few months. If you joined them, the benefits were enormous. A classmate of mine went from student to dean of the faculty in two years. Many others, however, were persuaded to join on grounds that were purely idealistic."

As the Communists gained, the democratic parties lost ground. Discredited by the occupation and the failure of the West in 1938, the non-Communist platforms had no great appeal, particularly to the young. Democratic politicians were forbidden to bring up certain topics, such as the concentration camps in the Soviet Union, although the Communists, with Gottwald as premier and with control of the police, were given the fullest freedom to agitate against the West. But even with all these advantages, by the end of 1947 the Communists felt their strength was waning. The February 1948 putsch was the result; although it has been defended since then as the exercise of constitutional rights, it was actually

an armed takeover, the leaders of which quickly ended further con-
stitutionality.

The takeover meant important new assignments for Hejzlar. His Youth
Union became all-Communist, and he was moved into the parliament,
the Party Central Committee, and the apparat then being run with great
skill by Rudolf Slansky, general secretary of the Party and number two
man to Gottwald, who had become president. The Youth Union played
a prominent part in all the campaigns that followed the seizure of power:
nationalization of industry, collectivization of agriculture, the purges in
the universities and the press, the attacks on the Church. Hejzlar's picture appeared frequently in the pages of *Mlada Fronta,* the Communist
Youth organization daily, accompanying some announcement of a new
success for the building of Socialism. From 1948 to 1952, Hejzlar served
on the Presidium of the Central Action Committee of the National Front.
This innocent-sounding body was actually the command center for the
purges.

THE PURGES

The first victims were the bourgeoisie, accused of collaboration, or
simply of resisting the new order by trying to hang onto their shops, factories, or farms. The purges filled the prisons, forcing the opening of new
ones or the return to use of old ones, including castle dungeons empty
for centuries. All in all, according to figures made public in the Party
press during the temporary frankness of 1968, 120,000 to 140,000 people fell victim to the postwar purges in the sense of being sentenced
to execution, prison terms, or forced labor. This is one out of every
hundred Czechs and Slovaks, and it does not include the hundreds of
thousands of others who lost their jobs, their professional standing, or
their health through the persecution of the new order.

The circle of the purged widened to include Communists as well as the
class enemy. The dividing line was the spectacular exposure, confession,
trial, and execution of Slansky, former foreign minister Vladimir Cle-
mentis, and other high Party officials. Slansky, fifty-one at the time of
his execution, had been a trusted veteran of Moscow exile and the Slovak
uprising during the war. He enjoyed Gottwald's friendship and confidence.
In the fall of 1951 the Party papers were full of congratulations and
praise for Slansky on his fiftieth birthday. In the fall of 1952 they used
even more space to tell the public how he had been a traitor and
enemy agent for years if not decades. A few of the thousands of sentences convey the level of the reporting of the trial: "The mask has been
stripped from Rudolf Slansky once and for all, and the face beneath it
is that of a cannibal." "Slansky—like a trampled snake that cannot
wiggle free." "To dogs, a dog's death."

Gottwald sacrificed his friend because the Soviets required it. Czechoslovakia, to prove its loyalty, had to reproduce Stalin's paranoia on a national scale. But there were also practical reasons for the purges. The 1948 revolution had not brought the steady march to Socialism that the idealists had predicted. Since nothing could be wrong with the system they advocated, there must be another reason. During the interrogations and the trials, it was found: sabotage. Scapegoats had to be found. Slansky was the ideal victim, since he was a Jew at a time of official anti-Semitism in Moscow (as were ten of the thirteen other defendants), he was unpopular, both among the people and in the Party, and he could be counted on to be loyal enough to his own shattered ideals to confess to whatever the Party wanted.

If he did not volunteer, there were ways of forcing the confessions. Karel Bacilek, the minister of national security during the trials, told an interviewer in 1968 that twenty-six Soviet advisers had worked in all departments of his ministry, and that the signal for the trials was given when Anastas Mikoyan, at the time a member of the Soviet Politburo, came to Prague in 1951 and put Gottwald under pressure to turn on his friends. Other accounts of the trials have told of the "scenarios" written by the Soviet advisers to be acted out at the trial by prosecutor, judge, witnesses, lawyers, and defendants.

The Slansky trial ended with the execution of ten of the defendants, including Slansky, but its effect on Czechoslovak Party and society was only beginning. The mindless circle of suspicion that had enveloped Slansky widened to include anyone who had had anything to do with him. Hejzlar had so many links to Slansky that it was only a matter of time before he was caught.

"They were both personal and political," he said. "First of all, my wife is from an old Communist family; her father was one of the founders of the Party in 1921. Until his death in a mining accident in 1935— although a Party official, he remained a worker—their home in Ostrava was the gathering place for Gottwald, Slansky, and the other Party leaders when they came to town. After the war, she worked in the office of Bedrich Geminder, one of the co-defendants. And I, as youth leader, was a member of the Organization Secretariat headed by Slansky, one of the key leadership groups in his Party apparat. Of course, I met with him several times a month. In October 1952 I was arrested and dismissed from all my posts, and expelled from the Party.

"The charges? The usual mixture of Titoist, Trotskyite conspiracy." Hejzlar is able to dismiss them now with a sweep of his hand. But the effects then were disastrous, not only to the career of a thirty-one-year-old Party official with what had looked like a promising future, but particularly to the careful structure of ideals he had built up.

Hejzlar was ordered to the "Black Battalions," the military punishment units of the Czechoslovak army, and sent to work in the coal mines in Karvina, near Ostrava.

"The work itself wasn't so bad," he recalled. "The intellectuals of 1968 are finding out, as I did then, that hard physical work is not bad at first. But after a time it wears you down psychologically. I was lucky. First, I didn't have to go to prison. Second, these special army units were dissolved after I had served two years. That was my good luck, because part of the punishment is the uncertainty. You are not sentenced; you never know when you'll get out."

Hejzlar was forced to stay in the mines for another two years as a civilian, then work two more in the Klement Gottwald Ironworks in Ostrava. Gottwald had died in Moscow after attending Stalin's funeral, and the cult of the personality was in full bloom in the land, with towns, a mausoleum, and countless factories named in honor of the leader.

Looking back on the period, Hejzlar remembers the climate of suspicion and mistrust as clearly and painfully as the hours he spent working in the mines and mills.

"For me, one of the worst things was how people stayed away from me," he said. "They believed, in those days. Today, the regime has to keep the discredited intellectuals out of the factories because it is afraid they will influence the workers. Then it was different. Now the majority of our people knows how things really are. In the fifties, they did not. They were still in the stage of what they thought was defending the hard-won gains of socialism against the class enemy. Ostrava's workers had been fighting that fight for decades. I had considered myself on their side, and still did in that period. But to them, I was the class enemy. They shunned me."

THE ROAD BACK

Difficult as it was for Hejzlar to accept this situation, his own personal sorting out of the rights and wrongs of the Slansky trial and his fall from grace posed a greater problem. He felt that he was innocent and had been wrongly accused and convicted. The workers, he felt, were wrong in shunning him. But yet if he was right, not only were the workers wrong, but the Party was wrong.

"At first, I believed that the Party was right," he said. "I didn't question its actions. It was beyond my understanding that a case like the Slansky case could be fabricated, simply made up. That part was perfectly clear in my mind. But another part did not fit. I knew through my own experience, through working with Slansky and Geminder, that some of the things that had been brought out at the trial simply did not conform to the facts. I also knew that I had done nothing criminal, although of course I had made mistakes.

"It was a long time before I could resolve these contradictions. In the end, I wasn't able to do it myself. It wasn't until several of us who were exiled in Ostrava got to discussing it, about in 1954, after Stalin's death, that I was able to sort them out. After Khrushchev's revelations about Stalin at the Twentieth Party Congress in 1956, it became clearer."

These little discussion groups, meeting in the corners of the dreary cafés and bars or in the one-room apartments of Ostrava and dozens of other Czechoslovak cities, were the birthplaces of the Prague Spring. Although always cautious and afraid of arrest, the exile groups grew in numbers and confidence after Stalin's death and denunciation. The events in the Soviet Union influenced Czechoslovakia positively, as they had influenced it negatively a few years previously, and Antonin Novotny, the arrogant and talentless bureaucrat who replaced Gottwald, was forced to open prison doors and ease conditions for exiles. For Hejzlar, this meant a chance to return to teaching, in an Ostrava high school, in 1958, and to commute to night school in Olomouc, 40 miles distant, to get a master's degree in history. But his main interests and energies were concentrated on the political groups.

"One advantage was that so many of us knew each other well," Hejzlar said. "My wife had worked with Smrkovsky in the resistance. Eduard Goldstuecker was an old friend. Later in the period, when the writers became active, it was a help to have been friends in the forties with two of the most active—Pavel Kohout, from the youth movement, and Jan Prochazka, who had managed an experimental state farm worked only by youth." (Josef Smrkovsky became Dubcek's top aide and ideologist; Goldstuecker head of the Writers' Union.)

The groups were limited at first to the separate towns and membership to trusted friends. Hejzlar and the other outcasts were watched closely by the security men after their release, and most of the meetings had to be made to look like social gatherings. But by the sixties, the dissidents were holding regional meetings; Hejzlar remembers one such occasion when the Ostrava group and a Slovak delegation led by Dr. Gustav Husak, who had just been released from a prison term of nearly ten years, exchanged ideas. Husak's group was most concerned about the neglect of Slovakia, just as many in Hejzlar's circle objected to the way the interests of the northern Moravian industrial region were being ignored by Prague. The protests of Goldstuecker, who had been Czechoslovakia's leading Germanist before his imprisonment as a Zionist, and of the writers concentrated on academic and literary freedom. One of the landmarks of their struggle was the rehabilitation of Franz Kafka's works, achieved by Goldstuecker, Kafka's biographer, shortly after his own rehabilitation.

The grievances of men like Hejzlar, however, transcended the narrow limits of regional complaints or professional hindrances. The central event of their history had been Stalinism. As victims of the senseless persecutions, but more importantly, as former members of the ranks of the oppressors, they wanted to make sure that Stalinism was exorcised from the nation and from the Communist movement forever. They realized that the death of Stalin and Gottwald had changed some of the outward characteristics of the system, but that basically the style of rule practiced by Novotny was no different from that of his predecessors.

The first task was to find out where the blame lay, and a large part of it, they knew, lay with themselves, as Hejzlar was to confess with considerable courage in his first reappearance in public in 1968. But if they had been wrong, or at best misled by their faith into doing wrong, they knew that the system had to be changed so that this could not happen in the future. The best way seemed to be to introduce some of the same elements of bourgeois democracy that they had been so energetic in removing in 1948. But there immediately arose the problem that was to complicate every action for Dubcek's leadership in 1968: how could they guarantee real democracy, knowing as they all did the enormous resentments that had built up among the people about their mistakes, without risking having the Communist Party thrown out of office? There were even those who thought this would not be a bad idea. As Communists, they were willing to try the role of loyal opposition for a while. But the argument of Czechoslovakia's well-known geographical position always convinced them that it would be impossible. The Russians simply would not stand for it.

Goldstuecker, one of the small group of theoreticians working with Dubcek, once formulated a solution to the dilemma in this way: "The revolution must go further. The Communist Party is the only power able to guarantee that it will go further. This is not to say that nothing has changed. The Party must now formulate its policies to satisfy the demands of the entire people; it must compete for the confidence of the whole nation. The time when these policies were decided within a small circle is over." The practical result of this policy was that even at the height of the Prague Spring, electoral lists were weighted so that the Communists could not possibly lose their majority.

The task of the opposition became easier in the sixties, when what Hejzlar calls a period of "repressive tolerance" was inaugurated by Novotny, who was worried by the stagnating economy and the continuing liberalization of Khrushchev, particularly the fresh wave of de-Stalinization at the Twenty-third Congress in 1963. "His idea," Hejzlar said of Novotny, "was to introduce a little freedom, but from the top, subject to recall at any time. It was because of this that we began to get the excellent Czech films, and that the writers and journalists began to feel more confident in what they could say. More importantly, this era permitted our plans for reform to be discussed more openly, although here there were setbacks, too."

One was Hejzlar's petition for rehabilitation. Since the Czechoslovak regime and all others had denounced Stalin's crimes, he thought it logical that their victims would now be listened to sympathetically. But he made the mistake of asking for the rehabilitations of a whole group of people unjustly convicted, not just his own. As he told an interviewer in 1968, he also "apparently did it in a matter totally unacceptable for conditions at that time—I didn't beg, I didn't refrain from criticism. I didn't hide my doubts of the honesty of the attempts of the regime to really solve the crimes of the fifties. Even at a time when the sparrows were talking about them in the trees all over Europe, the competent authorities were still pretending there was a mass of unclarity."

In 1961 Hejzlar was arrested by the secret police, taken to Ruyzne prison near Prague, where the Slansky defendants had been held, and interrogated one entire night. It was one of the periodic acts by Novotny's jumpy security service, and the excuse was standard: Hejzlar is supposed to have plotted with unnamed Yugoslav revisionists to deliver secrets about his country to the West. The real cause, of course, was the continuing work Hejzlar was doing in the growing reform movement.

"It is wrong to say, however, that there was any kind of opposition center," he said. "There was also no agreement on any kind of opposition program. It was a loose coalition of various interest groups, people who wanted change for their own individual reasons. What united us was a common opposition to Novotny and his apparat.

"There was a three-way generational problem," Hejzlar continued, "with ours, the forty-year-olds, in the middle." This was the generation that had built Communism as twenty-year-olds, seen it go wrong and often fallen victim to it, and yet now was unable to take any steps to correct its mistakes because the sixty-year-olds blocked its way. The third component of the problem was the contemporary twenty-year-olds, who had the same ideals and will for change but were even more distant from power.

BEFORE THE SPRING

In the summer and fall of 1967, as the other components of the coalition kept up their pressure for change, the youth and the forty-year-olds got their chance to force the pace. The Czech Writers' Congress in June turned into a revolt of the middle generation, led by Hejzlar's friends and contemporaries, Kohout, Prochazka, A. J. Liehm, Ludwik Vaculik, and many others. It was a congress almost devoid of literary themes, and almost totally devoted to politics. Half a year before the advent of Alexander Dubcek, it attacked Novotny and put forward a series of individual criticisms and recommendations that taken together formed the basis of much of what was done in 1968. Vaculik, son of one of the founders of the Party and a former worker in the Bata shoe factory, presented an indictment of the abuse of power that foreshadowed his *2,000 Words* of the following June.

Other speeches examined ways of combining socialism and democracy, of controlling the abuses of the regime, of how to involve the public in decisionmaking. At the end of this most unliterary of congresses, Novotny hit back: the Union's journal, *Literarni Noviny,* was taken from its control and put under the Ministry of Culture, and Liehm, Vaculik, and Prochazka were suspended from the Party.

In October, it was the twenty-year-olds' turn. On Halloween night, two historic events took place independently and without the knowledge of the actors in the other group. Dubcek rose in the Central Committee to demand the resignation of Novotny. And hundreds of students marched down the hill from their dormitories in the largest protest demonstration since Communist rule began. Dubcek's action was purely political; the students' was not. But the march had unexpected political effects that helped speed up the reformers' push against Novotny. The cause of the demonstration was one of the inevitable little faults of the system. The concrete block dormitory buildings on the windswept Strahov plateau had been put up too hastily because of the need to house students. The electrical system faulted, and to avoid further breakdowns, the bureaucrats in charge of the complex decided arbitrarily on a lights-out period just at the time the students needed light for reading, early in the evening. The heating system did not work at all. So the students marched with candles and signs. But their spontaneous complaint about facilities quickly turned into a political cause when police struck back so brutally with clubs and tear gas that dozens were injured.

The writers' and students' actions supplied an ingredient that the anti-Novotny coalition had lacked. It was possible to stir up part of the Central Committee on issues of Slovak or Moravian regional neglect, of course, and most of it on the issue of the economic failures. But the intellectuals were able to generalize from these separate grievances, and in this sense, their role was invaluable, as Goldstuecker, at that time chairman of the Writers' Union, said in a talk in the writers' pleasant clubrooms in the spring of 1968: "To outsiders, it may seem that the whole movement was a result of ferment among the intellectuals. This, however, is an optical illusion. They did play a big role. But objectively, it was only a secondary role, a catalyst to speed up the process. The great economic reforms simply couldn't be carried out without far-reaching democratization. This was the pressure of necessity. On top of this came the pressure of the intellectuals, who understandably wanted more freedom."

The economist Ota Sik's great service to the Party was not only in drawing up workable plans for reform, but in calling Party attention to the disastrous state of the economy as a result of the years of thoughtless central planning and control. In the late sixties, Sik was courageous enough to say bluntly in the Party councils what he said later in a series of television broadcasts to the nation: that Czechoslovakia, under Novotny, had managed to become the only developed industrial nation in the world since the second war to have registered an absolute decrease in the national income. This happened in 1963, and was the culmination of a long list of blunders that Sik pointed out. He criticized production for the sake of numerical fulfillment of the plan, while the goods piled up unsold in the warehouses. He found that wages in Czechoslovakia grew by about one-quarter between 1955 and 1965, while in Austria they doubled and in West Germany rose two and one-half times. Investments went into new plants, which often were not used to capacity for many years; meanwhile, the old plants were neglected, so that in 1963, 57 percent of the nationalized industries' machinery was obsolete. Even where investment was made, it was made for the wrong industries. The coal, steel, and electric power industries, the traditional mainstays of old-fashioned Communism, got 35 percent of total investment at the start of Communist rule, but more than 47 percent by 1963. But Sik found that this only created production for production: "In other words, the creation of heavy machinery production required more and more steel, therefore we had to build steelworks, and the building of steelworks required large construction works, which in turn required again heavy machinery. And as the heavy machinery industry increased, it again required steelworks, and so on." Managers, Sik said, were chosen for their abilities not to run the plants but to get along with their superiors.

The dozen years of underground warfare between the Party leadership and its opposition burst into the open in the fall and winter of 1967–1968. After Dubcek's October speech, the Central Committee was called into day and night meetings in December, which, after interruptions for the Christmas holidays, for which even Party business must wait in Czechoslovakia, finally resulted in Novotny's resignation January 5. The transcript of the sessions reflects the excitement of rediscovering democracy in the Party after a lapse of two decades.

Novotny began with the usual defense of the totalitarian. He attacked his critics as the helpers of the imperialists. But this time the opposition felt strong enough not to be frightened by the label of enemy agents. Speakers were able to stand up without the fear of Party expulsion or the secret policemen as the consequences of their frankness. At one time, 60 members of the 110-member Central Committee were signed up to speak, most of them to attack Novotny. The agenda got so crowded that some had to relinquish their right. In most Central Committee meetings under Novotny, it was hard to get anyone to speak. Sik led the attack, widening his criticism beyond economics. Democratization was needed, he said, in every area of society. The Party directed life in every detail, trying to replace all the other bodies of power and authority, from parliament to the unions. This stunted the other organs, and it left the Party unable to act as referee to solve the social conflicts. There would be no change, he concluded, as long as criticism was silenced and people threatened with the loss of jobs and liberty if they dared dissent.

THE PRAGUE SPRING

On January 5, there was a unanimous vote against Novotny, and a unanimous vote for Dubcek. The way was open for reform. But other Communist leaders have been overthrown by such palace revolts with little or no change, or perhaps even change for the worse; one need only cite the substitution of Brezhnev for Khrushchev or Honecker for Ulbricht. There are fresh promises and new phrases, but the end effect is not much different from that of a new set of colonels replacing the old in South America or Africa. In Prague, in January 1968, there was more. The change of leadership had been effected in a way outside the usual pattern, and the new men were also markedly different.

The first difference was the careful preparation for the reform period, the whole long process that had its beginning when the first political prisoners began to emerge from their cells in the fifties with the resolve that the system must be changed to prevent a recurrence not only of their personal injustices but of all the others, in politics, in the economy, in culture, and in the simple things of daily life. Dubcek was not the sudden choice of backroom politicians faced with the need to win a power play. He was the candidate of all those united against Novotny, not as a new boss, but as a man who would let these opposition forces have a chance to test their ideas.

The second was the means the reformers chose to loosen society from its rigidity. That means was free expression, a label that must stand for the great and wonderful outpouring of speeches, letters to the editors, crusading editorials, revelations, attacks, defenses, public meetings, political round tables, formation of political clubs, and even individual soapbox oratory that made Prague the freest Communist capital in history for those brief eight months in 1968.

Free expression was needed by the liberals because it was a lever to pry Novotny out of his Party and government posts, and even after this was accomplished in January and March, it proved necessary in preventing the Novotnyites from trying to reverse the liberal line. The free press also informed the new leadership of popular currents and gripes. It was an advantage the insulated dictators never had. But more importantly, it rallied the nation behind the reform program, explaining its goals and emphasizing its lesson by exposing the mistakes and abuses of the past.

The liberals, and particularly the journalists, writers, and publicists in their ranks, saw free expression as a necessary complement to the Party's goal of widening democracy.

More democracy, they were certain, would cure everything. It had enabled the Central Committee to end fifteen years of authoritarian rule, and now it could be extended to the other areas where it was needed. Loosened controls would mean that the economy could work as it ought to, with decentralized decisionmaking and the market, not the undemocratic ministries, running it. Factory democracy in the form of works councils and freely elected union leaderships would spread democracy further. More sensible solutions to the regional neglect in underdeveloped Slovakia could be found if the alternatives could be discussed openly, without fear of reprisal for "bourgeois nationalism," the charges traditionally used by Prague against the Slovaks who dared ask for more independence.

Democracy and free expression were first thought of as instruments for renewing the Party. But somehow, they quickly spread outside the Party councils. If the press and radio were to be used in the factional fight against the conservatives, then it was necessary to let the public in on it, as well as give the journalists more information and freedom to write what they learned.

"The Party had experienced real democracy between the wars," Hejzlar said. "This is what distinguishes it from most of the other Communist parties now in power, since they spent those formative years in illegality or as narrowly based groups. In Czechoslovakia, despite the periods of repression, and the trend after 1929 of subservience to Moscow, the Party was a broad-based movement. This was particularly true during the war, when it was the most active part of the resistance. By the war's end, this had given it genuine popularity.

"What we did in 1968 was open this phase up again, make use of the members' views in deciding issues. It was remarkable how effective it was, and how little of the tradition had been lost. It was also only natural for freedom of expression, once it was permitted in the Party again, to spread outside the Party councils."

Censorship really sort of stopped itself, in February 1968, and newspapers and broadcasts were free of censorship of any kind long before parliament got around to passing a law guaranteeing free expression in June. "After the fall of Novotny, the entire censorship apparatus had no idea of what to do," Hejzlar said. "It was used to taking orders, and to a system, and suddenly there was no one there to give orders. But the journalists were not too quick to seize their advantage. They had been prepared for this eventuality in the sixties, when they had a measure of freedom, and some of them had written some very good things. But in January and February, they could not seem to believe that they could write completely without restriction. It was a process of slowly getting bolder on the part of the journalists, as they saw that the censors were really not going to do anything."

THE TOWN MEETINGS

Hejzlar himself was one of the first to take advantage of the new situation. On March 3, at a time when very few people felt safe enough to speak out, he gave an interview to a reporter for *Prace,* the trade union daily, that was notable for its frankness. Since Hejzlar's ban from Prague dating from 1952 still held, the interview was conducted in Ostrava, and the headline said: "The Man for Whom Prague Is Forbidden." Accompanying it was an old picture of Hejzlar and Gottwald, in the standard profile view, with chins tilted upward as if to appear to be looking off into the glorious future of socialism. The interview, however, took a different line.

Hejzlar answered questions simply and directly, criticizing himself before he moved on to criticism of others. Like the hundreds of other interviews and articles that were to appear in the course of the Prague Spring, it was a startling departure from the bland generalities that Czech and Slovak readers were used to. He was asked at the start how he looked on his record as youth leader under Gottwald.

"A little sentimentally, as with everyone who is getting older," he replied, "and quite critically, as one who had helped push the carriage, and then fallen under the wheels.

"Like other members of my [Youth] Unionist generation, I was hit by the destruction of the national conscience after the Munich catastrophe. We formed ourselves in the resistance of the forced labor battalions and concentration camps of World War II. This foundation was a great strength, but also a great weakness. We had tremendous vitality, and a fantastic belief that the world could be changed according to our opinions. But we did not have a solid democratic training, and we had only a one-sided education by vulgarized Marxism. Enthusiastic with freedom, and with our part in the revolutionary changes—and later, with our participation in power as well, with all the bad that comes from that— we worked without respite for the realization of our conceptions. And because we were young, green, inexperienced, and uneducated, we accomplished, with tremendous perseverance, and with our fanatical certainty not only good things, but also mistakes."

Hejzlar's interview was the confession of a generation, and it was received as such, not only by the forty-year-olds, but by the young people of the day. They immediately elevated him to the select circle of politicians who received adulation in 1968 of the kind usually reserved for rock stars. Many of those politicians were invited to appear at a youth meeting that same month, and Hejzlar was included on the basis of his *Prace* appearance. The excuse for the meeting was an evaluation of Jan Masaryk, the son of the founder of the Republic and postwar foreign minister who died mysteriously in a plunge or fall from the Czernin Palace, the foreign ministry, shortly after the Communist takeover in 1948. Just to make it balanced, the youth also included an evaluation of Gottwald, who had died fifteen years before. But as it turned out, neither man got much discussion. The evening was spent on the present.

The site was the Slovansky Dum. It and the Lucerna, a similar combination of meeting hall, cheap restaurant, and bar, were the Faneuil Halls of the Prague Spring. Hejzlar's fellow panelists included Smrkovsky, Kohout, Vaculik, and Marie Svermova, a recently rehabilitated Slansky trial victim whose husband had died in the Slovak uprising (and to whose murder Slansky had been forced to confess).

The Man Who Could Not Enter Prague took the train from Ostrava the day before. There was, of course, no one waiting to arrest him; the secret police, like the censors, were maintaining a discreetly low profile, and even if they had wanted to harass Hejzlar, the thought of angering the youth would have discouraged them. Hejzlar walked over to the Slovansky Dum from the railroad station and looked it over. He imagined that one of the smaller rooms would be used for the meeting, but he still felt nervous, expecting some sharp questioning from the youth, particularly on the fifties.

The next evening, when the time came to take their places, the speakers could hardly push their way into the packed main hall. The aisles were full. Crowds stood in front of the doorways and filled the broad entrance hall. By the time the meeting started, they had backed up into the street, the main thoroughfare Na Prikope, and had halted streetcars for blocks. Smrkovsky had to go out and appeal to the crowds to disperse, warning them that the police might use the event as an excuse to crack down, provoke a riot, and then present the incident to the conservatives as proof of counterrevolution. The youths, showing the discipline that almost all displayed throughout 1968, went home after Smrkovsky had promised them a bigger hall and another chance.

It was an evening of drama, humor, and political action of the highest degree. Out of such meetings came the real spirit of the Prague Spring. They were proof to the participants that the people were being listened to, and their suggestions acted on. It was new to most of the younger audiences that high officials would agree to accept their controversial questions and then answer them in simple, nonbureaucratic, and honest language.

"Will this lead to another Budapest?" Prochazka was asked. "That would be a luxury for us," he answered, "because our cities are falling down even without our doing anything." There was laughter and applause. "What about censorship?" "It's gone," Prochazka said, to applause and shouts, and then added: "That's enormous progress. We last reached this stage fifty years ago."

Smrkovsky spoke eloquently about the changes being prepared under Dubcek's leadership, and argued against a move by militants in the hall to pass a resolution demanding the resignation of Novotny from his remaining post as president. When this was greeted with boos and whistles, he told the audience bluntly that the conservatives were waiting for just such a move to prove that the street mobs had taken control.

"Only parliament can recall the president," he said. "Illegality can't be solved with more illegality." The resolution was withdrawn.

When it was Hejzlar's turn to speak, he began: "Friends, before I get to the many questions, I really have great stage fright; I haven't spoken in Prague for seventeen years." He was interrupted with storms of applause, and then continued, amid laughter, "I'm not afraid."

After expressing solidarity with the Strahov students, he turned to his past. "There is not enough communication between our middle generation and the youngest one," he began. But it is not surprising, he continued, that today's youth do not understand those of his day.

"This generation of ours, of which the best ones went into the new Republic with clean hearts and clean hands, with warm dreams about the immediate construction of what was to be almost a paradise on earth, and who were disillusioned of those ideals in the 1950s, or partly accommodated themselves, should not be kept from playing a role now," he said.

"I think that precisely the members of our generation should now courageously cast out everything that, as the ballast of the past, makes hard the orientation toward the new. They should be among the first workers of the new, in all the sectors where they work."

He listed Kohout and Prochazka, and also Milan Huebl, the rector of the Party college, and Pelikan, director of the TV and former youth official, as among those who had spent the best part of the previous twelve years in trying to make up for their past mistakes, and he urged that they be accepted into the ranks of the new liberals. He did not mention Zdenek Hejzlar, but he did not need to.

A PARTY DIVIDED

Town meetings like the one in the Slovansky Dum played an important role in the Communist Party's attempt to win back support after nineteen years of injustice, totalitarian rule, and deep unpopularity. The Party was trying to do this while badly divided itself on its goals and tactics. In both Party and society, there was the added problem of resistance: from those who thought more should be done, or less, and finally, from the Parties and governments of the surrounding countries.

What happened in that long Spring was all the more remarkable because it was done without an agreed-upon plan or timetable. There was never a clear majority in the Central Committee in favor of much of anything, although most were agreed from the start that things could not continue as they had been before January. Broadly speaking, there were three main groups: those who opposed most of the changes, for personal or political reasons, and mostly for both; those in the center, who wanted change, but did not want to be pushed too far too fast, sometimes because of their own cautious natures, but often because of fear for their own positions, or of the limits to what the Russians would permit; and finally, the third group, constantly pressing for more, neither caring nor worrying about the geographical position of their country, and not wanting it to be used as an excuse by the timid to brake the reforms.

This division in the Central Committee was reflected in the nation as well, but there were even greater extremes: those who wanted to do away with Communism entirely, and who hoped that the logical end of the reforms would be exactly that; those who wanted to keep Communism, but who advocated reforms that would change it beyond recognition; and those fearful of any further changes.

The most influential group outside the Party hierarchy was the journalists of the radical right, as that term was understood in Prague. Their aim was to demand such wide-ranging reforms that the Party would be forced to go much further than it had intended in the first place. On the question of rehabilitation of political prisoners, for example, they wanted to expose the role of the Russian advisers; Dubcek wanted only to quietly make amends to those persecuted.

As much, indeed, was decided outside the Party councils as inside them. Vaculik's *2,000 Words,* published in June, had much more effect than the most startling piece of legislation or government decree. The reforms, he said, are "only an installment on the debt which the whole party owes to non-Communists. . . . No thanks, therefore, are due the Communist Party, only the recognition that it is honestly attempting to seize this last opportunity to save its own and the national honor." It was an appeal to the citizens, not the Party, to keep reform alive, through meetings, public pressure, signatures, campaigns. The manifesto was followed in July by Kohout's appeal for support for the Dubcek leadership in the face of the growing enmity of the Bloc. It was signed by nearly 2 million citizens, and had much more force than any diplomatic note.

One group argued actively for the establishment of a second Communist Party as a means of sharing power in the nation, either as a ruling coalition of liberals and conservatives or as a means of alternating between opposition and government without casting off the basic facts of Communist rule.

More popular—and realistic—was the idea that the writers and journalists had in effect already formed the second Party. The idea encountered strong resistance. To the traditionalists, in Czechoslovakia and the Soviet Union, it meant that the journalists had become a law unto themselves, able to make policy and influence the public without the control of the Party. They did not want a second Communist Party, and if they had felt the need for one, it certainly would not be formed from the ranks of the undisciplined journalists, who were ready to proclaim loyalty to Lenin in one breath and then suggest that the Soviets murdered Jan Masaryk in the next; ready to praise the Warsaw Pact as the guarantor of Czechoslovak security on one day and then to grant a sympathetic interview to the editors of Radio Free Europe the next.

But the period of free expression will go down as one of the recurring but rare golden ages in Czechoslovakia. Newsstands were often sold out by 8 A.M. during the spring and summer. People got up at dawn to buy the weekly *Literarni Listy*.

When Radio Prague's discussion programs came on in the evening in a wine tavern or pub, the noise at the tables would quiet and people would listen, pausing only to argue. Early in January, 118,000 copies of Prague's seven dailies were being printed, and many were often returned unsold. By March, circulation had reached 557,192, exhausting the capacity of the Prague printing presses. *Literarni Noviny,* the lively Novotny-era weekly of the writers, had a circulation of 56,000 in 1966. *Literarni Listy* reached a peak of 300,000 in 1968 and could have sold more if copies could have been printed.

Free expression gained momentum up to the time of the invasion. As people found they could say what they thought without punishment, and read what they had wanted to see in print, they were encouraged, and their own criticisms grew bolder. The number of town hall meetings grew. Three typical March days produced these: Party members in Moravian museums met in Brno to demand a greater role for the Moravian culture, said to be disadvantaged by the predominance of the Czech and Slovak. Old Stalinists met in Prague to draw up a letter blaming "Zionists" for the reforms. The Bratislava Party organization demanded an investigation of Novotny's role in the persecution of Communists. Smrkovsky addressed a district conference and criticized the old system of Party departments that took the place of ministries. There was lively questioning. The National Front demanded the dismissal of its chairman, Novotny. Students at the Catholic Faculty at Olomouc attacked the "peace priest" movement and demanded its dissolution. Students of Prague's Academy of Industrial Arts formed their own independent association. A thousand journalists signed petitions calling for a congress to rid their union of Stalinist leaders. The Presidium of the National Assembly and government met jointly and criticized the "aberrations in the work of both bodies in the past." Communists in the Supreme Court met to draft a letter of no confidence in the Stalinist minister of justice. Students of the Charles University held a meeting in the Vltava Students' Club, one of hundreds that year, to plan the first visit since the Communist takeover to the graves of Thomas and Jan Masaryk.

The press, radio, and television expanded these meetings from their physical limitations, the capacity of the meeting halls, and extended them to the nation. There were newspaper accounts (from which the preceding list is taken), live broadcasts from the Slovansky Dum, and debates staged on the air.

The removal of the old guard, the rehabilitation of those who long had to live in the shadows, the opportunity to speak one's mind and have access to the truth, and the attractiveness of the new leadership combined to create an atmosphere of good feeling and hope in Czechoslovakia. The change was obvious to a Westerner who had known the country in the Novotny days: for one thing, people in the hotels and on the streets smiled and were happy. The climate in Prague had no real parallel in the recent experience of American society. It was something like the enthusiasm of the first Kennedy months, but it was much more heartfelt, since the Americans, after all, were merely experiencing relief from the blandness of Eisenhower, while Czechs and Slovaks were rid of a regime that had engendered fear and hate in most of them for nearly two decades. They behaved as people engaged in a calm but deeply felt celebration of victory after a long and costly war. The feeling of joy was somehow in the air—in the noisy downtown taverns, where many more pale blue glass mugs of Plzen or Smichov beer were emptied than usual, in the busy editorial offices of the newspapers and Radio Prague, where young reporters rushed in and out with scoops as though they were in a movie version of journalism, and even in the solemn surroundings of St. Vitus's Cathedral on the castle hill, where the traditional performance of Dvorak's *Stabat Mater,* that most mournful of oratorios, somehow took on an aura of joy and affirmation during the Prague Spring music festival.

ALEXANDER DUBCEK

As it was in the United States in 1961, the feeling of solidarity and hope was bound up with the person of the leader. Alexander Dubcek was in many respects Czechoslovakia's John Kennedy. He was young, forty-six at the time he took over the nation's top post, compared to forty-three for Kennedy. He had the same talent for attracting intellectuals as his advisers, although he was not an intellectual himself. It would be pointless to try to extend the comparison too far; the son of a Slovak laborer who was schooled in the Soviet Union, fought in the Slovak uprising and became a provincial party functionary obviously was going to turn out a lot differently than the Harvard-educated son of a financier who became U.S. ambassador to Britain. Both men, however, had the same instinct for saying the right things to people, and both had the capacity for generating trust.

I had many chances to watch Dubcek in action in his fifteen months in power in 1968 and 1969, when he was speaking to student demonstrators in the light of their motorcycle headlights, arriving at the flag-draped Bratislava Castle to proclaim federation for Slovakia, meeting Party dignitaries in a Prague hotel lobby, singing the "Internationale" with tense face, surrounded by Soviet officers, a few weeks after the invasion. He was the same in every setting: dignified without the overbearing sense of importance that many Communist functionaries exude; self-effacing but also self-assured. In reading prepared speeches, he spoke without passion and often used clumsy or vague phrases, but this was a mark of his caution. If the style was dull, it was at least refreshing after the tirades of Novotny. The content was what mattered, although it often had to be read twice before it was quite clear just what new revolutionary step Dubcek was proposing. Dubcek made a typical speech early in March in Kladno, the mine and mill city near Prague, where the chimneys stain the sky with rust-colored smoke, and where the workers, secure in their jobs and Party sinecures, were apathetic to the reforms if not downright hostile. Apathy, Dubcek told them, was the greatest weakness of the Party.

"No organ, no institution, not even a group of deeply convinced individuals can push forward with socialist development without the participation of the people," he said. "But through this development, socialism can and must become much more attractive, and even directly challenge capitalism. Is that too bold? Yes, it is bold, but in Czechoslovakia, with its democratic tradition, one can do a great deal to accomplish this and, as a result, to make socialism more attractive to the world. For this reason, we're taking and planning steps to intensify the participation of the people in the administration of social affairs, in order to secure these ideas through the creation of adequate institutions and the exercise of an adequate influence."

This is hardly dramatic oratory, but in the middle of those involved phrases is the basic idea of Dubcek's program, the appeal to the people to participate, after their long exclusion from the political process, and the promise that if they do, they themselves will form the guarantee that the old abuses will not return again.

Dubcek was at his best when he spoke without a text and could make use of his sense of rapport with his audience. On a hot spring night in 1968, I joined a noisy student march through the streets of Prague, from the radio headquarters through the downtown, over the rickety wooden tram bridge (pedestrians were supposed to go around) and down to the Central Committee building on the Vltava embankment. The students were backing the presidential candidacy of Cestmir Cisar, the liberal ideologist whose own daughter had been arrested two years previously for demonstrating against Novotny. They chanted Dubcek's name outside the building for an hour. To their surprise, he appeared on the front steps. As it turned out later, he had been home and had driven back to the building when he heard of the demonstration. No Communist Party first secretary had ever done this before, but then, no student group had ever dared demand it. Dubcek responded with good humor. Cisar, he said, "is going to have a lot to do here at the Central Committee. At the castle, they'll be able to get along without him." He then explained that Cisar had been named a Party secretary to replace Novotny, and that the Party's choice for president was General Ludwik Svoboda, a seventy-two-year-old veteran who had fought alongside Soviet troops and had the Russians' confidence. "What about the Dresden conference?" a student shouted from the crowd. Dubcek had just returned from the summit in East Germany, where the first strong criticism of his program had been made by the Polish and East German representatives. "I think every country should solve its own problems and not mix into the affairs of its neighbors." There were many more questions in the session, which lasted until after midnight. At its end, the students left, laughing, cheering, and chanting "Dubcek, Dubcek."

Dubcek's decision to keep Cisar for Party work and to use Svoboda as the symbol of friendship with the Soviets was typical of his good sense and good luck in personnel policy. In a short time after taking over the Party leadership, Dubcek managed to surround himself with a leadership group far above the average in the Bloc. Oldrich Cernik, the self-educated miner's son who became an engineer and economist, was considered Czechoslovakia's most capable premier since the war. Svoboda showed unexpected strength after the invasion, first by refusing to receive the collaborators who wanted him to form a pro-Soviet government, and then by refusing to negotiate in Moscow until Dubcek, Cernik, and the other leaders were released from prison and could join the talks. In this, he probably saved Dubcek's life and did a service that no amount of justifying the invasion, as he was forced to do later, could take away.

As important as Dubcek's public appearance and choice of aides were, the real test of his ability was the Party infighting. In this he was a master, a graduate of the tough school of Slovak backwoods politics, where he rose from yeast factory worker to first secretary of the Slovak Party in fourteen years. Hejzlar often observed him at close hand.

"After January, and particularly after the invasion, we often heard some of the liberals agonizing over the choice of Dubcek," he said. "Was it a mistake to have chosen him, was he too weak, not liberal enough? I think he is the only man who could have accomplished so much. He was not an intellectual, although he does have that reputation in the West. But he was certainly not a primitive person, either, although we have had such people in high posts. He is smart, willing to learn, willing to listen. Most important of all, he has excellent instincts. Often I would see his instincts in action in political situations where an intellectual would have acted otherwise. In every one of those cases, he was right."

The situation that Hejzlar thinks best illustrates these instincts was the time of the Warsaw letter, the warning from the Soviet Union and the four nations that eventually joined it in the invasion. It was drafted after a summit meeting in Warsaw in July, and it was an awesome document, nothing less than a demand that the reform course be abandoned, backed up by a strongly implied threat of invasion.

"It was a serious crisis," Hejzlar said. "The Central Committee was divided, as it was in all of 1968, with a third of its members conservative, the men of Novotny, a third progressive, who would back Dubcek in everything, and a third"—he made a swinging motion with his hands—"who could go either way on a given issue. We were convinced that the undecided would be so frightened by the letter that they would capitulate. It is a very serious matter for a Party to be served such charges.

"Dubcek was not worried at all. 'They'll vote with me, and unanimously,' he told us. 'I know it.' We couldn't understand this. We expressed our doubts, and asked him how he could possibly hope to get the waverers to support him in such a dangerous situation. 'Don't worry,' he replied. 'They're cowards. I know them. They know that if they don't support me, I'll kick them out.'"

Dubcek was right. The Central Committee backed him without a dissenting vote. The conciliatory reply to the Soviets that he drafted with the help of his close advisers was doubtless a help. But that, too, showed one of his strengths.

Did Dubcek's instincts finally fail him when he was unable to read Soviet intentions accurately enough to head off the invasion? Did he overrate his understanding of the Russians, even though he had lived in the Soviet Union a third of his life? The subject is inexhaustible; the argument will never be satisfactorily settled. A review of the changing Soviet position in 1968, however, does shed some light on their later actions. It is a dreary history of charges, slanders, hasty trips, and conferences, of staff and troop maneuvers, inside Czechoslovakia and on its borders, and finally of the invasion.

THE STEPS TOWARD INVASION

Until March, the Soviets apparently were satisfied that nothing going on in Czechoslovakia was alarming. In that month, a summit meeting was held in Dresden. The stress there was the danger of ideological subversion from the West. Dubcek succeeded in calming the fears of his partners. But those with the most to lose by the spread of reform were not reassured. Only three days after the end of the Dresden meeting, Professor Kurt Hager, the East German ideologist, warned against unnamed countries where so-called Marxists had written off the leading role of the working class and considered "the intellectuals, particularly the writers, the actual or potential power factor." This was exactly what the imperialists were waiting for, he said, and he attacked Smrkovsky by name as the great hope of the imperialists.

The Masaryk case increased the tension. The philosopher Ivan Svitak reopened it in an article in *Student* listing thirty unclarified aspects of the foreign minister's death, and the federal prosecutor reopened the investigation, as more and more links to the Soviet Union were disclosed in the Prague press. The Soviets reacted angrily.

A May trip to Moscow was the result, with reassuring comments by Dubcek about eternal friendship, but within days, a new stage of the conflict opened. A military delegation under Marshal Andrei Grechko, the Soviet defense minister, arrived in Prague to check on the loyalty of the Czechoslovak army.

In June the troops came: first, the "Bohemian Forest" maneuvers of the Warsaw Pact, involving the Czechoslovak army with four of the future invaders, East Germany, Poland, the Soviet Union, and Hungary. On June 30, TASS reported the maneuver was ended, then retracted the report. A long series of conflicting announcements on the withdrawal followed. In fact, the last Soviet units did not leave the country until August 3, a date that gave them less than three weeks to come back again, this time with all roads and important centers clearly mapped and gone over.

In the meantime, the Warsaw letter had thundered its warning, and although its conclusion, an offer to come and help save Communism, did not mention troops or tanks, no one in Czechoslovakia needed to be reminded of the omission. The Red army seemed to be everywhere that summer: blocking off the main highway from Prague to Dresden while dusty armored columns passed, flying in helicopters along the Danube, camping in fields and chasing away the legitimate campers of the summer who came to watch. If the Spring had been a time of euphoria and high hopes, the military and diplomatic pressures of the summer had shaken Czechoslovakia back into reality. It had suddenly returned to the role of a small country, subject to the will of its more powerful neighbors, and its hopes of creating a model of socialism that would be an attraction for the world were reduced to simply salvaging enough of the existing reforms to make life a little better. The lines were still at the newspaper kiosks early in the morning, but the news was bad and the faces were tense.

July ended, with foreign troops still in the country, with the conference at Cierna nad Tisou, the little Slovak railway town just across the Soviet border, where for four days the combined Soviet leadership tried to call a halt to the reforms. It first tried to exact promises from Dubcek to restore the iron control of the Party, resume censorship, and demote the most prominent liberals. When this failed, the Russians tried to divide the Dubcek leadership, selecting its weakest members and subjecting them to pressure and promises. This tactic also failed, and Cierna ended with a compromise: agreement by Dubcek to rein in the press to prevent the worst excesses, if the Soviets would ban further polemics from the Bloc.

The compromise failed to hold. Czechoslovakia was too far along the road to reform to go back; the Soviets were too worried to let it continue. There is a set of rough working rules for getting along in the Bloc which specifies three ways in which the Soviet Union can be brought to think that its interests are being threatened. The first is to loosen up society so that the leading role of the Party is questioned, and other institutions are given a real part in the process of decisionmaking. The second is to permit free expression, so that open criticism, including that directed against the Soviet Union, is possible. The third is to institute independent foreign and defense policies. The working rules say further that it is sometimes possible for a Bloc member to get away with one of these actions, as Romania is getting away with independence in foreign policy, provided special efforts are made to tighten up the other two areas of suspicion. But the Dubcek leadership was violating all three at once. By the end of the summer, it had become clear that two distinct and conflicting kinds of Communism were being practiced in the Bloc, and that their differences were so great that one or the other had to be abandoned completely; coexistence was impossible. From then on, it was only a question of who would surrender—the 250 million population of the Soviet Union or the 14 million of Czechoslovakia.

Hejzlar's analysis of why the Russians invaded includes some additional observations from his experience in the provinces and at the radio station. "We suffered from too much democracy," he said. "Dubcek was too democratic in letting all the little district Novotnys remain in office. Even the most democratic of Western political leaders secures loyal supporters.

"Another thing that was out of joint was our political and technological development. We were in the state politically of an African country trying to find its independence. But as far as our communications media went, we were as sophisticated as Western Europe or the United States. Thus it was possible for the whole nation to watch demonstrations on TV, or to hear the confessions of Stalinists being forced out of their jobs, to hear the speeches of the leaders and react instantly to all this. Yet their reaction was that of the underdeveloped political creature. After twenty years of political inactivity, our nation wasn't prepared to handle the sudden explosion of democracy.

"We learned fast, but not fast enough. We made many mistakes. The main one was to overestimate the opposition in our own country—the factory militia, the Novotnyites—and underestimate the resistance of the Soviet Union. We knew that the Russians react slowly, but we guessed wrong, because they acted faster than we thought. We thought the Chinese issue would keep them busy. It only sharpened their fears about losing Eastern Europe. It would have been good to avoid some of the excesses, the Masaryk articles, the RFE interviews. The Social Democrats should not have been allowed to recruit. These steps would have been a restriction of free expression, but would have been justified had they prevented the invasion. I personally do not think they would have. I don't think you can say that if we had only not done this or that the Russians would have stayed out. I think the total impact of the Prague reforms was what brought them in, not one or another separate issue. Cracking down on individuals or excesses would only have alienated the liberals and helped nothing."

Hejzlar thinks this might have been done by introducing the reforms more slowly, but he admits it is hard to make political tacticians out of 14 million people. An alternative would have been to confine the changes to the Party. But that would have meant a completely different and weaker program. "It might even have been better to have gone from Novotny to Husak to Dubcek, instead of the other way," he said. "That way, it would have been more gradual. The Russians and our own people might have become more used to the changes we were trying. But you cannot use ifs in history or politics. Husak was not available in January; Dubcek was the logical choice and the right one."

INVASION AND OCCUPATION

On the night of the invasion, Hejzlar was contacted by the Bratislava radio staff. Fearing arrest, he sent his chauffeured car to Brno by back roads, then took a train, the last that ran, to meet it. "I was, of course, deeply disturbed, and disappointed, although not for the first time in my political career, because it was clear that the intervention meant our reform attempts had failed, and also because it wasn't yet certain how the occupation troops would react in the next hours and days—that the worst was to be feared. I was able to speak to Prague Radio briefly that night and the next morning, from Brno, and agree with my colleagues to keep the radio going at any cost, with the anti-intervention line of the Party Presidium of the twentieth as the basis of its appeals for unarmed resistance. On the morning of the twenty-first, I drove by back roads from Brno and Prague. This gave me the chance to talk to many people and get their views, and also follow the radio broadcasts with a transistor. It became clear to me that the strongest possible anti-intervention standpoint would be our best ammunition for the critical negotiations in Moscow, and that the radio had an especially important and unique task in the national defense effort."

The first broadcasts repeated two themes: the invasion was illegal, because no one had appealed for the troops, and therefore it should be resisted, but with nonviolent means. With the Soviet and allied troops closing in on the studios and transmitters, getting the message out became increasingly difficult. The account of a Radio Prague newsman (who cannot be identified because he is still in the country, although no longer a newsman) explains how it was done:

"On the night of the invasion, we all went to the station and organized. There were many more volunteers than we could use—not only our announcers, correspondents, editors, and engineers, but bookkeepers and janitors. We broadcast from the building as long as we could. For a time, we were using studios on one floor while the Russians occupied others. Then we moved out and went to the secret studios.

"We would meet on the street or in parks every day to find out the studio address for that day. Often we would have to change sites more than once in a day. We tried to get mixed residential and office buildings so that we could operate at night without suspicion. Some were around the corner from the guarded radio buildings; we could see the troops. Central Committee members and other high Party people arranged the broadcast places.

"On the technical side, the Warsaw Pact had provided each country with a system of emergency transmitters. The idea was that when the Germans invaded we could rally the country. Now we could use them against invasion that really came—from the Warsaw Pact. In addition, most radio people were army reservists in signal units. I was a jamming specialist. But the same equipment could be used for our purposes.

"On television, where we normally have one channel, we used five, switching from one to another to prevent detection. There was a saying in Prague in those days that if the secret stations had stayed on the air a week longer, we would have had color TV.

"The secret press operation was essentially the same. The Russians occupied the big printing plants, but there are dozens of small shops in Prague where the papers were printed, moving around just as with the transmitters.

"Newsgathering was not as difficult as you would imagine. Those Presidium and Central Committee members still free would contact us with the speeches and statements. Often texts would be passed surreptitiously in street corner meetings.

"Just as important as the broadcasts rallying the nation were those directed to specific actions. Once we got a report that kids with popguns were out in the streets. This would have got them shot down by the Russians. We broadcast an appeal to their parents, and they went inside. Other appeals got people to take down or switch street signs to confuse the Russians. The most effective was the call to disconnect the public loudspeaker system after the Russians gained control of it. Within minutes, all over Prague, you could see people climbing the light poles and tearing out the wires. The loudspeakers were silenced."

Hejzlar's activities were divided between directing this radio campaign and participating in the extraordinary Party Congress convened in the CKD factory in the industrial suburb of Vysocany. From the first day of the Congress, August 22, he was on the scene, directing radio coverage, relaying information to the delegates from the radio, and playing a political part. Most participants were not optimistic about the chances of the congress but nevertheless were willing to take the personal risk and make the effort to show the world the Party stood behind Dubcek and his program.

The fate of those elected to the Presidium at the Congress shows how great the risk was. An enlarged Presidium of twenty-seven men was chosen because of the uncertain situation. Dubcek and the other imprisoned leaders were included, as was Hejzlar. As could be expected, it was uncompromisingly liberal in character. Of that twenty-seven, only three remained in the Party under the "normalization" of Gustav Husak. Besides

Husak, they were Slovak Premier Dr. Peter Colotka and Miroslav Moc, a journalist who became editor of *Rude Pravo* after the liberals were purged.

The Vysocany Congress was the last stand of the liberals. When Dubcek returned from Moscow a week later with the terms of the Moscow surrender, the first waverings began. Soon four groups became discernible within the Party. Hejzlar believes that if a common front had been preserved a little longer, much more of the reform program could have been salvaged.

The first was the radicals, who resisted everything; the second the moderate capitulationists. Hejzlar belonged to this second group: "We had been defeated, just as a defeated nation in a war, and we had to accept this in the hope of achieving reasonable terms." But the formation of the third and fourth groups worked against this. The third was headed by Husak, who said that the country would have to accept everything the Russians ordered in the hope of being able to rebuild again someday in the future. The fourth was the former Novotnyites, who wanted revenge.

The confused situation in the early days of the occupation, Hejzlar believes, worked in favor of his moderate capitulation group. The Russians had clearly miscalculated gravely. They had expected to set up a collaborationist regime within hours, and apparently really thought they would be welcomed by the people with bread and salt, as they had been in 1945.

"They were victims of poor reporting, just as they were when the Germans were about to attack them in 1940," Hejzlar said. "There is something in the Russian mentality about unfavorable news being suspicious, and thus a reluctance to report it. There is also a tendency of the Russians still to believe that people everywhere are waiting for them to come and liberate them. This was the case in Finland in 1939, when they came with propaganda leaflets and were truly surprised to be greeted with gunfire."

The confusion of the early occupation days, the press, and the radio gave the liberals a chance to form a united front. It might have been maintained, Hejzlar thinks, if Husak hadn't broken it. The Dubcek group held out as long as it could, but Husak's group immediately began surrendering position after position, leaving no room for maneuver.

Hejzlar knew Husak well. The National Assembly is arranged in alphabetical order, so they sat next to each other from 1948 until both their arrests in the purges. To Hejzlar, Husak is living proof that it is possible to have suffered under the period of the personality cult and still have learned nothing. Husak's opponents find it difficult to condemn him completely; anyone who stood up to the pressure to confess crimes as long as he did in the fifties is worthy of admiration. He would plead guilty to anti-state activities under torture, then repudiate the confession in the court. After his nearly ten years in prison, he was back in the opposition movement, and Hejzlar saw him frequently.

"He wasn't much changed. He was a victim of Stalinism, but he remained essentially a Stalinist himself. He was hard to work with; he always had to have his way, and wouldn't stop until he had achieved it. He was for reform, but in a limited way, from the top. He wanted to get the economy going better, and he was particularly in favor of regional autonomy, as a Slovak. But his understanding of socialist democracy was limited. The free play of forces seemed foreign to him. He prefers the security of discipline, of being able to order things done and know that they will be done."

The Soviets guaranteed Husak this limited right, if he would concede them all higher rights, and the deal was made. It took them eight months in the spring and summer of 1968 to stop the reforms; a further eight months was required to wear down Dubcek and install Husak.

NORMALIZATION

Husak's normalization has taken on many forms, but in general it could be described as a negative print of Dubcek's reform program, with the bright areas turned dark, and those that were dark under Dubcek turned to white.

Normalization means, in the words of a liberal and now unemployed Czech intellectual, "modernized Stalinism." This man, active in reform movements even before 1968, belongs to the group forbidden employment even as waiters or streetcar conductors, because the regime fears its progressive ideas will contaminate those it comes in contact with.

"These are, in the term of the Russians, the 'former humans,' " he said. "The first step is expulsion from the Party. Then, accusations, self-criticism, charges against others, and finally release. They don't hang you anymore; they don't shoot you. They don't have to—they simply throw you in the sewers, and let you live like rats, and sooner or later, you will be like rats, so they think. And when you emerge, you're the outcast, the humans of yesterday.

"This is why they don't need the show trials, or the other Asiatic forms of the old Stalinism. Gottwald's gallows are gone, and this leads some visitors to think Stalinism has changed. It hasn't. Its basic goal was always to liquidate nonconforming ideas by means of the liquidation of their bearers. Only the method of liquidation has changed."

Any assessment of Husak's regime must start with this human cost— not only the 300,000 Party members expelled from its ranks and their jobs, or the 75,000 refugees, or those in prisons or awaiting trial, or those denied schooling or training because of their political beliefs or their parents', but also those put in to replace them. In this group Husak, the sixty-year-old former country lawyer and resistance fighter, seems moderate indeed. Those who have risen to prominence since the eclipse of Dubcek are, in large part, the men responsible for running the country down under Novotny, including his former close aide, Antonin Kapek, now Prague Party leader, the notorious secret police official Miroslav Mamula, now district leader in the Ostrava area, and the original Soviet collaborators and Dubcek opponents, Vasil Bilak and Alois Indra. Even Novotny has been taken back into the Party, despite the 1968 revelations of his direct role in sending innocent Party officials to their executioners.

Rude Pravo, the Party paper, allowed in 1970 that under Novotny and Gottwald mistakes had indeed been made, but "a great deal of honest and positive work" was also done, and although some of the trials were rigged, "many of them justly punished the real enemies of socialism."

Husak has proclaimed many times that there would be no return to the fifties, no "trumped-up accusations, rigged trials, or forged evidence." This is the lawyer and the victim of rigged trials speaking. But Husak has had to fight the trial battle on two fronts since he took office in 1969. On one side stand the moderates in both the Soviet occupation apparat and the Party who believe that show trials would hurt the image of international Communism, and point to the French CP protest against the political trials of 1972 as proof. At home, they say, trials would make it even more difficult for the regime to come to terms with the intellectuals and further lower the nation's morale, which in turn would be reflected in falling production. The ultras in the Party and in the Soviet Union, however, have never been satisfied with the escape of the leaders of 1968 from their just and inevitable punishment as counterrevolutionaries. Their view is that they were guilty of a serious crime and have gone free. This is a dangerous example to Czechoslovakia and the Bloc. Their hope is to work upward toward the former leadership through the trials and confessions of the lower-level progressives.

Because of this struggle, the trials of the summer of 1972, when Huebl, former head of the Party ideological college, and more than thirty others were sentenced to terms of up to six years, were a middle way out. Husak could point to the fact that liberals were being put in jail to satisfy the hardliners, but that they were being sentenced for specific offenses, mostly the distribution of forbidden political literature, instead of for their beliefs. The fact that some of the literature merely urged voters to make use of their constitutional right of abstention in the elections was not stressed.

Those punished through trials are only the tip of the iceberg. Some assessment of the cost of normalization to the hundreds of thousands who worked for reform in 1968, not only the one-fifth of the Party that was expelled, but the non-Communists, can be made through these examples of their fate: in 1948, when the Communists took power, eight or ten professors of the philosophy faculty of Charles University were forced to retire, with pension rights. Under Husak, more than seventy were forced out, and there were no pensions for counterrevolutionaries. The university's Middle East specialist had to find work as a reader for the blind; its two leading philosophers became translators. Others from the department became night watchmen or street sweepers. A professor from Huebl's Party college works as a janitor. A historian works in a factory in the same job he had under the Nazis. Other intellectuals wash corpses, repair the numerous fishponds that have dotted southern Bohemia since Charles IV's time, or simply look for work.

Many of these men were victims of Stalinism in the fifties and thus have gone through the nightmare of purge, rehabilitation, and purge once again. The Jews have fared the worst of all. Rudolf Slansky, Jr., now in his thirties, was barred from school and Party activity during the period of his father's disgrace. Rehabilitated fully in 1968, he was again dismissed from the Party in the new purges, fired from his managerial post in a Prague factory, and then fired again from a low-paid sales job.

This new Slansky case has been pursued without publicity, but general charges against "Zionists" are frequent in the Prague press and are usually linked with the Jewish background of a few of the Dubcek team, including Goldstuecker and Sik.

The official rehabilitation tribunals set up by Dubcek to restore jobs, pensions, and back pay to purge victims or, more often, their survivors were stopped in 1970, and new laws all but cut off any hope of further action.

The intellectuals have suffered not only individually, with loss of jobs, but collectively, with the disbanding or emasculation of their professional organizations and institutes. The political clubs, the Social Democrats, and the League for Human Rights were the first to go in the early months of occupation. They were followed by the independent students' unions. The Catholic and Socialist parties, which were gaining independence in 1968, resumed their satellite existence. The Journalists', Writers', Film, and Artists' unions have been disbanded; the leading publications of 1968, *Reporter, Literarni Listy, Student, Plamen,* and *Host do Domu* banned; so many films made in 1968 and 1969 have been withdrawn from circulation that the state film company was in serious financial difficulty; and plays, ranging from the contemporary to Molière and Brecht, banned from Prague theaters, on the basis of current or historical references to tyranny or foreign rule that might provoke public outbursts.

The journalists were the hardest hit. More than 1,200 have been expelled from their union or denied membership, without which they cannot work in their profession. Those expelled from the Writers' Union cannot publish, although officials say there is no censorship. But a few, among them Kohout, Vaculik, and the playwright Vaclav Havel, have the financial resources to exist and the courage to speak out. At the end of 1972, they and thirty-six others signed an amnesty petition for those imprisoned in that summer's political trials. They have also worked to encourage lesser-known writers to boycott the "normalized" Writers' Union formed by Husak; only a fifth of the old members could be persuaded to join the new union. Royalties from the West and fund raising by exiled writers kept the struggle alive.

The process of cleansing that the journalists' and writers' unions underwent is paralleled in all state and Party institutions; the 1970 purge in the trade unions, for example, was the most thorough in any body since the 1948 Communist takeover; all thirty-one members of the Presidium were dismissed. The unions' crime was the same as that of the writers, artists, and journalists: refusal to accept the postoccupation view of reality.

Reality in the age of Husak requires the acceptance of many ideas and concepts that to the average person would not seem to be true. A central role is played by the invasion, in which, all evidence to the contrary, it is held that the Soviet and other troops came by invitation of concerned Party leaders, and thousands of Party members, to save Socialism.

Thus through 1969 and 1970 the outside world was treated to the astounding spectacle of one organization after another, with its safely purged leadership, coming forward to retract its condemnation of the invasion and commend the Soviet Union for its brotherly help.

The other pillar of Husakism is the belief that all the nation's ills, from the low productivity to the shortages, can be blamed on the reformers of 1968—and, important for the years ahead—of "rightist" thinking among the populace, still infected by the disease of 1968. Anything that goes wrong under Husak is thus Dubcek's fault. And the cure for it all is not to ease up but to pursue more vigorously than before the ideological retraining in the schools, the factories, in books, films, plays, and in the press.

If Czechs and Slovaks will not accept the retraining, the regime will not accept them. Two out of three applicants for Bratislava's Comenius University have been rejected in recent years because of their answers to questions about 1968 and reform, or their record in that year, or their parents'. Those accepted are under constant threat of expulsion, not for demonstrating or striking, but often for giving the wrong answer in a Party-led discussion.

WE ARE WITH YOU; BE WITH US

Hejzlar was, of course, one of the first to lose his job. After a year's grace period, he chose exile to escape the imprisonment that would have been certain had he remained in Czechoslovakia. In October 1968 he was sent to Vienna as cultural attaché at the Czechoslovak Legation. But he was a political liability, even abroad, and the next October he was dismissed from his job and the Party and forced to ask for political asylum, first in Austria and then in Sweden, where he found work as an analyst at the Swedish Institute of International Affairs.

Hejzlar has no realistic hopes of returning to the nation he served as politician and prisoner, but he does feel strongly that Husakism is as transitory a period in Czechoslovakia as was the German occupation, Gottwald's era, or Dubcek's eight months. The grounds for his optimism are threefold: the general nature of political development in the world in the direction of liberalization; the specific changes under way in the Soviet Union; and finally, the continuation of the process he had been involved with inside Czechoslovakia.

"Political parties are born, develop, and die, and this also applies to the radical socialist parties, such as the Communists once were," he said. "The need for far-reaching changes in society remains—in West, East, South and North. Czechoslovakia, like all European socialist countries, needs thorough democratic reform, which must lead gradually to a new political system which gives full and real influence to the people in the exercise of politics and control of power. We must have a new model, probably a combination of the traditional system of representation and the forms of direct democracy and self-administration. Only in this way can a new pluralism of interests be created with enough integrative power to avoid the weaknesses of so-called bourgeois democracy and Stalinist dictatorship.

"We made the first step in this direction in 1968. Our defeat doesn't mean that we were wrong. All great emancipation movements, especially those of small nations, have been beaten down many times in history— but despite this, they have eventually been victorious."

In the Soviet Union, Hejzlar sees changes that encourage him: "It may not seem like much, but the fact that writers and intellectuals there can protest twice is a gain of immeasurable consequences. In the past, they could protest only once. There is also the great advance in education, not only in the U.S.S.R. but in the Socialist states, and there is the need for loosening of political controls because of the complexity of today's economic processes. This will at once free the economy and make the politicians less powerful. And, of course, only when more freedoms are granted in the Soviet Union can we be sure that they will be granted in Czechoslovakia."

But Hejzlar's final hope is based on his conviction that the young people in Czechoslovakia will not sit back and wait for change from outside, that they will take the initiative for reform in their own hands. The widespread purges of the men of 1968, ironically, are giving them more of an opportunity: young journalists and managers have been given duties far above their age because of the decimation of intellectuals and administrators. Along with these posts go benefits like apartments—often those abandoned by the exiles—and cars. With them go the obligation to be orthodox, to denounce Solzhenitsyn, to agree to act out the illusion that the Soviet invasion was beneficial and asked for.

They accept the benefits and the duties, because that is a fact of life in a small occupied country, but, Hejzlar believes, they will be no more willing than his generation was to accept them forever. Already the groups are gathering to work out how it will be done better the next time: not in the sense of formal plotters or counterrevolutionaries, as the uneasy men in the Central Committees believe, but with a common feeling that things are in serious need of change, from the economy to the hack literature, and that the power to bring change will eventually be put in their hands.

"They will make the next revolution, these twenty-year-olds, but they will make it their own way," Hejzlar said, "and they won't consult us.

"People want real socialism; they've never had it anywhere. When we worked our ideas out in the fifties and sixties, we knew what we wanted, but we were a little surprised after we emerged to find out it was so popular.

"What will happen will be a repetition of the fifties and sixties. They will need another crisis of the system to get support, but they will get it. It is inevitable. This system will have its own crisis, just as ours did. And then they will kick it out."

V

HUNGARY

Jozsef Bognar

The Prague–Budapest train leaves at ten after nine, and as it heads from Bohemia through Moravia into Slovakia, the three components of Czechoslovakia, there is a brisk business in the dining car, which is run by the Hungarian state railways with its usual mixture of dirty tablecloths, waiters with a flair for the dramatic, and goulash of a degree of fire that helps make up for the frequent lack of heat on the trains in the winter. The only passengers guaranteed comfort on East European trains are those in the through sleeping cars, because they have their own stoves, coal supplies, and porters to stoke them. On this particular train, the occupants of two Russian pullmans were comfortable, but the other passengers had to huddle in the dining car and drink Barack, the Hungarian apricot brandy. How did the Czechs, Poles, Slovaks, Russians, and East Germans in the diner that long cold ten-hour ride order their Barack? Hungarian, after all, is distantly related to Finnish but no other language in Europe; the Slavs could understand one another but not the Hungarians, and the East Germans, one might think, could understand and be understood by nobody. But here, as in so many situations in Eastern Europe, the common language was German. Decades of compulsory Russian and a generation of Soviet occupation have done little to make that language a part of daily life. Czech students used it to argue with Russian soldiers, and trade delegations use it in Moscow, and tour guides use it, but only for Russians, never as an international language. That remains the language of the Kaisers, the Eins and Zweis painfully learned at school, because it was needed in the town halls then and is needed today. The difference tells something about the changing forms of empire. Knowledge of Russian is certainly useful for an East European, if he is to be a diplomat or an engineer or government official in frequent contact with his Soviet counterparts. But the Russians have made no attempt to impose their tongue or their officials as the direct way of contact between rulers and ruled, as was done by the Austrians, by the three powers in Partition Poland, or by the Turks in the Balkans.

Budapest's lights recall the limits of the benevolence of Soviet rule. The western station, a lofty iron and glass building, is on the Lenin Boulevard, part of the arch through Pest, the main part of the city, and linked to Buda by bridges at either end. Budapest's bridges are like chapters in Hungarian history: the Arpad, the northernmost, is named after the tribal leader who brought his people west in A.D. 895. Margit, the next, and the island by the same name, commemorate a thirteenth-century princess. The most famous bridge is the Szechenyi or chain bridge, under the castle hill on the Buda side. Istvan Szechenyi was a reformer who tried to wrest the economic and cultural concessions from the Austrians that would permit his country to modernize. He was overtaken by the storm of 1848 and the fiery personality of Lajos Kossuth, who has no bridge but the main square behind the neo-Gothic parliament named for him.

Sandor Petofi, the other poet-revolutionary, who died at the hands of the Russian Cossacks (Kossuth died in exile), is commemorated by the southernmost Danube bridge. In between are the Erzsebet, named after a saint of the Arpad dynasty, and the Szabadasag or freedom. Freedom in Hungary is a two-edged word, and Budapest citizens asked about the origin of the bridge's name are not very sure. There are several kinds of Hungarian freedom, and all are discussed in one way or another when friends gather. There is the legendary kind of the Hunyadis, those remarkable fifteenth-century kings, warriors, and humanists who conquered Vienna, brought Italian and Austrian artisans to Budapest, and established a rich library. Or there is the blood and thunder of Kossuth, 1848, the "Arise Hungarians" manifesto, the battles that drove the Austrians from the country, until the Russians of the czar helped put down the revolt. There is the limited victory of 1867, when Hungary won freedom from Austria in all but foreign, defense, customs, and fiscal matters, or in the successive postwar dictatorships that followed the dissolution of the empire. Freedom might be best defined as those few days of excitement in 1956, when the names of Kossuth and Petofi were as current as those of Khrushchev and Eisenhower. Or perhaps freedom is what the Hungarian officials insist their countrymen have now, freedom from job loss and hunger, but don't question us about the occupation.

Revolution failed in Hungary, but reform is succeeding. Other East Europeans pitied the Hungarians after 1956; now they envy them. The crushing of the revolution left Hungary's capital in ruins, its government in the hands of pariahs, and its territory more firmly than ever in the control of occupying Soviet troops. The scars of the fighting have since disappeared from Budapest, but the government is the same and the 50,000 troops, although less obvious, are still in the country. What changed pity to envy was the remarkable rise in living standards Hungary has been able to achieve, and the beginnings of social and political liberalization based on the economic reforms.

Soviet Bloc neighbors which once deplored the emotions and excesses of the Hungarian poets and political leaders now send reporters from the Party press to Budapest to see how the Hungarians do it. They come back with reports of full shop windows, foreign investment, double the number of new cars every four years, traffic jams on the new, short superhighway to Lake Balaton, even a consumer magazine. They are equally interested in the innovations outside the field of economics: multiple candidates for parliamentary seats, the beginnings of trade union power, and above all, the idea of broad and national, not narrow and Party-oriented, participation in the running of the nation, best summed up by Party leader Janos Kadar's famous formula, "He who is not against us is with us."

There are many flaws in the political system, the main one being the impossibility of genuine opposition to the Party, and not a few in the New Economic Mechanism, as the reforms were labeled when they started in 1968. Since then, NEM has gone through several stages of revision. All the tinkering has one cause: the worries in Moscow and Budapest that using capitalist methods in the economy has injected too much capitalism into the society. The main fear of the Soviet and Hungarian leaders is the weakening of the Party that has accompanied the delegation of authority to managers. But the attacks have concentrated against another phenomenon easier to single out and combat. That is the fact that managers allowed to play the free market to earn money for the state also earn a great deal of money for themselves. They spend it, too, in the free market tradition of expensive cars, second homes, antiques, and fur coats.

The workers feel they have sacrificed the job security and slow pace of a Communist economy without really tasting the benefits of a capitalist, although their wages and bonuses have increased remarkably. But most threatened of all are the bureaucrats, who have seen the managers overtake them in earnings, status, and importance. This group has been able to attack NEM, restore a few of the elements of central planning, and say it is all being done on behalf of the workers.

But these are all problems shared by other nations of the Bloc, since all have undertaken some kind of economic reform, and all must grapple with the problem of Party control and wide variations in living standards. None of them, however, has the political flexibility and benefits of the marketplace that Hungary enjoys.

The two questions the visiting Communist reporters and television crews ask most frequently are: How do the Hungarians do it? And why Hungary? The second is harder for them to report than the first, because a large part of the Hungarian success was quite literally paid for by the blood of the 1956 revolution, melodramatic as that sounds, and East European audiences are not yet ready to hear officially that uprisings, successful or not, are bought off by concessions in later years. From the first shipments of Soviet relief goods and the generous loans that followed, there was an open intent on the part of the Russians not only to try to make up for the damage caused in fighting the revolutionaries, but for the economic toll of the previous ten years of exploitation. But this is not the whole answer by any means.

Other effects of the revolution have been more lasting. Kadar needed popular support at almost any price after his installation by the Red army, and the price has been to provide him with the popularity that a rising standard of living produces for the leader responsible, no matter how unpromising his beginnings. There is also the important fact that both Moscow and Budapest were convinced that the battered Hungarian nation, which had lost up to 25,000 dead by some estimates,* could be counted on not to try another act of defiance against the Soviet Union. The guarantee is thought to be good at least until the generation with direct experience in the revolution passes on. The thinking was that the Hungarians, having learned what happens to a Bloc nation that tries to restore capitalism, as they were accused of doing in 1956, are sufficiently inoculated against the danger to be trusted with the introduction of a little capitalism into the economy, whether in the form of Western investment or the market as regulator of prices and supplies.

To these explanations must be added another, harder to define but equally important. That is the Hungarian way with politics, an ability that seems to be shared by a disproportionate number of people in a nation of 10 million, which since World War II has seen three governments enter prison or exile and yet still manages to retain enough talent to keep the affairs of state and economy running more smoothly than those in neighboring Bloc countries.

Hungary has produced heroes, men like Kossuth, men like the anonymous machine gunners of Budapest, shot out of buildings by Soviet tank cannon. But it has produced more of those whose talents lay in trying to find a middle way, to reach a satisfactory compromise, to seek success in gradualism rather than grand slams. Imre Nagy was one of these gradualists, until he was swept away by the revolutionary dynamics of 1956. It is perhaps surprising that Janos Kadar is also a man of the middle, despite his advancement as Party strong man by the Russians. But Hungary's real treasure is the depth of talent; as a Western diplomat remarked admiringly, the experts in Party and government could fit in gracefully in any American corporate boardroom.

With the recurrent upheavals in Hungary's history, its citizens, more often than most others, must answer the question of whether to leave the

---

* The regime's death toll is 2,700; the 25,000 figure was the estimate of the defeated revolutionaries. The truth lies at an indeterminate point in between.

country to its misery or to stay there and try to alleviate it. There have always been exiles in Vienna and Paris, plotting revolution or parading in hussar uniforms. But there have always been many more of the smart and the able who made the difficult decision to function within the system, to try to make things a little better, whether for themselves or for the nation, or both. Such a man is Jozsef Bognar. Bognar belongs in the ranks of those who know that the techniques of survival, under Hungarian conditions, whether personal or national, have little to do with overt acts of heroism. It is not that Bognar has shunned high positions or controversy: he has been a part of every major social or political movement in Hungary since the thirties, from the populists to Imre Nagy's cabinet to the planning rooms of the New Economic Mechanism. Member of parliament and chairman of its planning committee, professor of economics at the Karl Marx University, director of the Afro-Asian Institute of the Hungarian Academy of Sciences and head of the council on world economy, member of the editorial board of the English-language *New Hungarian Quarterly,* Bognar is a man of many jobs, but he is best known as one of the principal architects of the economic reforms.

He is dark, short, with iron-gray hair brushed straight back above bristling eyebrows, and a broad face with prominent cheekbones, a face one is tempted to call a "typically Hungarian peasant face" until experiencing the variety of peasant faces in this crossroads of European migrations. Bognar wears elegant suits and tasteful ties, and talks to visitors in soft leather lounge furniture over the ubiquitous Turkish coffee, the legacy of another part of Hungarian history. I first sought out Bognar in 1968, the year the reforms started, for answers to the two standard questions, why Hungary and how. Was Hungary worried about the threat of intervention? It was a question asked often in those days and still asked in the seventies, whenever some new facet of the reforms is introduced.

He stressed moderation, equilibrium, the middle way, caution, and lack of haste. Czechoslovakia, he said, failed because it did not maintain a social and political equilibrium when reforms were introduced. Any reform, he emphasized, involves a redistribution of power among the various elements at work in the economy and the regime. Any equilibrium is chancy until the new forces are clearly in control.

"If you survive three or four hard years, you can make it," he said. "If you disturb the equilibrium from the start, you'll be out in the first year. The main problem is to maintain the equilibrium until such time as the upswing caused by the reform is apparent to most of the population. Only then can there be the fullest understanding for the steps being taken."

Hungary has survived those crucial first years of reform, as it has survived, during the life span of middle-aged men like Bognar, two revolutions, countless recessions and depressions, a procession of governments ranging from Fascist to Stalinist, wars with Romania, Czechoslovakia, Germany, and the Soviet Union, Red terror, White terror, inflation so uncontrolled that the banknotes lay in the gutters like leaves, famine, pogroms, purge trials, and the executions of two of its premiers, Nagy and the Fascist Arrow Cross leader Ferenc Szalsi.

It is no wonder that the heirs of Kossuth worry more about the very personal economic issues of a new East German car or a summer cottage than the broad political ones, and that those who do deal with policy emphasize the virtues of the well thought out and the gradual.

Bognar, as a participant in most of the history of his nation in this century, is clearly in the camp of the moderates. If he did not belong there by nature, his contacts with the ample patterns of extremism in Hungarian life would have put him there.

THE VILLAGE EXPLORERS

He was born in 1917, the last full year of the Austro-Hungarian empire, and grew up in a provincial town remote from the political turmoil of Budapest. During that period, Hungary shifted its course from extreme left to extreme right. In 1919 Bela Kun formed the first Soviet Republic outside Russia, but it lasted less than four months. When it was overthrown by Admiral Nicholas Horthy, a succession of rightist governments began under Horthy's "Regency without a King," starting with counts and landowners and ending in the anti-Semitic frenzies of the Arrow Cross as the nation crumbled before the advancing Russians in the last months of World War II.

In the thirties Bognar came to Budapest as a student and quickly was brought up to date politically. He had seen the appalling poverty of the Hungarian countryside as a boy. The great estates of the aristocratic families stretched out farther than a man could walk in a day: nearly 200,000 acres for Prince Pal Esterhazy, half a million acres for the entire Esterhazy family, which had been the patron of Haydn and, in modern times, was known for its efficient farm management. Estates like the Esterhazys' of more than 2,500 acres accounted for a tenth of a percent of the number of farms, but 30 percent of the nation's acreage. Eighty-seven percent of the peasants had fewer than five acres, the absolute minimum subsistence. One and one-half million peasants owned no land at all, and as late as the thirties, landlords were legally empowered to destroy their squatters' villages when the need for their labor was over. These were the rural proletariat, estimated by the populist writer Imre Kovacs to total more than 3 million in a nation of 9 million, including holders of dwarf plots, laborers, and estate servants. Their wages were seldom more than $60 a year; their diet, bread, pork fat, and paprika.

There had been attempts at reform; Count Istvan Karolyi, the first prime minister after the war, had been an admirer of President Wilson and democratic ideas. He divided up one of his own 50,000-acre estates among his peasants. But the movement did not get much further. Hungary remained an island of feudalism in the twentieth century.

Now, in the thirties, the political parties in Budapest were beginning to look again at the peasantry. The Socialists were barred, by a tacit agreement with Horthy, from trying to organize in the countryside. The Communists were a tiny group of perhaps two thousand, directed by exiles in Vienna and Moscow. But the pro-German followers of Premier Istvan Gombos and the Arrow Cross both were discovering honest peasant virtues and political power. They began to rally village and county town audiences with the simple but effective formula of blaming all the peasants' troubles on the Jews.

At the same time, the intellectuals on the Left, some based in Budapest, some from the country, were making a genuine effort to report and understand the causes of rural misery.

These were the Village Explorers, whose aim was to describe the life in the villages and smaller puszta settlements, and to use the data to advocate reforms. In 1938 they formed the March Front, named after Kossuth's 1848 movement. It included scientists, doctors, journalists, writers, political activists, and the composers Bela Bartok and Zoltan Kodaly, who had made many trips in the country to record and preserve the folk music.

A few of these men were Communists; most could best be described as populists, men who consciously or unconsciously modeled themselves on the Russian Narodniks who reached out to the Russian peasants under the czars. They used essays, poems, novels, and journalistic reports, such as Imre Kovacs's *The Silent Revolution,* to get the facts of village life to the public. Kovacs, who now lives in exile in New York, later organized the rural proletariat into the National Peasant Party.

Gyula Illyes, born in a puszta mud hut, wrote the best of all. In his *People of the Puszta,* he set out the stark economics of his people: "The total annual income of a farm servant under all possible heads—that is, including not only the wheat, rye, barley and firewood but also the lodging given by the estate—is about 350–400 pengoes [$35–40]. . . . These figures refer to the recent past and the present, to normal circumstances of peace. There are no complaints. But the young children scream, shaking and kicking at the locked bread bin."

Starting in 1934, the findings of the village explorers began to appear in the newspapers. It can be imagined what effect such reportage had on a young idealist like Bognar.

"I joined the movement for contacts with the Hungarian peasants from the very first," Bognar said. "The peasants were in the majority. We had lost our first revolution, partly because of the passivity of the Hungarian peasant. That's why the precondition of any democratization of Hungarian public life—or resistance against the threat of Hitler—was certainly support from the side of the Hungarian peasant.

"We started to go out into the village, to study ethnology, and at the same time to do political work. When the March Front was formed, I joined, in the university, in the villages, and later in the resistance movement during the war. The peasants and the Communist party, although it was illegal, had close ties in the resistance movement. I made my very first steps in politics through the March Front. This was a very radical movement, not for collectivization, but for land reform against the aristocrats and feudal elements, the estates, the foreign owners, the Church. More than forty percent of our land belonged to the landlords and the Church.

"How did we work? We had good ties to a large part of the peasantry. In every village, of course, the government party had its man. But there was also someone who knew who the leftists were in every village, and so we could get in touch with those who were for the new ideas. They advised us whom to see, how to go about it. The movement had great strength. These men were masters in their villages."

THE SZARSZO CONFERENCE

On summer days, the turquoise waters of Lake Balaton are speckled with white sails, and the highways leading down from Budapest are crowded with little East German Trabants, Czech Skodas, Polish Fiats, and sidecar motorcycles, most of them bearing the white and black Hungarian license plate and the "H" nationality sticker, and most of them heaped with beach toys, sleeping bags, and picnic supplies. The wave of cars crawls through Szekesfehervar, where St. Stephen, founder of the modern Hungary, was supposed to have been buried in the eleventh century, and where now Russian soldiers stroll along the main street or sit in the hot cabs of their shiny olive drab trucks. Mixed in the traffic are the Mercedeses and BMWs from West Germany, the Renaults from France, and occasionally a Warszawa or Volga. Balaton does big business with the foreigners, but it is essentially a Hungarian pleasure spot, unlike the Black Sea beaches of Romania, where the West German charter jets land on regular schedules and Romanian is rarely spoken. The lake, 40 miles long and narrow enough so that bathers can see across to the hillside vineyards on the opposite side, is a symbol of the new economic policy, its good as well as its bad sides. Hungarians intent on abjuring politics and finding private happiness have built so many little cottages and chopped up the shoreland into such tiny plots that there are regular editorials chiding their lack of environmental concern, and finally, a law has had to be passed to forbid the ownership of more than one vacation home.

The bright hotels, the crowded camping grounds, the outdoor restaurants that serve the tart white Balaton wines from slim green bottles—most date from the years since the revolution. Balaton was a quiet mixture of farmland, a few resorts, and villages before that. During World War II it was quiet enough to permit a remarkable gathering of Hungarian intellectuals, free from government interference or German supervision, to plot the nation's future.

The site was Balatonszarszo, on the south shore of the lake, and the date was August 1943, at a time when it had become clear that Horthy had chosen the losing side when he joined the Axis powers. The Soviet and German armies, at that time, were still fighting on Soviet soil, but the tide had turned that spring, after Stalingrad, and the Germans and their Hungarian allies had begun the long retreat westward.

Bognar and other members of the March Front were the leading participants of the meeting, which included about 500 persons: not only populists of different degrees of radical intensity, but members of the underground Communist Party (the bulk, and the leaders, were in Moscow), liberals, and Catholic intellectuals. A future prime minister, Ferenc Nagy, future cabinet ministers like Bognar, and a future president of the republic, peasant leader Istvan Dobi, were there, as were some of the leaders of the 1956 movement against the regime.

With the conditions in the country and the diverse views of the participants, it is no wonder that the conference produced disagreement on relations with the Soviet Union and Germany, whether a Marxist or a peasant-oriented course should be followed, and other matters. But Szarszo did bring out the general feeling that some kind of socialist development would have to come to Hungary after the war, that this was the only way to break out of the circle of feudalism and peasant poverty, that workers and peasants would have to cooperate, and that above all, the intellectuals would be active in the leadership for the first time since the brief period of Communist rule in 1919.

Szarszo was thus one of those rare opportunities in a nation's history when the general lines of a policy and the men with the ability to carry it out emerged at the same time, and at a time when both programs and leaders were sorely needed.

It is the tragedy of Hungary that the opportunity was missed. At the time of the meeting on Balaton, another leadership group was also setting down its thoughts on Hungary's future. Headed by Matyas Rakosi, a commissar in the Hungarian Soviet Republic who had served sixteen years in Horthy's political prisons, this group worked from exile in Moscow, and its ideas of postwar Hungary were, not surprisingly, identical with those of its Soviet hosts.

But Rakosi needed the populists, both the Communists and the non-Communists, for the present. After the Russian victory, Hungary went through the familiar first period of People's Democracy, with genuine multiparty governments. It could hardly be otherwise; the Smallholders' Party, which had been strongly represented at Szarszo, won 59 percent of the votes in the 1945 elections, and even the presence of the Soviet troops could not bring the Communist total past 17 percent. Ferenc Nagy, a

Smallholder, headed a coalition with the Communists, Socialists, and a left-wing peasant party. Politburo member Jozsef Revai admitted later that the other parties were tolerated for a time because "it was not correct to show our cards."

Rakosi's contribution to theory was his famous Salami Tactics, to slice away his opponents bit by bit, rather than taking them on all at once. He began by securing the control of the police. Bela Kovacs, the Smallholders' Party leader, was arrested for espionage, and premier Ferenc Nagy driven into exile. By 1948, the Party turned against its own, dismissing the minister of agriculture, Imre Nagy, executing the popular foreign minister, Laszlo Rajk, as a Titoist and spy, and, two years later, jailing Janos Kadar, a young man working his way toward the top of the leadership, on the same charges.

When Bognar discusses the days of People's Democracy, he is noticeably more enthusiastic about the early, gradual period, which is not surprising from an economist's view, because as the political climate got worse, the economy also showed the effects of Rakosi's mismanagement.

Bognar belonged to the minority left wing of the Smallholders, and when its anti-Communist leaders were jailed he and other members of the minority who cooperated with the Communists rose quickly to prominence.

"In 1945," he said, "I was a rather young man, twenty-seven, and was at first made mayor of Budapest." The city lay in rubble, the famous chains of the Szechenyi Bridge dipping in the Danube, the castle a shell, and multiple crises in housing, rations, and refugees, as well as the returning soldiers of the defeated Hungarian army for the young mayor to cope with.

He was soon to face problems on a national scale. Named minister of domestic trade, he was in charge of keeping some semblance of balance between supply and demand at a time when the needs of war relief and the demands of Rakosi's Soviet-model heavy industrialization were competing for priority.

Bognar had to do all this without training in economics. He owed his cabinet post to the need for balance with representatives of the cooperating peasant parties, not to any expertise: "I had no experience, I had no relations to economics before I became a minister," he said. "I was originally a professor of literature and not economics, after I completed my studies. But if you have a way of thinking which is orderly, in the scientific sense, you can learn. I needed three and a half years to learn domestic trade. By 1952, I knew that things had to change."

It was the last year of Rakosi's lunar economics, a time when the worried reports going to Moscow spoke of growing alienation of the Hungarian people. But as long as Stalin lived, what Hungary was doing had Soviet approval. It was not until after his death that the New Course, an easing of the consumer situation and the replacement of Rakosi as premier by Imre Nagy, was possible.

THE NEW COURSE

Nagy took office at the end of June 1953, less than four months after Stalin's death and ten days after the worker uprising in East Berlin. His program promised more political freedoms, legal guarantees, and above all a steady improvement in living standards. Collectives were permitted to dissolve; consumer industries benefited from Nagy's abandonment of the forced tempo of building up heavy industry. Nagy granted amnesties to political prisoners and abolished concentration camps. It was a populist program, not a Stalinist and hardly even a Marxist; it could have been the product of the Balaton conference ten years earlier.

But it was not an easy one to carry out. For one thing, Rakosi retained the post of Party secretary, and he soon began a program of systematic sabotage of the reforms. For another, it depended on the mood of Moscow. Only as long as Georgi Malenkov's concessions to the Bloc were the order of the day—which meant, among other things, as long as worries about the uprising in East Germany remained a factor in Soviet thinking—could Nagy and the New Course survive.

Bognar was caught in the middle those two years. As a minister in the Nagy cabinet, he was able to act with the approval of his premier. But as an official in a state where the competing power of Rakosi was also great, he could not do all he wanted.

"I knew that there had to be a change," he said. "We were going in the wrong direction. But change wasn't possible under the conditions of that day.

"After 1953, the relatively freer political atmosphere made it possible for me to explain my ideas more freely. I was always for reform. I started to deal with demand and supply relations. When we had shortages, I tried to detect why industry was not interested in production of consumer goods. I examined the effect that the lack of material incentives had on production.

"After a certain time I could understand that something was wrong. I made efforts to improve domestic and foreign trade and to influence decisions in the direction of change. In the very limited framework of a given branch of the economy, you could change something, but you had only a limited possibility of explaining your ideas about what was wrong—the predominance of heavy industry, for example. You were only asked about your own portfolio.

"When I became minister of foreign trade, that was better, because it is a mirror of the whole economy, and thus I could understand more."

But the New Course was not to last. Malenkov fell in 1955, and so did Nagy, charged with "right-wing deviationism," the same sort of charges that were leveled against the populists in the forties and were to be echoed after the revolution.

Bognar stayed in the new government and tried to save what could be saved of the New Course. But Rakosi was determined to make up for what he considered the mistakes of the Nagy policies. As if throwing a switch, he restored the campaign to build up heavy industry at the expense of the consumer. This time the effect was worse than if there had been no New Course, because Hungarian housewives and workers knew what they were missing. Rakosi lasted only a little more than a year, but contributed greatly in that time to the economic chaos and political division that exploded in revolution.

The events of the months before the revolution, the growing protests of the writers, the economic discontent, and the infection from Poland have been dealt with elsewhere in such detail that they need not be repeated here.

But the revolution is a vital mark in any discussion of the Hungarian economic reforms, because it symbolized the bankruptcy of all previous policies, whether command economy or liberalization attempts frustrated by central planning.

Bognar served Imre Nagy in the last cabinet before the Russians marched in, continuing as minister of foreign trade. After the revolution, he was dropped from Kadar's government. He does not discuss the revolution, but those familiar with the period say he did not play an active role in October and November and after the advent of Kadar chose to do his work behind the scenes. The first step was to gather with the shattered ranks of the economists and try once again to take a hand in planning Hungary's future.

"The general idea after 1956 was that we had committed a lot of mistakes in the economy—and not only in the economy—and that something had to be changed," he said. "At first it was a question of reducing our development of heavy industry and developing light industry and agriculture. The idea was accepted that you can commit serious mistakes in economic policy in a socialist country—this was new.

"It then became a problem of methods. The choice between central direction and influencing the economy through the managers and enterprises was not discussed very deeply at this time. Small groups of economists, however, began to discuss the idea that price, market, and money factors were more important than we had originally thought.

"We found out after 1956 that we had achieved a certain level of recovery, but the results were weaker than had been originally expected. Then the Party and government leadership were very eager and ready to analyze the system of guidance to see if it could be done through economic means. It was accepted that the old system of direction must be looked at, and that proposals be made on whether to replace it, to what extent, and with what."

And thus the New Economic Mechanism was conceived. But the time was not yet ripe for its birth. Kadar was pushing forward his program of conciliation as fast as he could. But there was a parallel program of arrests, deportations, and purges, in dealing with the defeated forces of revolution. Five years were to pass before the new Party chief felt strong enough to offer nationwide conciliation. Another six followed before the final lines of the reform could be worked out.

GOULASH COMMUNISM

Food plays such an important part in Hungarian life that the vocabulary of eating mixes easily with that of politics. Hungarians invented salami tactics. They called the New Course potato economics. And they have taken as their own Khrushchev's belittling description of the Kadar course as Goulash Communism.

But there is much more to Kadar's policy than extra helpings of goulash. Since the defeat of the Prague reformers, Hungary shares with Poland the title of the freest of the unfree, the Soviet Bloc nation in which the politicians, scholars, writers, economists, and ordinary people have to worry the least about the interference of the State and Party in their lives. The competing social forces are allowed free play, with the important proviso that their competition must not be directed against the Party. The apparatus of coercion remains, and is used when necessary, but persuasion is the preferred method. The watchtowers and barbed wire have not been taken down on Hungary's borders, but the state lets a quarter of a million tourists out of the country every year. It knows that hundreds will stay in the West, but that the great majority find Hungarian society attractive enough, and the refugee life unattractive enough, to want to return.

The attraction, Bognar stresses, cannot be based solely on more pay or the availability of goods.

"Not only the distribution of money, but the distribution of power, too, was not in accordance with the norms of a socialist society," he said. "This is why we must introduce at the same time, and we have introduced, a lot of political reforms. There is decentralization, more power in parliament, and a new role for the local councils.

"Local authority is much more important than it was in the past. The big change is that the ideas of many people will be realized, not those of just a few, in forming policy."

The new style of rule, Bognar said, is expressed in several different ways. Most important is the acceptance of the idea that a given problem can be solved by a variety of means. There is no longer one "correct" solution, imposed by the top man in that particular area of Party or government, with trouble for those proposing "incorrect" solutions. There is instead the selection of alternatives.

In addition, the decisionmakers measure the effects on group interests and the reaction of public opinion before they act. They try to prepare the public through discussion in the media. They delegate more and more of their work to the legislature and local councils, in order that the interest groups and public can register their protests or approval before a final action is taken.

This adds up to a considerable strengthening of democracy, Bognar believes: "Alternatives and different interests are taken into account before making important decisions, these are prepared with the participation of a wide spectrum of the best specialists, and the legislative is able to keep an eye on the executive."

This description of the new Hungarian Communism can apply as well to the process of drawing up the reforms. There was broad participation, and there were no "incorrect" ideas. This reversal of previous practice was the direct result of the failure of the old methods. Today's relatively liberal style of rule thus has its roots in the first postrevolutionary days, and the same is true for the reforms.

NEM was introduced because Kadar needed it as much as the economy did. Like Lenin at the end of the Russian Civil War, Kadar saw that the best way to popularity was through economic concessions. It is to his credit that he chose to consider the alternatives carefully and not be satisfied with the half-measures then being tried around the Bloc.

Any kind of rational planning was impossible in the first months of the Kadar regime. The Party was a wreck; nearly two-thirds of its membership of 900,000 had melted away. More than 170,000 refugees—2 percent of the population—had left the country. The Soviet Union was preparing to try and execute Nagy, in a period long after the Russians had been thought to have abandoned political killings.

Half a year after the fighting stopped, Kadar called a National Party Conference to find ways to run the country with such a depleted band. These talks shaped the alliance of Party and non-Party people that characterizes Hungarian society today. To hold an important job or be trusted, a Party card was no longer necessary: "loyalty to the Hungarian People's Republic and its constitution, the personal aptitude and qualities of the officeholder" were what counted.

By 1961, Kadar felt strong enough to present the alliance program to the people in his famous speech to the nation. "He who is not against the Hungarian People's Republic, the Party, the People's Front, is with them," he said. This was an appeal for unity on a new basis, reversing the classic Communist "he who is not with us is against us" that had been used to keep the Party pure but isolated.

The more than 9 million non-Communists in a nation of 10 million reacted to the Party first secretary's offer with caution at first, and later with some degree of enthusiasm. Kadar kept his word. It was not long before non-Party men and women were being given posts of importance in parliament, government, and in particular, the economy. Ordinary

Hungarians, too, use 1961 to fix the period of the upturn toward their present modest well-being.

THE NEW ECONOMIC MECHANISM

The most important use for the non-Party people was in planning the New Economic Mechanism. Kadar was able to call on the leading figures of the universities, the ministries, and the research institutes without regard to Party membership. They, in turn, were able to discuss their ideas in a genuine atmosphere of give and take. Bognar was prominent in the movement from the start.

"Ten or eleven committees of economists were formed, and worked on the various aspects of the problem for two years, in 1965 and 1966," he said. "The Central Committee of the Party accepted the new system at the beginning of 1967, and it went into effect January 1, 1968. This long preparation period, with its deep analysis of the past and of the potential, was very important. The accepted method of work was that it was not permissible to criticize the ideas of other persons without substituting their proposals with others. You can criticize our system, any system, easily from the negative side; it is easy to speak only of the dangers. The results we have achieved in the reforms are not far from what we expected in those committee study days."

Bognar was a member of the coordinating committee, which directed the work of the other committees and passed judgment on their ideas before forwarding them to the Party.

The committees went back to the roots of Hungary's economic problems. They found that the economy was still suffering from the effects of the early crash programs to build up Hungarian heavy industry on the Soviet model. Thirty-five percent of the national income had been skimmed off for use in investments for more expansion, usually in heavy industry. But Hungary had no real basis for heavy industry, neither iron ore nor coking coal. No one in Hungary, a visiting Soviet deputy premier once remarked, had ever stopped to figure out the price of a ton of steel made from imported materials.

But even after Kadar had restored balance between heavy industry and the production of consumer goods, and the nation had abandoned most of its grandiose projects, the problems remained. The experts traced the trouble to the inflexibility of the central planning system. They were not trail blazers; the Soviet economist Yevseny Liberman had come to the same conclusions in 1962. But the Hungarian suggestions for removing the restrictions of the plan went far beyond what was being practiced or contemplated in other parts of the Bloc.

The key to their thinking was that the directing role of the Budapest central plan authorities had to be done away with—not only in some industries, but all. Once that was done, then decisions could be made at the level of the economy at which the best information was available. And as Bognar makes clear, the lower the level, the better the availability of information.

"Our coordinating committee had not only close ties to the subcommittees, but a direct line—a hot line, as you would say—to the Politburo," Bognar said. "When we came to crucial points we could bring questions to the Politburo. After six months, we concluded that we must abolish all the so-called plan indicators. We went to the Politburo and said: 'If only one indicator remains, the logic of the system will bring back all the others. Can we continue to work in the supposition that the Politburo will accept this elimination?' In two weeks, we got our answer, our go-ahead."

Cutting the controls from the center was drastic, but necessary. Otherwise, the economic misery would continue. There would continue to be shortages of some items, surpluses of others, and wasted investment funds. Under the reign of the central planners, enterprises could not cope with the scarcities until the Budapest offices got around to revising the targets. Sometimes this took only months; often it was years.

Yet at the same time, unwanted washing machines, hair curlers, and carburetors would be piling up in the stockrooms and warehouses, and the enterprises that produced them would be rewarded by Budapest for numerical fulfillment of the plan. There was a similar lack of reasonable controls in investments. Plants were not charged interest on loans for building construction or machinery purchases, with the result that projects lingered unfinished for years.

NEM lets the market solve these problems. The plan remains, partly as a means of placating the Soviet Union and the orthodox critics in Hungary, but it sets out only the general lines of the economy. The bureaucrats in the ministries no longer have the job of detailed supervision. This has passed to the lower levels, to industrial groups or individual enterprises.

In the place of the plan, the managers rely mostly on the market to regulate their production by telling them which items are scarce and which are not wanted. Prices are set according to supply and demand, with the exception of a large number of basic items, from bread to clothing, which are price-controlled to protect the consumer. Profit, not a certain number of tires or pots, is the enterprise's gauge of success, and an instrument of future successes. The factory now gets to keep about a third of its profit, for investment or production bonuses.

Investments, too, follow capitalist laws. The government bank, which used to be confined to administering loans and counting money, now has wide powers of discretion. It can, and does, reject poorly conceived projects by attaching high interest rates on investment requests for them. The result is that little capital is left lying idle, and the moonscape of unfinished projects and lonely excavations that once characterized some of Hungary's industrial areas has vanished.

The authors of the reforms had given them three years to take hold. If by that time inflation, widespread unemployment, or other major troubles had developed, a cautious recentralization would have been called for. As it turned out, NEM breezed through the critical years and has continued to perform better than the economists had expected. The growth rate, which had been expected to be between 4 and 5 percent a year, actually had been between 5 and 6 percent, with price increases held to no more than 3 percent annually. The results have been more pay for the workers, and considerably more for most managers, more goods in the stores, better selection and quality. NEM also permits greater flexibility and encourages the role of small private enterprise. Some of the results of the reforms can be seen in the Budapest shop windows and the growing rows of little private cars outside the apartment complexes on the city's edges. But for a closer look, it is necessary to drive out to a village we will call Sajokezsi, not far from the northwestern industrial city of Miskolc.

IN SAJOKEZSI

The villagers do not want to be identified more closely; they consider that they have had enough trouble with the Budapest authorities and those who have occupied their nation. A Soviet army barracks is a few miles from the village, but the only contact the villagers have with the troops is when late at night Russian soldiers tap on their windows, offering to sell bootleg military gasoline. There is an exchange of jerry cans and a few forints—considerably fewer than at the state gas pump in the village—but that is all.

Sajokezsi is off the main Miskolc–Budapest highway, down a gravel road that could serve as a particularly tough proving ground for new cars. The potholes and puddles the size of small ponds are not much of a hindrance for the 3,500 villagers, because they drive tractors or horses and wagons, not cars. The village is suspicious of the authorities because it has experienced two mass deportations since the end of the Second World War. The first took away men who had fought on the side of the Germans against the Russians. They were told they were going back to Russia to rebuild the farms and factories they had destroyed. Only about ten of the four hundred came back. The village got permission to send a delegation to the Soviet Union to look for the men, but it returned without success.

In the 1956 revolution the village was a local center of resistance. After the Russians deposed Nagy, a general strike was proclaimed in the area, which has industries as well as farms. The revolutionaries set up a machine-gun post on the dusty main crossroads and enforced the strike by shooting at anyone who tried to go to work. They, too, were defeated in the following weeks, and many of the leaders were taken away. The chaos of the period made it hard to keep an accurate count. But most of those men are now either back in Sajokezsi or known to be living elsewhere.

The Communist Party has about thirty to forty members in Sajokezsi, about 1 percent of the population. There are also about ten members in the large collective farm on the edge of town. Since there are two separate Party organizations, there is considerable rivalry. The number of Party members is not a public matter, but is generally known through gossip. Under the Kadar formula, membership is no longer necessary for success, and the villagers who consider all the angles often would rather be classified as loyal non-Party members.

To create the appearance of popularity, the Party opened a tavern in the same dirt courtyard where village headquarters is located, and set the price of beer and the sharp Barack apricot brandy at slightly below that of the other taverns. Now the workers and farmers cluster there in considerable numbers, and even young people have taken to the place. The Party secretary makes use of this audience to discuss the latest materials he has received from Budapest on Leninism, the current Party history project, or the economic reforms.

The reforms have affected the village in three ways. Those workers employed in the nearby industrial complex are earning more, both in bonuses and in monthly wages. Their pay before NEM was around $65 a month. Now it is near $100. In addition, their share of the profits now stands at a full month's pay. The price controls coupled with the reforms have held inflation down, so there has been a real increase in living standards.

The second improvement, at least for a half-dozen enterprising villagers, was the relaxation of restrictions on private enterprise. The economic reforms included many provisions to help the neglected private sector, including state loans, generous tax write-offs, and the sanctioning of moonlighting through a regulation permitting an artisan to work both for a state enterprise and for himself. The private sector now performs almost half the nation's service work, and some private artisans even contribute to the national export drive.

Sajokezsi's contribution to free enterprise is a TV repair shop that has branched out into the picture-frame business. Lajos, the young proprietor, got his electronics training in a Budapest factory and took advantage of the two tax-free years allowed under NEM to get the shop started. Almost every house in the village has a TV set, but until he opened up, villagers had to take their sets to the next town and wait three or four weeks for the state repair shop to fix them. Lajos would do the job in a day or two. Soon the people from the next town began coming to Sajokezsi with their sets, and Lajos took on hired help. Since the ideologists would say that this constitutes the exploitation of man by man, it is forbidden, but the objections can be got around by calling yourself an artisans' cooperative.

The next step, after some experiments with scrap metal, was to start making little brass picture frames when the TV repair business was slack. The frames, for family photos or pictures of soccer or movie stars, sold well because no state enterprise seemed to be making them. Lajos applied for a loan from the National Savings Bank and bought a metal shear, a foot-operated machine that bends and cuts the frames. The village factory now has six employees and a modest export program: "We can sell some of our frames to West Germany when the quality is good," Lajos says. "When it isn't, they can be sold to Russia without trouble."

The biggest change that the reforms brought the village, however, was the great leap forward from agriculture to industry on the local collective farm. The farm, just beyond the village limits, has expanded and shrunk in time with the changes of agricultural policy in Budapest. It was formed in the forced collectivization campaign of the immediate postwar years. When the New Course restored voluntary membership, most of the members quit. After the revolution, there was a speedy reorganization.

Neither collectivization drive had the desired effect. The land around the village is not particularly fertile, and incomes on the farm were considerably below the national average of about $50 a month. They were able to supplement their incomes by selling milk, eggs, and produce from their private plots, but they still lagged behind the industrial workers in earnings.

For some collective and state farms, the reforms have brought spectacular rises in profits. The Babolna State Farm borrowed money to buy $350,000 worth of American chicken processing machinery and $500,000 worth of Western farm machinery. It now sells tens of thousands of broilers wrapped in plastic bearing colorful Hungarian peasant designs in the supermarkets of Vienna and Munich, and its workers earn about double the national farm average.

But to Sajokezsi's collective, NEM offered a way of changing from unprofitable farming to what was hoped would be profitable industry. The collective borrowed $17,000, bought an East German textile printing machine, and had East German mechanics install it in an abandoned feed storage barn. There were problems at first; the two East Germans had the machine working well, but after they turned it over to the Hungarians, it began to break down, and none of the peasants assigned to the new project knew how to fix it. Finally the farm found a free-lance master mechanic in Miskolc to check it once a week, and since then production has climbed. The collective concluded a contract with a Budapest department store, which promised to take all the material it could print.

Now the machine clacks away on two shifts, under the supervision of a manager, paid $105 a month, an assistant, paid $90, and several farm women, who earn about 20¢ an hour. They do not know much about the workings of NEM; the collective farm's Party secretary decided to put in the machine on the advice of the village secretary, who had returned from a Budapest Party meeting full of enthusiasm about the reforms. There is no profit-sharing as yet from the textile venture, since the series of breakdowns eliminated any profits. But all those concerned with the project are making more than they would from farm work. The peasant women got pay raises of 20 percent or more by becoming industrial workers, and they consider the work much easier.

Such clearly measurable gains are rare under Communism, in contrast to promises of a better future, which are plentiful. There are many injustices that the reforms have not removed. But Hungarians, on the whole, have been pleasantly surprised by NEM. They were suspicious of it when it started, as they were of so many other promises. Here, however, was a case of promises being fulfilled.

THE CRITICS

The economic reforms have brought Hungary the highest standard of living in its history. But with so much wrong in the way the economy was being run for so long, there is bound to be much that still needs reforming. Some of the problems are going to be easier to solve than others. The decentralization, for example, has left a lot of room for sloppy and even criminal methods of accounting. One export-import official devised a fake price scale and for two years put the difference between actual cost and what he was charging in a Swiss bank account. The economists do not worry unduly about such headline-making cases, because spectacular theft is rare in the Communist system, compared to the daily little swindles of time, material, and money. But they do worry that these little thefts will add up to a major problem unless a new system of checks is brought in to replace those done away with when the central planning died.

More of a problem is equality and inequality. NEM has spawned two groups of the dissatisfied. One wants an end to the differentiation in incomes and bonuses, a return to egalitarian Marxism. The other not only does not object to the different scales but wants its own share to be greater.

"In any reform, some parts of the population must suffer," Bognar said. "Everyone wants flexible prices, but no one likes to pay more. Everyone proclaims more freedom for managers, but if they become too powerful, then the trade unions or the ministries feel hurt."

Those who proclaim egalitarian views, he believes, ought to look back into what really went on in the forties and fifties, when prices, rents, and wages were rigidly leveled and controlled, but when nevertheless the favored managed to live far better than the majority.

"Many artists, writers, and similar people are value-centered, are shocked that things depend on productivity more than on the value system. Some people believe that we are creating a consumer society, and that there are conflicts between the inherited value system of socialism and the idea system, if it exists, of a consumer society. But this is not completely true. Many things were hidden in the old society and are happening in an open way now.

"For example, if you have fixed prices and shortages, a black market will exist. You can call this a fixed price system and not admit there is a black market, where people who can afford are paying more. But now, thirty percent and more of our prices are free, and they sometimes go up if the demand is greater. People call this instability, and say it is dangerous to a socialist society. We say the black market was even worse."

The other problem, inequities in the distribution of the pie, is more difficult to deal with, if only because more people are complaining about it. Bognar's solution to the swollen bonuses and profits of the managing class sounds more like John Kenneth Galbraith than Marx.

"If you want to give higher incentives, you must change income differentials," he said. "This will cause social tensions. Some people will move into more favored positions and some into relatively less favored—I say relatively because they will improve their positions, but not as much as the others.

"We expected social tension from this. The difficulty is the inherited structure of industry, which the trade unions are fighting very much to maintain, and it is not very easy to change.

"We have achieved very significant results. The living standard is up. But at the same time, you must strengthen the character of the redistribution of income; otherwise you will create differences that are intolerable in a socialist society. We are giving the taxing function more power than in the past. Through this, we can moderate the differentiation. The ratio between a skilled worker and a manager should not get beyond four or four and one-half to one. Socialism is not only an economic but a political and value system. It is based on equality of opportunity. But people measure equality very frequently on the basis of incomes."

Thus it is that there are frequent warnings in the Party press against the moneygrubbers, those who drive conspicuous foreign cars or live too conspicuously well in villas in the Buda hills.

THE POLITICAL EFFECTS

The most important problem laid bare by the reforms is that caused by the growing decentralization of society, the release of competing political and social forces and ideas. It was not wholly expected, and the regime has had some difficulty in dealing with it. Bognar welcomes the broadening of democracy on the purely pragmatic grounds of an economist interested in seeing the system work efficiently, and does not concern himself unduly with the problem of controlling the side effects, which in Hungarian history have so often become the central effects, of permitting more of the people to have more of a say.

The economic reforms played a double role in this process of broadening democracy. Criticism and more open discussion were officially encouraged as a valuable source of information to a regime exploring uncharted areas, and they are still welcome at a certain level. "Keep criticizing us," Deputy Premier Gyorgy Aczel once told a private meeting of journalists and social scientists. "We need it." But neither the criticism nor Aczel's reaction was ever made public.

NEM also provided a great amount of material for discussion. Its measures revived the old dispute between the egalitarians and the consumer advocates, at a time when the Chinese were making inroads in some Party circles with their purist ideas. Its provision of conflicting roles for union and management did away with the artificial unanimity that had characterized labor relations. Its weakening of the central authority in the economy raised the natural question of why political controls could not be weakened.

Kadar and the other political leaders were put on the defensive. They made it a point to invite discussion, partly as a way of showing that the political rules were loosening up, partly as a means of heading off more serious criticism among the youth and intellectuals. At a 1969 visit to the university in Budapest, Kadar spoke frankly with students and later reported to the Party newspaper *Nepszabadsag* that he had been asked why greater freedom in cultural matters could not be granted, "similar to the freedom guaranteed by the reforms in the industrial-economic context." In politics, as in culture, Kadar said, the Marxist ideology will win in open debate. But for the present, it needs some help; it "must develop and become stronger, from season to season, as plants do, which are first supported by sticks which can be removed when the plant is strong enough to stand by itself."

Hungarians in the universities, the professions, and the factories have testified about how these ideological support sticks work. Among the students, Maoists, New Leftists, and other dissidents are quickly weeded out. Some get mere expulsion from school, but many have been imprisoned.

Precensorship was never reimposed on journalists and writers after the revolution, although there are many institutional safeguards against the publication of unwanted criticism, from the Party committees in the writers' and journalists' unions to the controls of the editors and publishing houses. Since the 1961 release from prison of the noted novelist Tibor Dery and other 1956 rebels, no one has been jailed for what he has written, as another writer noted with some pride and satisfaction. But much has been kept from publication. If something controversial does slip through the system of gates, then the Party's correctional process is called for.

As described by this writer, who has experienced it, the process goes like this: Aczel invites him over. Aczel, whose former career as a minor Shakespearean actor is the subject of much mirth among Hungarian intellectuals, pours French cognac, offers cigars, and opens the discussion with comments on Goethe or Shakespeare, from his own experience.

Then to the point. He reads selected passages from the writer's latest work. Sometimes it is already in print; usually it has only reached the manuscript stage and is still safe from the public. "We didn't think much of that . . . was it really necessary to say this? . . . Couldn't this criticism have been handled in a more positive way?" There follows a little lecture on the constructive role of the artist in the building of socialism. Then the rewards are offered. The main one is further publication. Visas for Western trips and hard currency grants to participate in writers' conferences or do research abroad come next. Extra editorial or translating jobs are promised. It is not formal censorship, but it would be hard to find a more effective method of control.

THE UNIONS

The workers get the control without the cognac. Union-management conflicts cover many areas of labor relations, but their main rubbing point is the distribution of profits. The managers usually win.

How profits are divided up was illustrated by an official analysis of 7,600 state enterprises. It found they paid about 66 percent of their profits back to the state in the form of taxes. This is enough to make a Western entrepreneur gasp, but it must be remembered that land, buildings, machinery, and everything else that the enterprise uses to make money were in effect a gift from the state on the day that the reforms went into force. Since then, investments have had to be paid for.

The 34 percent remaining stays with the enterprise, which divides it up in the proportions of 67 percent for investment, 10 percent for reserve, and 23 percent for bonuses for the workers, managers, and office and technical staff.

In the first year, there was a further breakdown, allowing the managers to get up to 80 percent of their base pay in bonuses, the technical and white-collar personnel 50 percent, and the workers 15 percent, the theory being that the men at the top should be rewarded the most.

Workers who stopped to figure it out discovered that the profits would be almost nonexistent by the time their share came around. After the state took its two-thirds, and the plant its three-fifths of the remainder, their supervisors would be skimming off most of the rest. In practice, the differentiation was nowhere nearly as great. The distribution system only set maximums; it did not say managers *had* to be paid bonuses of 80 percent of their wages. As it worked out in 1968, the three categories got bonuses that averaged 7.8 percent, 7.4 percent, and 4.7 percent of their wages. But the idea of the topheavy system of rewards remained unpopular.

"It is difficult to make people understand and accept the fact that the share of those in leading positions seemed to be ten to fifteen times greater," a Party official complained. "Many people considered categorization itself to be a civic classification. This unfavorable atmosphere caused a setback to the very aim of the categorization system—namely, to increase incentives."

As a result of these widespread objections, the three different classes of rewards were abandoned, and it was left to management to decide how to split profits. But the unions, too, had to be consulted. The role of the unions had been strengthened at the beginning of the reform period through legislation designed to make them more of a bargaining agent and less of an accomplice to management. The law gave the unions five basic rights: consent, which means that safety regulations, working, and living conditions must have union approval; decision, which permits unions to distribute social and cultural funds after consulting with management; control, which means checking on whether regulations are followed; opinion, which gives the unions a say in managerial appointments, promotions, or dismissals; and veto. The veto power is the most important. All the other rights are more or less advisory. With the veto, however, an enterprise's union leadership can block a management decision that is contrary to law, the contract, or "socialist morals and ethics." It must then be decided at the next higher level between government and union representatives.

After decades of acting as transmission belts for Party decisions, the unions have proved to be unsuited to their new role as more aggressive advocates of workers' rights. Each year, official figures show, there are about 100,000 labor disputes in Hungary, but only about a hundred reach the veto stage. The most celebrated example was the 1969 dispute in the Gyor Railroad Carriage and Machine factory in western Hungary. Management had introduced new machinery and imposed a fresh schedule of production norms, involving more work and a loss of incentive pay. It was the kind of ill-considered measure that was common in the days before the reforms. But this time it had national repercussions. The enterprise union leadership vetoed the norm increase, the dispute brought Kadar to the scene, and the higher authorities eventually sided with the unions.

But even if such dramatics in labor relations are rare, there are other encouraging signs. Sandor Gaspar, chairman of the trade unions, was a model functionary by the old standards, insisting that the union organization be used to make the workers work harder, since in the end they would benefit—after all, they owned the factories. Party, state, and unions, he said in a 1967 speech, all have different roles in the common task. The unions give advice on what goals should be followed, but after the Party decides, their job is to use their "organizational strength and political influence to mobilize the people to attain these objectives."

But during three years of the give and take of labor disputes under the Mechanism, Gaspar's conception of the role of his unions underwent a change, and his speech at the Party Congress at the end of 1970, for all its hedging and qualification, was the statement of a spokesman for a pressure group.

"We are equal, but different," Gaspar said of the competing groups within Hungarian society. "Contradictions, although not antagonistic, also exist in Socialism. Therefore it is necessary that the trade unions shall represent and protect the interest of the workers. The rights of the workers and the implementation of the principles of Socialism are ensured by law and regulations—nevertheless, they do not become realized automatically."

Gaspar was careful not to demand equal status with the Party. In the division of labor, he said, the Party is not "a" force, but "the" leading force.

Nevertheless, in the pecking order below the Party, the unions will yield their place to no one, not even the state apparatus. They have equal rights with management and the ministries in deciding wage, production, and other disputes, Gaspar said. Agreement is not always possible, however: "Differences in views are caused by the fact that the trade unions, during their daily activity, can sense better and more directly the situation and realistic requirements of the various strata. The government, on the other hand, more adequately views the realistic financial position."

The unions, in other words, know that the workers want more money, and management knows that it wants to hold back profits for investment or other uses. If the setting were American, this could be the plot for a play about the class struggle. In Hungary, however, Gaspar insists, other standards apply.

"The state and unions are not rivals, but only serve the working class with different means," he said. "But it would be a mistake to put an equation mark between the tasks of the state and trade unions and erase their independent profile. The unions have to support and criticize the state administration at the same time."

This theme of simultaneous support and criticism takes up much space in the continuing debates on how conflicting interests can be resolved in the Hungarian system. The unions are the first in stating their case, but the organizations of the peasants, the youth, the women, the writers, and even the consumers, through their own critical magazine, also make themselves heard. For the most part, the protests are faint and the points they make often ignore the real issue. Youth leaders complain about lack of dedication to the building of Socialism, not about the fact that there is a serious shortage of schools. The peasant organization's plea for higher prices and more subsidies never takes in the issue of collectivization. The young writers say they do not have enough opportunity to get published, not that they cannot write what they want.

Nevertheless, the fact that these interest pleas are being made in more forthright fashion is one of the most important effects of the Hungarian reforms to date, and one of the most interesting trends for the future, because the forces that have been released are going to be hard to control.

THE LIMITATIONS

Enjoying NEM's benefits without having the reforms get out of control is the number one problem of the Hungarian regime, and it is not only the concerns of the Soviet Union about the danger of incipient capitalism that it must worry about. The centrifugal process that has been started will continue. All agree to that. Only the rate of change is at issue.

The main danger is that NEM has created rising expectations but has only a limited capacity to fulfill them. It is true that Hungary has reached a level that will take Poland and Czechoslovakia five years to reach. But the very success of the Hungarian economy carries with it the seeds of trouble.

It works well enough, the Hungarians say, so why not better? When there was inflexible planning, shortages, and all the other abuses of Stalinism, no one bothered to ask. But now they do. Not only can Hungarians ask; they can see. The reforms are providing increasing numbers of Hungarians with the cars and the Western currency to travel to the West. The government's confidence in the growing attractiveness of Hungarian society permits more and more to leave. But while they are driving or taking the train through Austria, where the living standard can be compared from the old days, they get strange appetites for more progress. If the Austrians can pave village roads, or have such attractive new flats, why can't we?

Thus there seem to be both structural and time limits on NEM's efficacy. The reforms may have gone about as far as they can without bumping up against the leading—which means interfering—role of the Party, and against the need for much closer cooperation with Western industries, with all its political dangers.

The time limit being suggested is the early 1980s. By then, the fifteen-year plan to build a million dwellings will be completed, the cars increased at 50,000 a year or better. It will be the end of the initial phase of reform. But there is every likelihood that the East-West gap will have increased, and along with it the dissatisfaction. The Hungarians cannot be isolated from the West. They are too close and too sophisticated; they know what is going on outside their borders. Another important time factor is direct knowledge of the revolution. By the eighties, the young revolutionaries of Budapest will be in their fifties, and most of the country will know the dangers of defying the Russians only through tales and history books.

The reforms in the economic sphere will also be increasingly tied to democratization. NEM, for all its limitations, did at least sweep away one of the greatest impediments to rational conduct of the economy when it knocked out the central command headquarters. Bognar and his associates did the economy a real service when they replaced this with a system allowing true choice and true alternatives. If it makes better sense to concentrate on petrochemicals instead of steel production this year, then the leaders can make up their minds on the basis of a full analysis of the choices and consequences, helped by the computers that went into service in 1971 and the opinions of some of the best-trained economists in Eastern Europe.

But there has been no reform of such basic importance in the nation's political life. Here, the dead hand of central planning has its parallel in the dead hand of the leading role of the Party, which means that however the national sentiments, public opinion, the facts, add up, the situation is subject to Party veto. Just as the most eminently practical economic solutions were not possible before the reforms if they clashed with the artificial directives of the plan, so are practical political solutions impossible if they seem to be endangering that artificially nurtured leading role.

The two main experiments in democracy since the inception of NEM have been greater worker participation and a better role for parliament. Both are limited by the Party's role as ultimate decisionmaker. Gaspar, the union chief, has talked a great deal about "factory democracy." This means frequent meetings with union representatives, where gripes can be expressed, but no possibility of overruling the unions. Gaspar, it must be remembered, is appointed by the Party, and at the same time sits in the highest Party council, the eight-member Politburo. All the key posts below him, from the chairmanships of the different branches of the unions to the factory representatives, are either filled by outright appointments from above or results of Party-controlled elections. The prevailing direction of power remains from top to bottom, not the reverse.

The same is true in parliament, despite the advantages of multiple candidacies in 49 of the 352 races in the 1971 elections, a great gain from the cautious nine contests permitted in 1967. It is clear that if 49 red-hot insurgents were elected in these districts, the overwhelming majority would still back the regime. And the system makes no allowances for red-hot insurgents.

Bognar is very much in favor of the legislative reforms, particularly the work done in the parliamentary commissions and by the local councils. This is a broadening of democracy that ties in well with his wishes for decentralization of the economy. He does not say so, but the impression is also that parliament and the councils are much less likely to get out of control. That is clearly not the case with workers' councils. Hungary had them once, like Poland, and they formed spontaneously across the nation in 1956 as a rival to the Party, not an underling that recognizes the leading role. As long as the Nagy government lasted, the councils pushed it into more and more radical steps, and finally survived it until arrests and executions put them out of business.

On the subject of workers' councils, Bognar, usually the most impassive commentator on political affairs, becomes abrupt, brusque, annoyed: Absolutely out of the question—no question at all. Not being considered. End of discussion. The impression is both the practical economist's rejection of utopian ideas and the worry about the spread of democracy in uncontrollable patterns.

Nor does Bognar discuss the Soviet role in the nation's political or economic development. He usually makes wide circles around the subject, using terms like inherited value systems when he is describing the Stalinist excesses imposed on Hungary against the wishes and advice of its best minds, his own included. There are occasional acknowledgments of the Soviet influence that everyone in East Europe must pay attention to, but they are never direct: "We must be prepared to take into consideration the situation in the nation. This relationship means compromises."

And yet the Soviet Union casts its shadow over the reforms in Hungary in the seventies, just as it did over the decisions of the Szarszo conference in the forties. Nothing could be done then against the wishes of the Soviets, and nothing can be done now. The populists of Szarszo and the experts of Budapest have the same problem: their freedom of action is limited. They must not risk the steps that set uncontrollable forces in action in their nation. The reason is clear. The first target of these forces would be the Soviet Union.

Thus, although Kadar may be sincere in his belief that the majority of Hungarians would vote for him, given the free chance, this is why he does not permit them to, and why the controlled majorities have ranged only within the 100th percentile in every election since the forties.

What is the way out? Thoughtful Hungarians speak of a change in Moscow, as do others in the Bloc. They aren't looking for miracles; just a return to the Khrushchev-like pragmatism that loosened up the Bloc before Brezhnev froze it again. "Separate roads to socialism" is their slogan, but when questioned closely, few are willing to set a date on which the roads can safely diverge.

Bognar believes that his nation's future prosperity, in every sense, must be founded on a thickening network of trade, and that means trade to the East, to the West, to the developing nations. But it must involve investment as well as exchanges, he stresses, to make the institutional bonds greater.

He wants Hungary to cooperate as closely as it can with Comecon—a reformed Comecon, capable of flexibility like Hungary's—but also with the Common Market, the United States, GATT, and the developing countries, his particular interest now.

Under this heading comes not only Hungary's cooperation in Eastward and Westward directions, but the growing realization on the part of the competing powers, China, the United States, and Russia, of the value of establishing trade and cooperation in manufacturing, investments, and licensing. This is the final linkup, as in NEM, between economic progress and political liberalization, and the key to Hungary's hopes for a future in which it will be permitted to develop unfettered in the sunny climate of improved East-West relations.

The reason, Bognar said, is not difficult; and it applies to Hungary's position vis-à-vis both East and West as well as the larger issues of East-West trade: "If there are common interests, economic cooperation, investment, trade—this means that the political atmosphere that made cooperation possible in the first place will continue to improve."

Therein lie Hungary's hopes, and they do not stop with the hope of selling more paprika to the Americans, but in gaining freedom at home.

VI

ROMANIA

Silviu Brucan

The train from Budapest, the Balt-Orient Express, leaves at dusk, when the lights are beginning to go on on both banks of the Danube: the soft illuminations of the old pastel buildings on the castle hill and of the intricate Gothic-style parliament, the bright points of light outlining the bridges and the roads winding up into the Buda hills. Waiters are bringing coffee to the customers who have lingered since afternoon at the marble tables of the Hungaria and Vorosmarty cafés, and the first bottles of Balaton white wines are being uncorked on the elegant terrace of Gundel's restaurant, in the People's Park out at the end of the little antique subway line. The gypsy violinists, in embroidered red vests, prepare for an evening of the joys and sorrows of their music. Budapest at dusk. It is the highest expression of the city's sophistication, its civilization, which has endured through half a dozen different kinds of governments and triumphed over all of them.

At dawn, it is still Hungary, but not Budapest. The train was due to cross the border into Romania sometime during the night, but there was trouble, and now, in place of the lights of Budapest, the sun is coming up at the edge of the vast, flat puszta, first an orange-red bar, like a strip of iron in a forge, and then, as it gradually takes its spherical shape, a brighter orange that quickly lights the high, cloudless sky. Off in the distance are the well sweeps and the clusters of thatched, whitewashed mud huts. A shepherd, in sheep-skin cloak as shaggy as the coats of his flock, watches the train. Three track workers crouch in a ditch by the roadbed. They have built a fire and are cooking goulash in a smoky iron kettle. It is the original, the prototype of the little kettles on stylized wrought-iron stands in the Budapest restaurants, and you wonder if the food is also that much better than restaurant fare.

It is still early morning when the train enters Romania. A poll of the Hungarians aboard would probably produce a unanimous denial that any border had been crossed, because this is now Transylvania, the home of the one and one-half million Hungarian minority, and a territory Romanian only since World War I, with an interval of six years during the second war when it was again Hungarian. Transylvania's towns have such split personalities that they bear three names, Romanian, Hungarian, and German. The border also means a change in landscape, from the great plain to the Transylvanian alps, pleasant low mountains, and then the Carpathians, more craggy and forested. All day the train threads through tunnels and over viaducts. It takes six hours to negotiate the 200 miles between Cluj and Brasov, or Kaloszvar and Brasso, or Klausenburg and Kronstadt, depending on the language. There are unexplained stops between towns, while the trainmen get out and crunch along the gravel and converse, and the engineer sends out whistle signals from the cab. Then there is time for the passengers to lean out the corridor windows or get out of the train to survey the scene.

In the high valleys of Transylvania, the wheat has ripened, and peasants are cutting their way down the long, narrow fields with systematic swings of their scythes. A few hours before, the big silver metal harvesters had been clogging the roads in Hungary. Romania has harvesters, too, but in many fields not only the hay but the wheat is cut by hand, as in an eighteenth-century rural landscape print. The scythemen's dress, too, is eighteenth-century or older. They wear creamy white woolen pants, black-embroidered white cotton blouses, open deep at the throat, and lace-on Balkan moccasins. A smart pony rig rattles past one field, with a prosperous-looking peasant on it. A German, someone on the train remarks, because the road leads to one of the ancient Saxon towns where the Germans still live, preserving a few of the rights and much of the language of their colonization of 800 years ago. The pony rig is nineteenth-century, and soon the twentieth century appears. A Party or government official drives past in a gray Russian Volga sedan, driven by a chauffeur in suit and tie, but no cap, since this is an egalitarian society. No one can see what the official is wearing, because there are bright blue curtains covering the rear windows of the car to protect his privacy. Or are they to shield him from the sun? The curtains seem to be in use summer and winter, in town and out.

By early afternoon, the train is in Bucharest, a city of parks and lakes and gardens, so much so that the transition from country to city is not nearly as abrupt as it is in most places. The rural encroaches on the urban in dozens of ways. The cobblestone streets on the edges of town, the big gardens and huts, show that Bucharest, like other cities, has absorbed villages but, unlike others, has swallowed them practically unchanged, grazing cows and all. Even in the center of town there is a peasant presence that must remind the citified Bucharesters of their rural background: kerchiefed women watering flowers in the parks at dawn, or sweeping the streets, or clipping shrubbery. The greenery cools and beautifies. Downtown Bucharest has many oases to escape the searing summers, and they are sorely needed in a land where air conditioning is practically unknown. On the ragged edges of town, a few seeds or plants set in by the roadside quickly spread to form screens to hide the storage yards and hovels.

Romania has been called a nation with rubber borders. Its territory has stretched and contracted many times with the fortunes of war and politics. Not only Transylvania to the west, but Bessarabia to the east and Bukovina to the north have been subtracted, added and subtracted. When French President Charles de Gaulle's state visit in 1968 was limited to the cities and countryside around Bucharest, some in the official party conceded that the purpose might have been to keep him in the only territory indisputably Romanian.

The Galati steel mill rises out of the flat lower Danube landscape 10 miles from Romania's border with the Soviet Union. Its towers appear suddenly on the horizon when the highway from Bucharest swings into the marshes on the outskirts of Braila, the Danube port 15 miles upriver. Through the haze of the subtropical skies, Galati's great brick blast furnaces and tall smokestacks look like a complex of mosques and minarets. It is an illusion, although a plausible one, because the Turks ruled the area for nearly three hundred years. From 5 miles, the illusion is gone, and the structures in the distance can be seen for what they are: a huge metallurgical combine, pouring gray smoke and a rusty-edged cloud of white into the sky, polluting Romanian territory, past and present. The lands beyond the river Prut have been called the Moldavian S.S.R. since 1940, but to Romanians, they are still Bessarabia, and one of the many causes of disaffection with their Soviet neighbor.

Galati is another cause, and at the same time a monument to the success of the careful Romanian policy of detaching itself from Soviet control. The mill is huge, but that is not the only reason for the impression it makes. The steel plants in Pittsburgh or the Ruhr are much larger; their surroundings, however, are also industrial and more in scale. Galati's impact comes from its setting. Its towers seem to rise directly out of the Danube wetlands, where the fields grow high reeds, sunflowers as tall as a man, and two crops of corn. The only buildings to compare with it are the whitewashed mud brick cottages with their thatched or tin roofs. Everything in the foreground is in scale, both in size and in time: the wells with bucket and crank hoists, the horsecarts, the naked boys splashing in the irrigation ditches, the old men looking after tethered cows by the side of the road. It is the background of steel, brick, and smoke that is out of place. The Galati combine does not belong in this nineteenth-century rural landscape.

That is what the Russians told the Romanians in 1960, when plans for the mill were completed. It was a time of "socialist division of labor," when the old autarky theories of Stalin were being discarded, and each nation in the Soviet Bloc was supposed to begin specializing in the production it could manage the best. Since Czechoslovakia and East Germany were developed industrial nations and Poland and Hungary were well on the way to development, it became the lot of the two least-developed nations in the Bloc, Romania and Bulgaria, to stay in that ranking. What Romania had done best for a hundred years was to grow grain and pump oil. It had the only dependable surplus of wheat in Eastern Europe, and the only oil reserves worth mention. But it did not have enough iron ore and coal to supply Galati's appetite, which eventually was to reach 4 million tons a year in a nation that mines only 3 million tons of ore.

The plan was not unreasonable; there seemed no justification for Romania's having to invent or import all the technology that its more advanced neighbors had and try to produce from scratch the cars, machine tools, and rolled steel they had been producing for years. But being reasonable takes on different meanings when it involves dealing with the Soviet Union, and the Romanians, with a long history of exploitation from their neighbor, knew the costs of being tractable. They had paid them not only with the loss of Bessarabia and northern Bukovina, a territory the size of Vermont and New Hampshire with a population, 65 percent Romanian, of 2.8 million, but with the notorious SovRom companies, which milked the land in the postwar period, and in complete subservience to Moscow in running the country until the mid-fifties, whether it meant purging popular leaders or paying relatively more reparations than East Germany, an enemy state, although Romania had been an ally in the closing months of the war.

Within five years after Galati's cornerstone was laid, Romania managed to defy the Soviet Union without either the military intervention that Hungary and Czechoslovakia suffered or the economic blockade that Tito's defection cost. At the same time, it gained China's backing, political and economic, managed to maintain trade and political relations with both Israel and the Arab States, and most important of all for the future, made a spectacular opening to the West that put a billion dollars' worth of modern technology in its factories and brought Richard Nixon on his first presidential visit to a Communist country.

When Nixon, the Communist fighter, embraced President Nicolae Ceausescu, the revolutionary, during his visit to Bucharest in 1969, the irony was not lost on the American correspondents, but it was also shared by their Romanian colleagues. Ceausescu uses a cast of characters ranging from Chou En-lai to David Rockefeller in his attempts to go outside the usual connections of the Bloc. There is no indication he enjoys rubbing elbows with the class enemy any more than Nixon did. He docs it because he has to. Ceausescu probably would have been much more comfortable if he had stayed loyal to the Soviet Union, had obeyed the directives from Moscow. It was certainly a safer and easier course, as both Ceausescu and his predecessor, the late Gheorghe Gheorghiu-Dej, could testify from the days when they followed it. But paradoxically, it was the Soviet Union that forced them to abandon the course. This came about because of the growing unpopularity of the policies Gheorghiu-Dej was carrying out with Soviet approval in the fifties. Until World War II, the Romanian Communist Party was a splinter group of about a thousand members in a country of 19 million. Its ranks swelled with the Soviet victory, but whatever popular support it had was quickly dissipated in the occupation atmosphere. By the mid-fifties, Gheorghiu-Dej realized that he had to change the policies or lose the people.

The point of change, as for so much else in Soviet Europe, was the Hungarian revolution. It showed the Romanian leadership the cost of trying to ignore nationalism. At the same time, it forced the Soviet leaders to grant many more concessions to the other nations of the Bloc, the most important of which was Nikita Khrushchev's promise, made at the height of the revolution, of much greater freedom of movement for the individual regimes. From that point on, it was a question of how much freedom to accept from Soviet hands, how much extra to demand, and where to stop.

Romanians are used to this kind of game; in the five years of World War II, they progressed, with the progress of the fighting, from lukewarm ally of the Germans under King Carol to active combatant on the side of the Germans in Russia to disillusioned noncombatant and finally to active ally of the Soviets.

The progress in the sixties was nearly as startling, and certainly more in the control of the Romanians. In that decade, Romania changed from the most loyal of the satellites to a nation that spurned international Communist conferences, voted independently in the United Nations, withdrew as much as possible from the Warsaw Pact, was friendly to the heretical Chinese and Albanians, not to mention Western politicians, and, most important of all, switched the direction of its foreign trade from a 70–30 preponderance with the East to a 55–45 one.

It is a policy of nationalism, but that is a word that finds little favor in the briefings in the staid old foreign ministry building in Bucharest. There, a litany of noninterference, respect for sovereignty, and equality is repeated. It is the same theme that appears in Ceausescu's speeches and those of the others. "Bourgeois nationalism" is, after all, a dangerous charge used by the guardians of orthodoxy, and Communists of such impeccable credentials as Mao Tse-tung and Gustav Husak have been found guilty of it. The Romanian talent is for taking the terms and promises of Moscow and making a use of them that Moscow never intended.

"We are good chess players. We never make one move without trying to foresee the consequences. It is the secret of our success." The speaker was Silviu Brucan, one of the best of the chess players.

SILVIU BRUCAN

Brucan has been Romanian ambassador to Washington and the United Nations, editor of the Party daily, foreign policy adviser to Gheorghiu-Dej, writer, professor, resistance fighter, and Party censor. One of that thousand-member Communist Party that came out of the ruins of Bucharest at the end of the war, he has been both the chronicler and a participant in the long and difficult match with the Russians.

"Galati," he said, "was the turning point." (The Romanian pronunciation of the word makes it sound like Galatz, because single final *i*'s in Romanian are dropped; this makes it easy to pronounce Bucuresti, the capital, but not Ploesti, the oil center.)

"We saw in the fifties that our steel production was about three million tons a year, and discussed whether it should stay at that level. We needed more for a machine tool industry—that was the key to our planning, and the key to whether you have an industrial nation or not. We went to the Russians, since the manganese ore would have to come from Krivoi Rog, and told them we wanted to raise production.

"What for? they wanted to know. To establish a machine tool industry, we said. What do you want to do that for? they asked. We'll sell you plenty of machine tools. But we went ahead with ore supplies from India, Algeria, and Brazil, and we shopped in the West for equipment. My embassy staff looked in the United States, but it was too early at that time, and your restrictions prevented us from buying American."

The Galati project, nevertheless, had an auspicious start. When it was first announced in 1960, Nikita Khrushchev, honored guest at the Romanian Party Congress, offered "technical help," and soon the mill was being praised in the Party press of both nations as an example of fraternal socialist cooperation.

But the first five years of the 1960s were crucial ones for Soviet-Romanian relations, and the progress of the plant reflected their uneven course. In 1961 construction began, with the assurance that the Russians were contributing a blooming mill of 3.3 million-ton capacity and a sheet rolling mill of 1.5 million tons as well as the forge and foundry section of the mill. Only the latter equipment was ever delivered.

Two important events changed the situation in 1962. The first was Khrushchev's declaration that the Council for Mutual Economic Assistance, Comecon, was now going to be truly integrated. The decision was in part a response to the growing integration of the European Common Market. It was also caused by the Soviet conviction that Comecon had not gone much beyond its origins as a trading post for bilateral business in the Bloc. It was time to carry out the socialist division of labor, and Romania, under the division, would suffer.

Hints of the Soviet stand had been made as early as 1961, so that the Romanians were not caught unaware. But their response shocked the Bloc. Instead of going through with the Soviet agreements, they went West, accepting British, French, Austrian, and West German contracts for the multibillion-dollar task of equipping the bulk of the Galati complex.

"After we bought the German and Austrian equipment, and after the Russians saw we were going ahead, they, too, supplied a rolling mill. The Russians simply couldn't have a major steel plant going up in a Socialist country without participating," Brucan said. "After Khrushchev was ousted we were able to get more ore out of Krivoi Rog. But that is a delicate situation. It can be cut off any time."

The Romanian response to the Galati crisis—simply to shop in the West—was successful, but it was clear that such answers to individual problems with the Russians were not going to serve the Romanians in the long run. Policy needed constant review and rethinking; allies had to be found, insurance and reinsurance policies taken out. In all this period of rethinking, Gheorghiu-Dej proved to be a master tactician, preparing the way for Ceausescu's later triumphs, and Brucan, as Gheorghiu-Dej's policy adviser and confidant, played an instrumental role.

"I knew when to say no to him, to contradict him. He would get angry, but he was intelligent enough to realize that he needed such men around them," Brucan said. "Ceausescu certainly was such a man.

"He was the only one of the top leadership that would dare go against the top man. That made him angry, too, but long before Dej's death we all knew that Ceausescu would succeed him."

Gheorghiu-Dej and Ceausescu met in prison during World War II. The site, Doftana, an hour's drive from Bucharest, has since been made a national monument. It was one of the most distinguished gatherings of prisoners in Romanian history. The list of prisoners read like a who's who in postwar politics, with the future Presidium members Gheorghi Apostol, Chivu Stoica, and Alexandru Draghici sharing cells with Gheorghiu-Dej, even then head of the small underground Party, and Ceausescu, then only twenty-two. Later, another postwar leader, Ion Gheorghe Maurer, rescued Gheorghiu-Dej from the Targa Jiu concentration camp, to which he had been moved. Maurer, a lawyer and member of the Communist underground, is said to have simply put on an air force captain's uniform and walked out of the camp with Dej. Ceausescu and Maurer both enjoyed Gheorghiu-Dej's protection after the war, but after his death, the prison solidarity weakened; Gheorghiu-Dej was severely criticized for some of his Stalinist actions, and most of the old jail gang were removed from their Party and government posts over the years.

Brucan was also in his twenties during the war, already a member of the Party. He worked as a journalist in the underground, and in this way got to know Gheorghiu-Dej, who, although in the concentration camp, still managed contacts with the resistance, to the extent of once meeting an exiled Presidium member sent to see him in Moscow. Without much formal education, Brucan became a professor at Bucharest University in the closing days of the war, when the presence of Soviet troops in the land made it safe to emerge.

From there, he went to *Scinteia,* the Party daily, becoming foreign editor, deputy editor, and acting editor in chief. The paper, which had been a clandestine resistance operation during the war, soon grew into a modern daily newspaper with huge pressrooms, correspondents all over the world, and a modern, ugly building on the edge of Bucharest.

Silviu Brucan does not look like a former resistance member, any more than the paper resembles its underground predecessor. Walking on the grounds of the hotel at Poiana Brasov, the mountain resort north of Bucharest, or at a terrace restaurant in the capital, he could be taken for a Western European tourist, in open-neck shirt, suede-front cardigan, crinkly gray hair, and a completely casual manner in discussing sensitive issues that most Romanian officials have not managed to acquire. Brucan has been in trouble for saying unpleasant things to the leadership, but he has been permitted to travel and even spend a period at the Center for the Study of Democratic Institutions in Santa Barbara writing a book about power blocs in which neither the Soviet Union nor the United States emerges without criticism.

NATIVES AND MUSCOVITES

The period of wartime resistance, Brucan said, was the real start of Romania's policy of independence, although it would be years before it could be realized. Without a popular base, the Romanian Communists were the party that never should have come to power. Under normal political circumstances, they would have been, at the most, a minor coalition partner in 1945. But with a country full of Soviet troops, circumstances were not normal. Being pushed to power by the Soviets, however, had its drawbacks. With Moscow's support went Moscow's direction. The couriers were Ana Pauker, the Comintern veteran and foreign minister, and others of similar type who had been exiled under the Iron Guard dictatorship years of the thirties and spent the war in the Soviet Union.

Opposite these forces were the native Communists, those whose politics were learned without Soviet support—and indeed against the Russians, during the Nazi-Soviet pact, when the Russians were friendly to the Iron Guardists and King Carol.

Gheorghiu-Dej, Brucan said, had many qualities that made him the natural choice to lead his country on its daring and dangerous postwar course. His chess playing has already been mentioned. In addition, although limited in education, he was highly intelligent, and he had excellent organizational talents, dating from his days as a railway unionist in Dej, the town he added to his name after being jailed there.

"But above all, he was a native, a national creation, someone who spent his time here in the class struggle and the liberation and was not trained or living in exile in Moscow. The entire story of postwar eastern Europe is the struggle between these two groups."

Gheorghiu-Dej got rid of Ana Pauker, who was Jewish, during the 1952 wave of Soviet anti-Semitism. He admitted later, rather ruefully, that he, the nominal Party chief, had actually been a minority of one of the Pauker-controlled Politburo.

"Gheorghiu-Dej had enormous capacities for good judgment," Brucan said. "He was also trusted by the Russians for many missions, including Cominform duties and contacts with the Greek Communists. One such mission, never made public, was to go to Budapest in November 1956, during the crucial days of the revolution, to help install Kadar. He entered the capital in an armored car. He returned deeply impressed by what he saw."

What he saw was the awesome power of national feeling, finally released after having been pent up by the Soviet Union and the Hungarian Muscovites. It was striking how national and emotional issues played more of a part in the Hungarian uprising than those that might have seemed more important, such as the nation's economic misery. The Hungarians were marching, fighting, and dying for their national coat of arms, their flag, their heroes, their anniversaries, even their own army uniforms.

When Gheorghiu-Dej returned, he told Brucan, who was in Bucharest from the United States for consultations: "We've got to turn our policy toward the Russians around by 180 degrees."

The first obstacle was the presence of Soviet troops in Romania. They were not occupation troops, as they were in Hungary, since Romania had been an ally at the close of the war. But the Romanian leadership knew this distinction would be meaningless if Soviet control were in danger.

There are a number of versions of how Gheorghiu-Dej went about getting rid of the Soviet troops. Brucan limits himself to saying, "The way Gheorghiu-Dej got them to remove the troops was nothing short of masterful."

One version contends that Gheorghiu-Dej was rewarded for helping control Hungary after the revolution. Hundreds of Hungarian secret policemen took off their uniforms and refused to function, or they fled to the West. At this point, Gheorghiu-Dej is said to have entered the picture with an offer of the loan of his own Hungarian-speaking security force, which could be borrowed from Transylvania, where most of Romania's Hungarian minority lives. But in exchange, Gheorghiu-Dej is supposed to have demanded the removal of the troops from his soil after a suitable period of time. The Transylvanians were effective, and the Russians held to their half of the bargain. After all, by 1958 no one could have had any inkling of Gheorghiu-Dej's plans for the 180-degree turn. He was the most loyal of the satellite chieftains.

Another version says that at the time of the revolution, when Khrushchev made his concession of more freedom for each loyal member of the Bloc, Gheorghiu-Dej carefully held him to it. He argued that the troops' presence in Romania was a sign Khrushchev lacked confidence in Romania. In addition, there were no borders with the West, as in East Germany and Hungary, and no need for guarding supply lines to troops in adjacent countries, as in Poland. The Soviets always answered that there was a threat from Yugoslavia, because Tito could not be trusted to hold back Western influence. But Tito's stature rose and fell periodically in Moscow, and Gheorghiu-Dej took advantage of one of the high points to argue that with such a strong Socialist neighbor, the troops could be safely removed. They were, and Gheorghiu-Dej was free to pursue his policy of independence with less concern.

Whatever the role of the revolution in the troop issue, its role in setting Romania on its new course cannot be stressed enough, Brucan believes: "After Hungary, it became clear to us that copying the Soviet Union in every detail would not work, would lead to explosive situations like that in Budapest. The Hungarians ignored and neglected every national feeling and tradition in following the Moscow model in every respect, and the revolution was the result. The people could not, in the long run, be expected to accept having everything of their heritage wiped out. It is enough to build a new social order, but there must also be native roots. The Hungarian Party was particularly shallow in this respect; there was no resistance link. Every Socialist country, however, was the same as far as copying the Soviet model went. In every Party there was a wing that had returned home from Moscow determined that from collectivization to the establishment of ministries, there would be no swerving from what they had learned in the Soviet Union. It was an eminently safe policy, or so it seemed at the time, because direct copying, without the need of imaginative application, does not take much leadership ability or intelligence."

EAST AND WEST

Other currents in international affairs, particularly in the Communist world, were to come to the aid of the Romanians. The most important was the growing dispute between China and the Soviet Union. The Romanians played the issue with all the delicacy and passion of an Enesco gypsy rhapsody. The bridge-building policy toward Eastern Europe followed by the West, with Gaullist France in the lead, and the adventurism of Khrushchev's final years, as expressed in grand schemes for Comecon integration, an economic plan that would have gobbled up a major part of Romanian territory, even the Cuban missile crisis.—all were used by Romania.

Romania needed allies, and the trends outside the country in East and West made it possible for it to gain them. The ties to the West began with trade. Business with the West rose steadily from less than 20 percent in 1955 to 23 percent in 1958 to 35 percent in 1965, Gheorghiu-Dej's last year. Early in that period, Gheorghiu-Dej sent Brucan to the biggest target of all, the United States, to see what could be done.

"I was really made ambassador to the United States by an Iowa corn farmer, the famous Roswell Garst," Brucan said. "He was here as a guest in 1955 and I was his interpreter. In his direct farmer way, when Gheorghiu-Dej asked him how relations could be improved, he said, well, Mr. President, you can't expect to have good relations when you've got an ambassador in Washington who can't even speak English, and what's worse, interpreters who can't, either. Why not send Brucan?"

Brucan laughs at his own mock version of his start as a diplomat: "Garst didn't really send me, although his presence here was a sign of improving East-West relations. I was sent because Gheorghiu-Dej wanted me to take as many soundings as I could for him and effectively represent my country in a period of change. I went to Washington in 1956.

"What a time to have such a post! Imagine, my secretary of state was John Foster Dulles, with his famous policy of rollback and liberation. I had to deal with American opinion during the Hungarian revolution; then at the U.N., where I went in 1961, there was the question of seating the Hungarians, the Khrushchev shoe incident. The Kennedy era brought such a change to Washington and the U.N.! I knew Stevenson well and liked and admired him tremendously. I was privy to some of what he had to go through during the Cuban missile crisis, when for the first time he had to read a speech written for him by the State Department. He was nearly in tears.

"It was at this time that American companies began to be interested in trade in Eastern Europe, but there was still too much preventing it. A deal like the Corning Glass one we have now was impossible from both sides. You had the embargo restrictions on practically everything we wanted, and we had investment restrictions."

When the opening to the West had exhausted its possibilities for that period, the Romanians turned to the East. The widening split between Moscow and Peking made it a propitious time. The Romanians never broke contact with the Chinese as the other nations of the Bloc did; in fact, when the others were reducing their trade with Peking at Moscow's behest, Romania was increasing hers to take advantage of its neighbors' canceled deals.

"We Romanians rode along with the China conflict from the start," Brucan said, "seeing in it a way of giving us much more room for maneuver. In a two-power world, we had had it; it was one side or the other. In a three-power world, the divisions are much less clear."

Brucan is usually not guilty of understatement, but to say the Romanians rode along with the conflict comes close to this. Both Gheorghiu-Dej and Ceausescu saw the Sino-Soviet split as a unique opportunity, and their policy, at least to outside analysts, seems directed to take active advantage of the dispute, rather than passively riding along with it. There have been times, in fact, when 20 million-population Romania worked actively in the belief it could influence relations between the 800-odd million Chinese and Soviets.

Room for maneuver was the key to the Romanian view of what the dispute could do for them. There has never been any question of Romanian admiration for Maoist policy; the Party leadership and the government have worked as hard as they could to point the country in exactly the opposite direction. The only exception might have been Ceausescu's miniature cultural revolution, launched in the summer of 1971, after his return from a long visit to Peking. Ranging from the cutting of beards of television performers to a scuttling of Western films and plays, its aim appeared to be a Chinese-style proletarianization of cultural life. But it is probable that it was launched to convince the Soviets of the tightness of domestic controls rather than to emulate Chinese ideas.

If the Romanians did not accept the substance of Maoism, they made great use of its effects. They followed the example of Albania, which in the late fifties had left Russia's side for China's. But, unlike Albania, they stopped short of a break. The signals, beginning in 1963, were clear: Romania restored relations with Albania, increased its trade with China by 10 percent, began boycotting Bloc conferences, refused to reprint the Moscow attacks on the Chinese, and began printing the Chinese versions of arguments, which neither the Soviet Union nor its faithful allies made public. All this was only the preliminary to the Romanian adventure in diplomacy of March 1964, when Ceausescu and four Politburo members broke the Bloc boycott and went to Peking.

The Romanians' aims could best be described as keeping the wounds open. If they were healed completely, and the Soviet Union and China once again began to act in concert, then the scope for independent policies in the lesser countries was going to be drastically limited. If they proved fatal, then Romania could never again play off China against Russia. How much influence a small country like Romania would have in this contest of the giants is problematical. Romanian officials tend to overestimate it. But whether or not the Romanians were really pushing the two big powers around, the split benefited the Romanians. If they tended to write their role in it larger than life, that gave them the confidence they needed to be bolder. And bold they were.

Flirting with China also produces tangible economic results. It took a decade for the alliance to pay off in large-scale projects, but by 1970 Romania was the recipient of a surprisingly generous $100 million in relief aid for its floods, the worst in its history, and had the added nationalistic advantage of being able to compare China's generosity with the few tens of thousands of dollars of Soviet aid. Longer-term economic aid was agreed to during Ceausescu's trip to China in 1971. Chinese technicians were promised to Romania to help build glass, asbestos, and other complete factories worth $371 million, with repayment on generous terms. It was more money than the Soviets had given the Romanians in a decade.

But the Party leadership needed more than distant allies. It is not strange, in the Communist world, that one of the last places a leadership looks for support is its own people. In the sixties, this is what the Romanian regime did, building on the firm foundations of nationalism, which has been at once the glory and the curse of the peoples of Eastern Europe since the time of the Turks.

NATIONALISM

The Romanian leadership did not have to create nationalist feelings. It had only to remove the restrictions it had itself placed on them in the forties and fifties.

A walk through the streets of Bucharest illustrates how the nationalist policy has worked. It starts at the university, where visitors would inquire in vain for the once famous Maxim Gorky Institute. Until 1963, the institute's autonomy was so complete that students called it a state within a state. Formed to train the Slavic language specialists needed to staff the thousands of posts throughout the nation during the days of compulsory Russian, the institute answered to the Soviet Embassy, not the university. Its rector was independent of the university rector, its students had bigger and better-furnished living quarters, its canteen was better, its holiday camps were fancier and bigger. Gorky students had their own library and could also use the university's. The reverse was not true.

But in 1963, the Romanian government stopped the compulsory teaching of Russian, and the Gorky Institute was quietly abolished. Its students all but vanished, and its faculty was absorbed into other jobs. In both Bucharest and Jasi universities, the removal of compulsory Russian caused a reversal of the proportions of Russian and English language students from about 5 to 1 to about 1 to 7. Often those who changed had to lose an entire year of study. They were glad to do so.

The walk continues through Bucharest. Its streets are a pleasant gold and green; the green from the boulevards and many parks that replaced the Balkan-style city that existed until about the turn of the century. The golds come from the stucco buildings, which have a kind of architectural unity in their designs from different periods. It is expressed in the former royal palace and adjacent Atheneum, which brought cultural events to the new capital a hundred years ago, and in the crumbling villas that house institutes and minor government offices.

In one of the villas is *Magazine Istorica,* which has given Romanians a month-by-month account of their own and the world's history since its establishment in the nationalist wave of the sixties. The role of the Soviet Union is put in Romanian perspective in its pages. The same period brought *Lumea,* an excellent weekly of news and opinion that replaced the Romanian-language edition of the Soviet *New Times. Lumea* is written and edited in Bucharest for Romanian readers. The local edition of *New Times* was largely written in Moscow for Romanian readers. There is a world of difference. But *Lumea* is more than local patriotism. "It opens our eyes to the world," one of its editors said. "In it, we have been able to show our readers that there is more than one version of the events they read about, more than one kind of right or wrong." If the Soviet Union fares badly in its pages, so does the United States, but it depends on the issue. In both *Lumea* and *Istorica,* some of the Bloc's fairest accounts of events in the West, past and present, can be read. This frankness does not extend to current events at home.

Films, too, have improved. At about the same time the huge Russian bookstore disappeared from the Calea Victoria, the main boulevard, with the excuse that the building had to be razed, the movie theaters in the downtown area began to get new names. The First of May became the Union, and the Maxim Gorky the Excelsior. Their diet also got a little richer, and typical cinema fare ranges from Romanian-produced detective stories to Western love and music.

Nothing can be done, however, about the Casa Scinteia, the publishing palace that houses everything from the Party daily and government news agency to Hungarian-language youth magazines for the Transylvanian minority.

The Casa is Stalinist monumental in style, and its size, although not as great as some of its sisters, such as Warsaw's Palace of Science and Culture or Prague's International Hotel, is enough to dominate the main approach to the city with spires, masonry curlicues, and red star, straight out of the planbooks of the Stalin School of Architecture. "We've thought desperately of how to remodel it," an editor long resident in the building confessed. "It's actually not a bad place to work in, with balconies and parks. But it's an architectural horror, and besides, its symbolism is anathema to us as Romanians. But there's no reasonable way it could be changed."

Not far from the Casa Scinteia is the impressive restaurant on the Kiseleff Road. It was one of Bucharest's prewar landmarks, but for fourteen years it was run as a private club for Russians. In 1963 the government announced it could no longer be justified to keep the restaurant open for seventy or eighty guests at a loss. The Soviet Embassy was displeased. It was equally displeased when party education courses that same year were shifted from emphasis on the history of the Soviet Party to the much shorter and less distinguished history of the Romanian Party.

How that history is taught is shown by a film the Romanian Party prepared and screened on its fiftieth anniversary in 1971, after an evening of peasant dancing and strong-voiced worker choruses. Its artistic quality was uneven, but it deserves critical praise as a masterpiece of the art of the cutting room. From the turbulent strikes of the twenties to the underground conditions of the Antonescu dictatorship, there was never a hint that the Party was nothing more than a minor splinter movement with little influence. But in the war period, the film's editors really got their test. The Romanian army is depicted in battle and victory scenes fighting its former allies, the Germans, in a campaign that pushed as far as Banska Bystrica in Slovakia. All this is historically true. But the Romanians are shown doing it all by themselves. Not a single Russian soldier can be seen in the film.

Films, bookstores, language teaching, movie theaters, monuments, magazines, architecture—some of these changes meant a great deal to the Romanians, some were only of nuisance value to the Russians. The major nationalist issue of the period, however, posed a real threat to relations between Bucharest and Moscow, because it dealt with territory and people, sovereignty and aggression. The issue was the annexation of Bessarabia.

BESSARABIA

The best look at the issue can be obtained in Jasi, which is known in English as Jassy and pronounced Yash. Once the capital of a principality that stretched to the Dnieper, Jasi "lost importance," as the history books say, when Moldavia, its principality, and Wallachia were united in 1861 to form modern Romania, despite the opposition of the great powers.

Modern Jasi was in the middle of a more serious kind of big-power politics. Fought over by the Germans and the Soviet army, it was all but flattened, and now great patches of green space out its Byzantine Orthodox churches and buildings in the rough-hewn Romanian public style, a mixture of traditional stonework and stained timbers and overhanging roofs.

As in Galati, the Soviet border is a few miles away, and it is as easy to get the Romanian-language station of the Moldavian S.S.R. as it is the local broadcasts. Jasi residents say it is more of an irritant than a source of information. But occasionally it does bring the latest bulletins in a border war that has been fought in the press and on the airwaves of the two countries for more than a decade.

The issues are much the same, although the level of acrimony is lower, than in the Soviet-Chinese border dispute, or indeed, any other, like Guatemala's with Honduras or Poland's with Germany. The scenario goes like this: "It's ours." "Yes, but it was ours before it was yours." "Yes, but it was *ours* before it was yours before . . ." and so on.

To begin only with recent history, the 17,000 square miles of territory were awarded to the czars in 1812, at the end of the Napoleonic upheavals on the continent. Romania got them back from the weak Soviet state in 1919. A strong Soviet state seized them in 1940 after giving King Carol twenty-four hours to surrender them voluntarily. Romania, with German help, got them back in 1941. The Soviets returned in 1944, and the Communist leadership of Romania was delighted to confirm the "voluntary" ceding of the territories, even though its most recent pronouncements describe the transaction as "the results of an ultimatum of the Soviet government accepted by the Romanian government."

In late 1964, Romanian readers were startled to find the Bessarabia question opened again, and this time by Karl Marx. The rewriting of Party and national history sent researchers far afield, and in the Marx-Engels Archives of Amsterdam's International Institute of Sociology, the historian Andrei Otetea found Marx's unpublished *Notes on Romania,* four manuscripts in a variety of languages. They were translated into Romanian, edited, and published in an edition of 25,000 which sold out practically overnight.

Marx's other attacks on the Russia of the czars are well known and often are used in current criticism of Soviet rule. The *Notes on Romania* quite simply corroborated the Romanian view that their powerful neighbor has taken advantage of its strength to seize territory and carry out economic exploitation, whether czar or Party secretary sits in the Kremlin. The date was 1812, but it could have been 1964.

But there are two sides to the territorial question in Romania. The other is Transylvania, where 1.6 million Hungarians live, part of a minority problem as large and troublesome as any in the United States. Eleven percent of Romania's population is Hungarian, German, or, in smaller numbers, Bulgarian, Yugoslav, or Ukrainian. By and large the policy toward the minorities has been liberal, with education in their languages possible from grade school through high school. Hungarian youth can study in their language through the university level, although the separate Magyar university in Cluj was abolished in 1967.

The Hungarians are more of a problem for Bucharest than the other minorities for a number of reasons. Like the Germans, they settled the area in the Middle Ages, and had been the minority ruling the Romanian majority until the First World War. Many of them live on territory contiguous to Hungary, and have experienced border shifts in their lifetime that made them real Hungarians. Romanian nationalism is famous, but Hungarian is legendary, and there is a tendency that comes out very quickly in conversations with Hungarians on either side of the 1945 border to look down on the Romanians. Romania's minority policy has been one of ebbing and flowing of concessions. The Hungarians once had an autonomous region, centering in the mountains around Turgu Mures, their attractive main city. Now it is only a cultural capital, since autonomous region smacked too much of Soviet style and was considered an impediment to national unity. The ancient Hungarian university at Cluj was merged into the Romanian for the same reasons the previous year. But in 1968, worried by increased Soviet pressure, Ceausescu began courting the minorities again, granting widespread concessions in cultural affairs and more of a voice in national policy.

No one understands Romania's minority problem better than the Soviet Union, of course, with its own vast edifice of so many minorities. The Soviet leaders also know how to exploit the problem with the willing help of Hungary, which despite its subscription to proletarian internationalism, still harbors feelings of injustice over the loss of Transylvania. Moscow made use of those feelings in the tense summer of 1971, when its campaign to tone down Ceausescu was at its peak. Through a speech by Hungarian Politburo member Zoltan Komoscin, warning the Romanians of the fate of their Hungarian minority in case of too bold adventures, the Russians managed to return Central Europe to the nostalgic atmosphere of between-the-wars jingoism. The issue is one the Soviets can make use of any time they want, and they and the Romanians both know that. The knowledge is so deeply ingrained that radical Romanian students in Jasi admit they never voice their feelings on Bessarabia, knowing that the Soviet would exploit any protest or demonstration.

"Bessarabia isn't much of an issue," Brucan contends. "Remember, it was our most underdeveloped part of the country and is still very poor. More important is the fact that if we reopen that question, then the Transylvanian question can be reopened, and that would be very undesirable. Transylvania is very rich, Bessarabia is very poor."

But nationalism in the general sense, Brucan believes, is another matter entirely, and one that should be exploited to the fullest.

"When I was in Washington and New York, we were seeking ways of making the best use of these national feelings," he said. "We knew that following the Russian model wouldn't work, and we were trying to find a Romanian model we could follow." He was reminded that most officials avoided terms like nationalism, preferring the standard "noninterference" formula. "Nationalism? Why not use the word? That's what it is," he said.

"It was under Khrushchev that our policy of independence took shape

—not that he was particularly generous. He was a remarkable man, though. After all, it was his grand integration scheme that started things. And yet he could see that nationalism was a force. They do it themselves in the Soviet Union. In all the republics, they let it have a lot of scope, although they always keep a Russified national on top of things, or a Russian, because they know its potential. Nationalism is an enormous factor, especially in this part of the world."

ROMANIA AND INTEGRATION

Khrushchev's grand integration scheme had both economic and territorial aspects. The first was to be carried out through a closer knitting of Comecon; the second through a plan to "internationalize" some of the Bloc. Romania's resistance forced the modification of the first aim and the abandonment of the second.

All the paths of Romania's move to independence are so intertwined that it is often impossible to separate the various individual actions. These paths crossed and recrossed in the crucial year of 1964. The first venture by a delegation to Washington, the Ceausescu visit to Peking, the first overt quarrel in Comecon, the first boycott of a Bloc meeting, the territorial controversy, and finally, the release of *Notes on Romania* all followed each other by weeks or days in 1964.

In April 1964, the month after the Peking trip, Romania issued its first open criticism of Comecon, although the dispute over its right to industrialize had been smoldering behind the scenes, expressed only in veiled exchanges of criticism in the Party and economic journals, since 1958. The issue in that Moscow meeting of the executive committee was nominally a broadening of Comecon. But in fact, it was a reply to the Khrushchev plans for integration, announced in 1962. "Under current conditions," the Romanians said, "since there are fourteen Socialist countries in the world, of which only a part are members, it would be desirable that all would take part" in Comecon. This quotation is typical of the Romanians' favorite policy tool, the multipurpose statement. It sought first a return to the sharing of Comecon technology and trade with China, which was feeling the effects of the Soviet-led boycott. Second, since there would have to be ideological compromises if China were to get in, it was an appeal to heal the split. But most importantly, from the Romanian viewpoint, it called for a change in the shape of the Comecon leadership pyramid, to get away from the system of Moscow at the top and Romania and the others at the bottom. The entry of China, Vietnam, Cuba, and other states that would supposedly turn socialist later would give Romania allies in its fight for national sovereignty in the trade Bloc.

Moscow replied that Romania was wrong to contend that "Comecon seeks to put certain member states in a subsidiary position." At the same time, however, it said that "only in a closed community can the socialist countries develop their economies in the most rational and effective ways." And then, as a final aside to the Romanians, "it is remarkable that those Communist states that want to be left to their own devices get technical help from the capitalist countries."

The history of Romania's quarrel with Comecon is long, and is still being written. It began about 1955, when the more developed states, East Germany and Czechoslovakia, began questioning the Stalinist idea that every state in the Bloc should have its little, self-contained national economy. By 1958, they had come out with the means to do this—plan coordination. The arguments were conducted in Aesopic language for years.

The developed countries used arguments that were both self-serving and economically sound: If Romania, Bulgaria, and to a lesser extent Poland and Hungary are encouraged to become industrial nations on the Czechoslovak and East German level of development, several bad things will result all at once. Our aid, technological and financial, will be needed, and we would rather spend it where we can get greater political advantage, such as in Africa or Asia. It will also cost Soviet aid that we will not get. But what is worse, if Romania makes its own machine tools, it will not buy ours. This will have two related and equally undesirable effects. We will have to seek other markets, and although it would be nice to sell in the West for dollars or marks instead of Romanian lei, our quality may not always be of that level. In addition, if Romania does not buy from us, it will not have to sell to us, and its oil and grain are raw materials we need and can obtain from Romania at the artificial Comecon prices, much lower and with no foreign currency problems.

Then comes the ideological justification. Of course, the theorists said, we want Romania and Bulgaria to undertake the historic transformation from agricultural to industrial nation, because only through the formation of a strong proletariat can the future of Communist rule be assured. But let us look at the agricultural-industrial proportions in the Soviet Bloc as a whole, not in the individual countries. If Romanian farmers are providing bread for the workers of Brno and Karl-Marx-Stadt, and Romanian machinery purchases are expanding the industries of the more developed northern neighbors, then the industrial base and hence the proletariat of the Commonwealth as a whole is growing, whether or not this is reflected in the individual countries.

After the arguments came the institutions. The result was the "Basic Principles of the International Division of Labor" adopted by Comecon in 1962.

It should be noted that all members, including Romania, signed the agreement; it was still too early to try defiance. The "Principles" were tough. The document called for the coordination of the national plans on the basis of the most advantageous chances for investments in each. There was a sop to the Romanians in the promise that this policy would not be applied in such a way as to do harm to the employment situation, the balance of payments, or the national defense position of each country. But the emphasis was clearly coordination. Worst of all was the ruling on iron and steel production. It sounded to Romanians like it had been drawn up expressly for Galati: "Metallurgical plants with a complete cycle should be developed first of all in countries that are fully or in large measure supplied with domestic ores and fuels, or at least one of these."

Romanian officials wavered between anger and despair. Despite the apparent concessions, the "Principles" had forced on them everything that they feared: integration, restrictions in national economic decisions, the possibility of being doomed to the status of the Bloc's gardeners and oilmen. It was particularly rankling to think that not only the Russians had the power to decide what was good for the Romanians, but that Czechoslovakia and East Germany, like apple-polishing pupils, could also dictate to Romania's disadvantage and their own advantage.

At this low point, the ebullient Nikita S. Khrushchev landed in Bucharest on a good-will tour to convince the Romanians the right thing was being done for them. The effect was exactly the opposite. It helped convince the leadership that Khrushchev's course was dangerous and should be stopped at all costs.

Khrushchev was taken on a tour of the nation's industry, to show him that underdeveloped Romania was indeed moving forward. The tour was carefully arranged to include those few factories which had been equipped with Western machinery. The message was plain: industrialization would continue without and even despite the Soviets.

Khrushchev apparently avoided the Galati site, where the first structures and towers were then slowly rising, because that would have put him in a position of either endorsing or condemning the project. But, Brucan said, he was not a great deal happier during his visit to the Electroput plant, which, like Galati, was plunked down in a landscape of mud roads and one-cow farmyards on the outskirts of the pretty Balkan-style provincial city of Craiova. The factory, using mostly imported machines and technology, turns out huge electric turbines, locomotives, and industrial motors.

"Khrushchev personally didn't want to see us doing things like this," Brucan said. "I was with him when he visited Craiova, where we had a new locomotive plant we were proud of. They were producing on a new Swiss license. 'Why do you have these locomotives that we can't get?' Khrushchev wanted to know of Gheorghiu-Dej. He was angry. 'You don't need these plants,' he told us.

"A group of workers approached him with a model of the factory, as a gift. It was plain that they had worked on it a long time and were proud of it. He turned his back to them, refused to accept it. They were humiliated. But that was his attitude toward the smaller countries going ahead on their own. We simply weren't entitled to that."

Romania's response to this and other humiliations was to use all the skill it could muster in manipulating the various levers, political and economic, still left to it. Sometimes the lever was pushed full ahead, sometimes to stop; more often it was somewhere in between. In those early years, Romania would not send a top official to Bloc meetings, but usually did not boycott them completely. When it alone of the Bloc published Chinese polemics against the Soviets, it did so only in paraphrase, and it stressed those points that coincided with Romania's views on Comecon.

The Declaration of the Central Committee of April 1964, however, was issued with the lever full ahead. The Declaration of Independence, as it came to be called in Bucharest and abroad, covered a great deal of ground, but kept returning to the theme of Comecon and the loss of national rights: "The idea of a single planning body for all Comecon countries has the most serious economic and political implications," it said. "The planned management of the national economy is one of the fundamental, essential, and inalienable attributes of the government of the socialist state . . . transmitting such levers to the competence of superstate or extrastate bodies would turn sovereignty into a meaningless notion."

The shock that the declaration touched off in Moscow was to be matched a few months later by shock in Bucharest over a Soviet plan that seemed exactly designed to build the superstate the Romanian nationalists feared. The plan was made known by a Soviet geographer concerned with the potentialities of the lower Danube area for international economic cooperation. E. V. Valev wrote that the labor supply and raw material of the Soviet Union, Romania, and Bulgaria "would help solve these problems in common" with the use of iron ore from Krivoi Rog and various industrial plants in the three countries, including Galati. But existing borders could not remain as they were if the economic area were to be truly efficient. Each nation would have to contribute to the common good.

Romanians learned about the plan in an indignant article in the Party economic journal, *Viata Economica.* "Romania would give up 42 percent of its area on which 48 percent of its people live, for the complex," it said. "We must ask if the term 'border area' is not too broadly used. If one answers that the Soviet Union and Bulgaria have also given land, Romania is giving 67 percent of the 150,000 square kilometers; Bulgaria, 38,000; the Soviet Union, 12,000.

"The area would be treated as no man's land, and not parts of sovereign states, as though state borders, in the alleged interests of the Socialist world system, could be violated. If these plans were realized, Romania as a state and the Romanian people as a nation would be liquidated through simple administrative methods, on the pretense of economic necessity, in the name of simplistic Marxism-Leninism."

Moscow realized immediately that it had gone too far, and punctured the trial balloon. It chastised Valev for "narrow scientific perspective."

THE TURN TO THE WEST

As these skirmishes with the Soviet Union continued, Romania was turning more and more to the West, first for trade, and then for political agreements. Brucan focused on the main target, the United States, as soon as he reached his Washington post. But for some time before that, Romania had been extending its contacts with Western Europe.

The results of this spread of trading patterns are so remarkable that a traveler to Romania might wonder if the nation even belongs to Comecon at all. He or she arrives at the new Otopeni airport on a British Aircraft Corporation jet flying the red, gold, and blue Romanian colors. The planes, Romanian officials like to relate, were bought in a barter deal that sent a good part of the Romanian grain crop to Scotland's distilleries, from whence some of it has presumably returned to the luxury stores on the Boulevard Magheru.

From the airport, the traveler rides into town in a British Leyland bus built under license in Israel and traded to Romania for oil, or in a West German Mercedes bus built under license in Iran and bought for tractors. Or perhaps he or she rents a Dacia, the little cars named after the ancient peoples that dwelt in Romania before the Romans. Dacias are built under license from France's Renault, which also supplied the factory. The hotel could be the new Intercontinental, built with American financing, and with Austrian, German, British, and French touches in the air conditioning, elevators, and engineering. There would, of course, be Pepsi-Cola on the menu, and also Italian vermouth and Danish aquavit, but there would also be traces of some of Romania's other trade adventures, such as the heavy, sweet Albanian cognac or the floral-patterned Chinese towels.

More striking, however, than these surface indicators is the extent of Westernization in Romanian industry. Galati and the Craiova electrical works are not isolated instances.

Any tour of Romanian factories shows up an amazing variety of Western equipment. When Soviet Premier Alexei Kosygin chatted with Romanian lathe operators on a visit to the First of May machine tool plant in Ploesti, the Made in West Germany label was prominent in the background. The chemical combine in Craiova has equipment from no fewer than 371 foreign companies—130 different suppliers for manufacturing equipment, 101 for the power plants, and 140 for measuring and control devices. On the Iron Gate project on the Danube, where

Yugoslavia and Romania are building a power and navigation dam, yellow and chartreuse American construction equipment competes with Soviet, and both compete with the antlike labor of the youth construction battalions. The equipment list is practically endless. One final item, however, is the management training center of the United Nations, in a pleasant setting a few miles from Bucharest. Here the managers of the state-run plants are taught modern management, and this means Western. There is no Marx or Lenin in the center's library shelves, but there are many books with the imprints of the business schools at Columbia and Harvard.

The turn to the West was soon reflected in the foreign trade figures. In 1958 the Soviet Union accounted for 51 percent of Romania's trade, and the West 17 percent. By 1965, Russia's percentage was 39 and the West's 30. Trade with the rest of Comecon remained at about 21 percent.

"My days in Washington and New York were at the beginning of this reassessment of Romanian policy," Brucan said. "We knew that following the Russian model wouldn't work, and we were still trying to find our Romanian model."

The quest took Brucan into some strange byways, including that peculiar American institution, the TV talk show. Only forty when he took over the Washington job, fluent and colloquial in English, and frank to a degree rare in Communist or any diplomats, Brucan soon found himself an attraction for reporters and cocktail party hostesses. This was fine with Gheorghiu-Dej, because he had sent Brucan to Washington not only to make soundings, but also to show the United States that Romania was loosening up, that it would be easy to deal with. But the bureaucrats back in Bucharest were not quite prepared for the new style, as Brucan relates: "The first time I was invited to take part in a round-table discussion on American television, I cabled back to the foreign office for permission. This was normal practice. But they insisted on seeing all the questions and answers ahead of time. This, of course, was impossible. When I came back on a visit, I explained to Gheorghiu-Dej how impossible it was, and told him that if I were to go on American TV I would have to have a free hand. He gave me the green light. Go ahead, he said, and you'll make some mistakes—but try not to make any big ones."

Brucan's imagemaking and the concurrent efforts of the Romanian officials and diplomats in Bucharest and the other Western capitals did a lot to restore confidence in Romania as a marketplace, even among those who had been stung by the expropriations and imprisonments of the forties. In the sixties, the traveling salesmen began to come and go with greater frequency. They were a familiar sight on the sunny terraces of the Lido and Athenee Palace hotels in Bucharest, with their unrolled blueprints and open briefcases among the ice buckets of Romanian wine and Tuica, the ubiquitous plum brandy. The visit of one such figure,

Richard Nixon, at that time an attorney representing Pepsi-Cola, soon resulted in new bottles in the ice buckets.

It seemed all very simple. The graphs showing trade with the West pointed uphill, with the incline ever steeper; those showing trade with the Russians pointed downward. Trade agreements were signed with the regularity of international soccer matches, and almost every day the Romanian press carried a new account of Western equipment purchases or technical aid. Most of the announcements were in the future tense, however: France or Germany was delivering a plant or technology that would eventually enable Romania to make such and such a manufactured product, which could be exported to pay back the cost of the equipment. In the meantime, while the new machines were tooling up, the traditional export pattern of grain, oil, hides, wood products, and fruits and vegetables continued.

The result was trade deficits, ever widening. Here the graphs made some spectacular patterns. The debt to the West was estimated at $300 million in 1966. Two years later, it was $800 million. In 1971 it passed the billion-dollar mark. There was concern among Romania's business partners, but not of the magnitude that might be expected; political considerations were as much a factor for the Western governments as the expansion of trade. French aluminum plants and car factories helped the French economy, but they also supported the Gaullist policy of creating a third force in Europe. In like manner the Krupp machinery backed Ostpolitik, and Mr. Nixon's Pepsi-Cola was an aid, first to President Johnson's bridge building, and later to his own.

But even if the political considerations made the debt easier to live with for Bucharest, its immense size eventually presented a problem. The trade gap could be cut in several ways, but all were difficult. If machinery imports were reduced, then the industrial development that was counted on to eventually pay off the debts with exports would be stunted. If consumer goods imports were reduced, there would be problems of worker morale. If Romania turned back to the Soviets, where loans and soft-currency deals were available, that would mean a surrender of hard-won independence, and lower-quality imports besides. As it turned out, the Romanians decided to adopt a little bit of all these courses. As a result, there were soon indications that the deficit had passed its peak. But in the meantime, the old cycle that plagues so much of Eastern Europe's economy continued its revolutions: shoddy goods are produced because of poor technology and worker morale. They cannot be sold in sufficient quantity in the West to pay for the imports of machinery and consumer goods. Thus the machinery deteriorates further, as does the morale, the sales suffer more, the import purchasing power is further restricted, and so on.

Are there ways to break the cycle? One is by selling the Romanian sand and sun to Germans, Britons, and others who have hard currency but uneven weather in their home countries. In 1956 only 5,000 foreign tourists visited Romania—100 a week. In 1969 the 2 million mark was passed. There is a Miami Beachlike complex of hotels and beaches and restaurants stretching from the mouths of the Danube to the Bulgarian border.

This may have nothing to do with Marx's added value theory, but it does help balance the books. A more promising development, in Brucan's view, is the setting up of cooperative manufacturing ventures with Western companies. In this way, markets are assured, if not in the West, then in third countries, such as the Middle East.

"This involves fifty-fifty sharing, and co-production for export wherever the American partner wants to sell," he said. "Some of the plants are run by an American manager. But Romanians are being trained, on a very long-range program, to take over in twenty years. We supply the plants and the working force. You supply the machines and the know-how. This is the way our credits can be paid off. Exports have never amounted to much, and won't, even if we're given most-favored-nation status. But cooperation is the way of the future for us."

The Corning Glass Works agreement is an example of the new kind of cooperation. Corning concluded a $7 million contract to build a plant in Romania to make the glass housings for television tubes. Twenty Romanians were trained from two to six months in Corning's New York state plant. Over a three-year period, Corning sent about fifty technicians to Romania to supervise construction and help in training. The plant started operations in 1970, and by mid-1971 all the Corning employees had trained their Romanian counterparts and left. The plant will not cost Corning any business, since it did not export the television tube housings to Eastern Europe, and it has put Romania into the export market.

The key to the arrangement is export to third countries. It puts the American investment into areas like the Middle East where it might not otherwise be welcome. And it earns the Romanians foreign currency without forcing them to compete on the American domestic market.

There have been many other steps forward in Romania's efforts in the United States. Restrictions are being lifted, Export-Import Bank credits are forthcoming, most-favored-nation status is on the way. U.S. corporations are planning joint oil drilling ventures in the Black Sea and the construction of new refineries in Romania to handle both domestic and Middle East crude. There is regular Pan American air service between Bucharest and New York. Trade rose spectacularly in the space of a very few years: from $11.8 million in 1965 to $79 million in 1970, and, of course, the deficit rose, too, to $116 million in that same five-year period. The 1970 figures show why: Romania exported only $13 million worth of goods to the United States, from which it bought $66 million worth. The Export-Import Bank, however, guarantees payment for nervous creditors. There are also Romanian guarantees, permitting

American and other investors to hold as much as 50 percent of the venture and to expatriate profits.

All these agreements are quite an achievement for a nation still very much in the Soviet Bloc and without any sizable pressure group of American relatives to lobby for it. Part of the credit must go to the Nixon administration, which saw Romania as the most suitable target for a foreign policy initiative toward Eastern Europe, and backed up the successful 1969 visit of the president with the dull business of setting out agreements and concessions. But most credit must go to the Romanians, who after all wanted the Nixon visit badly—as badly as the Chinese and Soviets did three years later—and who followed it up with some handshaking of their own in the United States.

CONDUCATORUL

The central figure in this sales campaign, surprisingly enough, was the ex-resistance fighter and apparatchik Nicolae Ceausescu, not only in laying down the policy, but in unexpectedly expanding a short visit to the United Nations in 1970 to add on a salesman's itinerary of bankers and businessmen on both coasts. He lunched with David Rockefeller, chairman of the Chase Manhattan Bank, and guests that included the top men of Atlantic Richfield, Allied Chemical, General Foods, Standard Oil of New Jersey, Anaconda, and A.T. & T. In 1973 he was back again, promising joint exploitation of Black Sea oil to help the U.S. energy crisis. If Ceausescu looked a little out of place in the boardrooms of the American corporations, it could be that there was also a certain distrust of the capitalists on the part of a man who had joined the Communist Party's youth organization at fifteen, become a Party member at eighteen, spent two years in prison between eighteen and twenty, was back in prison at twenty-two, and held a variety of government posts after the war, ending up as a thirty-two-year-old major general and deputy minister of defense at the height of the cold war in 1950. There was a parallel rise in the Party: member of the Central Committee at thirty, of the Politburo at thirty-seven, and, after the death of Gheorghiu-Dej, first secretary—later general secretary—at the age of forty-seven, a remarkable achievement in a movement dominated by older men. (At the time of Ceausescu's becoming Party chief, he joined a group of Bloc leaders whose average age was sixty.)

But in Bucharest, far from the towers of lower Manhattan, Ceausescu is very much at home, and very much in control. With all the ritual of religious processions, the Romanian Communist Party regularly celebrates the many anniversaries and conducts the many conferences that make up its year. The capital is frequently draped with banners and flags—the red, gold, and blue national flag and the red Party banner, never the Soviet flag, as in neighboring Bloc countries.

The cars pull up before the steps of the great domed auditorium built behind the former Royal Palace, now the home of Conducatorul—the leader. Pecking order is meticulously observed: Mercedeses, black and well kept, for the top men, and then the Russian Volgas for the middle ranks, and finally, a shabby collection of Polish Warszawas and even Romanian cars.

The occupants of the cars are also mostly standardized: their stature, short; their age, in the forties and fifties; their suits, a brown-gray-blue monotone, with only a slight variation in tone to distinguish one murky color from another. They wear drab green-gray shirts, with ties of a similar but muddier hue. There are a few exceptions to the pattern; the generals and the drivers are usually older, and sometimes the red ribbons of Party medals brighten the drab suits. But almost everyone else seems to be about the size and age of Comrade Ceausescu, and everyone seems to be dressed like him. How this is possible in a country of so many minorities and ethnic backgrounds is puzzling.

The women are among the minorities. Outnumbered perhaps twenty to one, they have token posts on the presidial dais, and get token mention, along with the young, in all the speeches. Their dresses, however, are a clear match for the men's in drabness. While they wait for the event to begin, both men and women study the pages of the Party daily or, more often than not, the all-sports paper *Fotbal*. *Fotbal* is also popular with the security police waiting outside, sitting on padded benches in the backs of trucks.

On the stage, the two huge flags, Party and national, are draped dramatically behind the dais, with the use of about 250 yards of material 20 yards wide. There are banks of flowers, and large, gilded symbols of the occasion—the Party Congress, the Anniversary of the Party, the Liberation.

There is a sudden quiet in the hall, although there has been no perceptible signal, and suddenly Ceausescu strides on stage from a door below the flags. He arrives on the minute of the scheduled opening, leading the other Politburo and Central Committee members. The applause, which begins when the top of his head is detected above the dais, rolls over the 5,000-seat auditorium in great waves. There is much standing up at peak applause times, then sitting, then standing again. There are cheerleaders who convert the applause into rhythmic "Ceauses-cu" clapping. Sometimes the crowd's behavior is the subject of precise reporting by the government news agency, Agerpress: "At the conclusion of the report, all those present stood up and cheered for minutes on end. Ovations and cheers responded in the hall, and 'RCP-RCP' and 'Ceausescu-Ceausescu.' It was a strong manifestation of profound love for the tried leader of our people." Other reporting is more extravagant. There are references to Ceausescu as "the most-loved son of our people, a Marxist-Leninist leader steeled in the revolutionary struggle, closely bound to the masses." There is even a school of poetry around Ceausescu, with lines such as these: "I know a man who is the symbol of this country. I know a man whose soul is afire, and the man is Comrade Nicolae Ceausescu." *

Ceausescu speaks often and long. New listeners think he is about to finish when, at the two-hour mark, he slows down and signals a lieutenant to take the chair. But if it is a major address, two hours is only halfway. The speeches cover a great deal of ground, always including the familiar lines about independence, sovereignty, and noninterference in internal affairs, but Ceausescu also offers, often in fatherly fashion, compulsory advice to the nation's bureaucrats, managers, scientists, artists. He gives instructions on the design of the new national theater. He lectures the writers on their task of "presenting the wonderful picture of the future that stands before Communism." He draws on the past, linking the heroes of the anti-Turkish struggle with the contemporary Party. He supplies detailed criticism of industrial shortcomings. He manages to play on nationalism while at the same time hailing the achievements of the Russian revolution.

Despite the cheerleaders, the poems, and the hyperbolic tributes, the applause is genuine for the most part, or at least the sentiments behind it are. It is difficult to measure popularity in a dictatorship, but from four years of soundings at all levels it is safe to say that Ceausescu has it. There are degrees and variations, of course: his standing up to the Russians is universally welcome; his domestic policies, especially the shortages and the police state restrictions, are universally resented, but the balance remains favorable.

CRISIS MANAGEMENT

The best test of how the Romanians really feel about Conducatorul was the afternoon of August 21, 1968, a few hours after Soviet and other troops of the Warsaw Pact—but not Romania's—invaded Czechoslovakia. It was the most serious crisis in Soviet-Romanian relations since the start of independence. But it was not to be the last; Bucharest and Moscow go from periods of warmth to periods of coolness, and often the change is so precipitous as to constitute a crisis.

Romania did not join the invasion forces because of the convergence of three policies it had been following throughout the sixties. The first was friendship with the reform and liberal elements in the Communist movement, not only in Prague, but in Belgrade and the Rome headquarters of the Italian Communists, the most innovative of the Western parties.

The second policy was built around the Romanian insistence that there could be no center of the Communist movement, whether in Mos-

* As reported by James Feron in *The New York Times*.

cow or Peking, and that each Party was best able to decide for itself how to build socialism. A logical consequence of this thinking was refusal to interfere in the affairs of other parties and reluctance to take part in movement-wide attempts to direct the affairs of others, whether it be in Comecon or in the moves then under way to organize a Communist summit. Romania had walked out of the main preparatory meeting for that summit in Budapest the previous February, objecting to the way the Soviets tried to stage-manage the conference and use it to condemn the activities of other parties, including, by inference, the Chinese and the Romanian. Romania was to attend the Moscow summit in 1969, but to sign the final document only on condition of a long list of exceptions. After successfully resisting the Soviet-dictated integration of Comecon, Romania managed to pick and choose, agreeing to join the Comecon Investment Bank, Interchim, and other international organizations only after being assured that only unanimous decisions, not majority ones, would be binding on members.

The third policy that had kept Romanian troops out of Czechoslovakia was the growing reluctance to take part in the Warsaw Pact. Romania never got to the point of withdrawal, as some Western commentators had predicted. That would have been too dangerous.

But it was clear even in the early sixties, Brucan said, that unquestioning allegiance to the Pact was also dangerous: "Khrushchev was a formidable man. I was with him many times. But he became too dangerous and had to be removed. If Hungary was one turning point for us, the Cuban missile crisis was another. At that time, Gheorghiu-Dej and our delegation had arrived in Moscow on our way back from Indonesia. We had heard about the crisis en route. But the two Politburo members who had come to the airport to greet us had not even been informed. It was only Khrushchev and his generals. We were convinced from that point that Romania must have a military posture that was as independent from the command of others as possible. It is difficult, and dangerous, but it was done before 1968."

It was done, as is everything else in Romanian policy, in slow steps. To start out with, Romania persuaded the Warsaw Pact not to hold any further maneuvers on its soil. Ceausescu has stressed his opposition many times to manuevers on the territory of other states, but Romanian staff officers have found it impossible to avoid them altogether. Thus it must have been clear to the Pact generals that they could not realistically include Ceausescu's forces in any invasion planning for Czechoslovakia.

Romania also successfully resisted integration of the Warsaw Pact command; it was no more willing to have military policies made on its behalf than economic or political. For this reason, there were frequent boycotts by the Romanians in the sixties of the Pact's military and political conferences.

Soviet pressure has continued, but Ceausescu and other officials spare no occasion to reiterate their views on the desirability of keeping troops at home. In this, the Imperialists are a useful foil, as they are in almost every other policy stand the Romanians take. It does not take much imagination to fill in Soviet where the speaker might seem to be referring to the United States.

This, then, was the background for the August afternoon when Ceausescu, after emergency conferences with the Central Committee, county party chiefs, journalists, union leaders, and women, went outside to address the crowd.

While the conferences were going on, the 100-yard-wide square between the Central Committee headquarters and the presidential palace had begun to fill, and by noon the crowd had passed 100,000. When Ceausescu appeared on the balcony of the yellow Central Committee building, there was no need for cheerleaders. A roar of shouts and applause went up, and it died down only for a few seconds at a time, the time needed for Ceausescu to finish a sentence, and then surged again.

Ceausescu began with a promise not to change Romania's course. He was there, he said, "to express our full confidence in the Romanian people's resolve to ensure the peaceful construction of socialism in our homeland." Then, after this opening sentence, he went directly to the point, a style of speaking not usually practiced by Communist leaders.

"It is inconceivable in the world today, when the peoples are rising to the struggle for defending their national independence, for equality of rights, that a socialist state, that socialist states, should transgress the liberty and independence of another state. There is no justification whatsoever and no reason can be accepted for admitting for even a single moment the idea of military intervention in the affairs of a fraternal socialist state."

As the crowd roared, Ceausescu applied the lesson to Romania. Prague's road, he said, had the approval of the people, and Romania's does, too. If there was ever a need for stressing the principles of noninterference, it is now: "Nobody can pose as adviser, as a guide to the way in which socialism has to be built in another country."

But this was only talk, and the Romanians knew it. The twenty-first of August was a turning point for Romania. From Gheorghiu-Dej onward, policy had been based on the assumption that things had changed a great deal in the Bloc, that Ceausescu and the other leaders could rely on the whole list of factors that would enable them to go their own way: Russia's impotence because of the Sino-Soviet split, its image in the Third World, the influence of the Western Communist parties, and finally, all the justifications used by reasonable men to rule out the use of naked force to win a political argument.

But naked force had been used, and there was a whole new Fotbol game for Romania to face. Ceausescu faced part of it in that same speech. He organized a home guard—"armed patriotic detachments of workers, peasants, and intellectuals, defenders of the independence of our country." Had the Soviet mechanized divisions in Moldavia wanted to cross the Danube that same afternoon and roll across the flat countryside into Bucharest, neither this home guard nor the Romanian army could have even slowed them down. But its formation convinced Romanians they were all part of the same venture, and that they must defend it from danger. They rallied around Ceausescu, even those not particularly pleased with his domestic or foreign policy.

But once the cheers had died, the Romanian leadership had a difficult choice. Clearly there must be a damper on unnecessary manifestations of independence. But to bend too far backward would be tantamount to abandoning Romania's most cherished principle: to avoid the dictation of policy from the outside.

Ceausescu's response went through several stages. Before the end of August, Radio Bucharest and the Party newspapers noticeably softened the volume of their outrage over the occupation. At the same time, Ceausescu increased his defense of Romania's course. But he did cautiously assure the Soviets, through a *Scinteia* editorial, that Romania would remain faithful to its Warsaw Pact commitment "so long as the Pact lives up to the mission for which it was created."

The 1969 Moscow summit and its attempts at institutionalizing the center of the Communist movement in the Kremlin was another challenge. It would have been needless provocation if Romania had not gone, and perhaps if Ceausescu had not signed the final communiqué. But he did make it clear that Romania did not accept the closing document without reservations, including those on Middle Eastern policy and the criticism of other parties.

A new period of pressure began in 1971, at a time of the renewed diplomatic offensive of the Chinese in the Balkans. Yugoslavia was received back in the good graces of the Chinese, and Peking's friendship with Romania was sealed with Ceausescu's visit. To Moscow, this meant an ideological invasion of the Balkans, and, since it could reach neither Albania nor Yugoslavia, its target became Romania. The pressure this time took two forms: another attempt at Comecon integration, and vague threats of invasion or subversion of the Ceausescu leadership.

The Romanians kept cool while the Warsaw Pact held maneuvers across their border in Bulgaria, and Ceausescu politely turned down an invitation to "vacation" in the Crimea with other Bloc leaders to discuss Romania's behavior.

Correspondents rushed to Bucharest, and the Vienna press, that faithful barometer of the extent of jitters in Eastern Europe, was filled with rumors of troop movements and plots to overthrow Ceausescu and establish a regime loyal to Moscow.

The crisis subsided, but there will be many and repeated long hot summers in Romania in the years ahead; its course is bound to continue to run counter to Moscow's, and Moscow is bound to try pressure, wars of nerves, and finally the threat of armed force to get Romania to give in.

Romania's great strength against crisis is Ceausescu's tight system of control. When one talks about Romanian independence, it is almost exclusively a reference to external independence, freedom of action in foreign affairs. No groups form soapbox audiences to denounce or applaud anything in Bucharest; it is a police state so complete that some streets around Party headquarters are even off limits to pedestrians. With one executive act, Ceausescu can eliminate American films and TV series, order the shaving of beards of TV announcers, and institute daily columns of "good news" about the Bloc in all newspapers. All this helps convince Moscow that with all the looseness in the conduct of foreign policy, things are under control at home.

Early in 1972 there were suddenly favorable articles in the Soviet press on Romania's economy, and less praise of China by the Romanians. A series of diplomatic soundings apparently convinced the Russians that Bucharest's loyalty was not endangered. The crisis was over.

Brucan believes there will be many more crisis cycles, starting with a new Romanian initiative, continuing with Soviet pressure, and ending with reconciliation, but with the Romanians giving in much less than the Soviets in the final compromise.

"Will they invade?" he asks. "I don't think there's the slightest risk. What they worry about is internal control, and there's not the slightest doubt about that here. Dubcek was naïve!" (He dismissed him with a wave of his hand in the general direction of the Carpathians, the chain of mountains that ends in the West near Bratislava, Dubcek's place of exile, a gesture that showed both the impatience of the professional politician and the surprising lack of sympathy East Europeans often show for each other.)

"He was naïve; things got out of control," Brucan continued. "They were returning to their parliamentary democracy of between the wars." As for the Russians, "they wouldn't do anything that wasn't absolutely necessary, and not before evaluating every possible consequence. That is what they did in Czechoslovakia in 1968. Their evaluation here showed them that there is no danger."

THE PRICE OF INDEPENDENCE

But independence has a high price. The tight internal controls, the censorship, the sealed borders, the secret police, are only part of it. There is also the need for a sort of Stalinist primitive accumulation to pay for Romania's foreign policy ventures. Romanians have to stand in line for meat and fruit in a country of such agricultural riches because Romania's best cuts of meat and best peaches are going to the export market for sale for hard currency to buy lathes and automated measuring equipment. The people are told that it is only temporary; but they are now in the second quarter-century of having heard this. The Germans eat the peaches and the meat, and then send the Krupp plants and Siemens electronic data processing in exchange. The Romanians can be pardoned for asking themselves occasionally how it is possible that the Germans can enjoy both. But such thoughts must be private. Not only can there be no public criticism of Ceausescu's list of priorities; there must be public praise in every piece of journalism and literature that they read.

This control is the Ceausescu anchor, the assurance to the Party conservatives in Bucharest and Moscow that all is well. If once it is accepted, then Romania can branch out into the world, make ties with everyone, try to mediate the Israeli-Arab conflict, praise the Chinese, rub elbows with the Rockefellers. With the lid on at home, all is permitted abroad.

Brucan disagrees with this domestic stability theory, insisting, as the other officials do, that Romania is in no sense a police state, and it is liberalizing. It is true that the concrete watchtowers along the highways are manned less than they used to be, but at times they still do block traffic; that censorship loosens from time to time, but it is still pervasive.

But if domestic policy is to liberalize, is there not the danger that foreign policy will return to cautiousness to maintain the balance?

Brucan does not think so. His reasoning is at the same time an explanation for Romania's success in independence to date.

"The Russians will not do anything to us because of the limitations of power. Even a superpower is limited, as you found to your sorrow in Vietnam. The fact that a small and poor nation like Vietnam could hold off the technologically vastly superior United States has its results, and not only in Asia, but in other parts of the world—South America, for example.

"The Soviets, for all their size and overwhelming power in this part of the world, are subject to the same limitations, and their leadership is smart enough to realize it. This is why we, as a small nation, feel safe.

"As a sociologist, I look at the changes that began at the end of the fifties and start of the sixties as the change from class-ideological to power-strategic interests. This means the camps are not fighting each other, but that there are fights within the camps. They are exemplified by France against the United States and China against the Russians. For the first time, power confrontations were not based on ideology, but only on national interests. As the weaker partners began to get stronger and be no longer so dependent on the big power in each camp, the divisions were inevitable.

"The independent nations in Western Europe, by giving up some of their independence, will create a fourth power. And that is what we want, a dividing up of world power. The Common Market has the potential. But Comecon is different. It is a bloc dominated by a large power, and that is why we resist so much the surrendering of any of our independence to it.

"Small nations must fight. That is what Romania has been doing for more than a decade. We are not against integration; it is to our advantage to be able to borrow money from a joint bank, jointly exploit our resources and markets with other nations. But the basis must be equality. Only when nations are treated as equals can there be true supranational integration—the big not dominating the small, the white and developed not dominating the colored and underdeveloped.

"If we achieve this, then we can proceed with what has been in preparation since the sixties. It is wrong to call it liberalization. It is remaking socialism in our own way, in accord with national peculiarities and political traditions."

VII

BULGARIA
Vutsidei

The Danibius Express, from Bucharest to Sofia, is the last train of the trip, and its ten-hour run includes the obligatory hour-plus at the border and a spectacular Danube crossing. The bridge connecting Giurgiu, Romania, and Ruse, Bulgaria, was completed in 1954, replacing the ferries and sleds that once were used summer and winter to get train passengers across. Up until World War II, in the winter, when the ferries were iced in, passengers were dragged across the ice in flat-bottomed boats by crews of men. Larger ferries that could carry the train cars replaced the boats, and then came the bridge.

Bulgaria's landscape changes from Black Sea fishing villages to Balkan mountain forests, from wheat fields to the famous Valley of Roses, where mile after mile of roses are grown for their oil. But throughout the changes, one element remains the same: the working women. They are everywhere, along the highways, whitewashing the trunks of trees (a process that seems to have been nearly completed all over the nation), or bending over, weeding, harvesting, planting, in platoons and regiment-sized crews of collective farm workers. They wear flowing dresses and kerchiefs almost completely shielding their faces in the old Turkish way, or they wear shorts or jeans, depending on the area of the country and their age. There are men in the fields, of course, but usually they are driving the trucks or tractors, or supervising.

Another constant of the Bulgarian scene—and indeed, the East European scene as a whole—is a naive disregard for the environment. The factories on the edges of the towns spewing dark smoke into the air with all the heedlessness of nineteenth-century capitalism out of Dickens, the diesel trucks on the highways, the open sewers in the towns, the refuse pits, where garbage lies in heaps for gypsies and other scavengers to poke through—all are marks of an age of innocence of things environmental.

In Bulgaria, it doesn't matter too much, because the land is not overpopulated, and the smoking chimneys are not joined by too many others, so that the clouds they emit soon disappear in the clear sky. But other more developed areas are in real trouble: the coal-steel basin of Silesia in Poland, for example, with its neighboring smog-generating area around Ostrava in Czechoslovakia, or the area of the Leuna works, producer not only of synthetic fibers but of a vicious acid smog that sometimes covers 60 miles of East German highways, or Budapest, its lights extinguished by the brown coal smog that sometimes presses down on the city for days. Bulgarians are not only less bothered by this, but display a perverse kind of pride, equating smog and traffic with development, industrialization, and progress, something they worked for so hard, before and after Communism.

Sofia has had three names, marking successively the Roman, Byzantine, and Slav occupants of the city, but many more conquerors than that. The main facts of its life, and Bulgaria's, are attested to by the architecture of the capital. Old mosques, surrounded by modern buildings and looking out of scale and even on the wrong level, are left from Turkish days. Then there is the architecture from the brief period of national revival: the theater patterned on those in Berlin and Vienna, the opera house, the statue of the czar liberator, and the splendid domed Alexander Nevsky Orthodox church. Finally, dominating all of this, the marks of Communist rule: the downtown Party headquarters, topped with tower and star, the monument to the Red army liberation, of generous proportions and heroic design.

But Sofia is a beautiful capital, set on a 1,500-foot plateau and surrounded by mountains. On week nights, the official cars crowd the parking lots of mountainside restaurants that overlook the city. On weekends, the mountain paths are full of hikers, families who take the streetcars to the end of the line for a nickel and spend the day in the wilds.

Beyond the streetcar tracks, the Iskar River valley leads up into the Rila Mountains, where the white peaks, the highest on the Balkan peninsula, reach 9,500 feet. The weather often changes half an hour out of the capital, from sunshine to sudden snowstorms, or the reverse. The landscape changes radically, too, and within the space of a few miles illustrates better than any statistics Bulgaria's postwar development from peasant to agro-industrial economy. Impressive new factories and warehouses share the outskirts of Sofia with dreary apartment complexes. There is a general air of progress, but there are also marks of the disorder that resulted from Bulgaria's rush into industrialization, and of the social dislocation caused by transforming peasants into industrial workers in a single generation.

In 1952, eight years after the Communist takeover, 78 percent of the population still made its living off the land, only 2 percent less than the prewar figure. But by 1970, the figure had been cut to 45 percent, and for the first time, industrial production accounted for half the national income. Sofia expanded to take in the new workers, trebling its prewar population of 300,000, and the poured-concrete factory halls and prefabricated housing blocks began to ring the capital, facing each other across treeless vacant lots. Many of the apartments, although new, have broken windows, littered front yards, and Cyrillic-alphabet graffiti on their freshly stuccoed walls.

A few miles into the hills, and industrial Bulgaria is left behind: the fields and forests flank the road, first the broad, unfenced acres of the collective farms, and then, as the road goes higher, the timber lots, grazing land, and smaller fields of the mountain peasants.

The peasants of the Rila Mountains, the Shoppi, have a history of being difficult to rule, whether the rulers in Sofia, at the foot of their mountains, are the Turks who governed the nation for five hundred years or the Communists who have done so since the war. When the Turks were finally driven out, in 1878, Bulgaria's peasants got full title to their small family farms and became easier to deal with. After 1944, when the Communists began forcing the family farms into collectives, their resistance reappeared.

Vutsidei stands out as an individualist even among his fellow Shoppi. In Samokov, 8 miles down the valley from his home village of Govedarci, passers-by know his name. In the nearer villages, there are grins and knowing looks when directions are asked, because these peasants know Vutsidei personally, not just by reputation. One of the peasants, a white-haired old man with stainless steel false teeth flashing among his own, tells why Vutsidei is so famous locally: "Aha. You want to see the fellow who stayed out of the collective."

But Vutsidei is also well known to tens of thousands of other Bulgarians who have never been to the Shoppi country and are probably not certain whether he is real or fictitious. This is so because of a remarkable book about the village and its people, published in 1958 and reprinted twice since, by a remarkable writer, Asem Khristoforov, who shared the life of the villagers for many years under remarkable circumstances. *Vutsidei* was a book that nearly did not get into print, but when it did, it became a best seller. The name itself is a nickname, earned by Vutsidei in his youth as a shepherd. He was known in the neighborhood then for his piercing cries to keep the wolves away, whether the danger was real or not. *Vutsi* is Shoppi dialect for wolf, and *dei* means go away.

Govedarci's plain little houses are spaced along the mountain stream that bisects the village and on the dirt streets that connect the Sofia road and the communal fields. Vutsidei's house is not much larger than the others, but it stands out. It is square and white, with a red tile roof, pale blue decorations along its fluted corners and lime green window frames. The house is stucco over brick, the barn a frame and stick affair with a stucco coating. A covered wooden walkway connects house and barn, because the snows are deep in Govedarci, 3,000 feet above sea level. It skirts a small garden, where Vutsidei's wife tends vegetables and grows plums for the slivova, the golden brandy that they offer guests. The barn is like a rural museum, except that its tools and facilities are in daily use: a handwoven basket to feed the chickens, a handcarved hay crib for the calf, homemade wooden rakes, handhewn beams. A sheepskin stuffed with hay hangs on the side of the barn, curing. There are a few marks of modernity, including a water tap in the farmyard, which sets the village off from many others in Bulgaria with their communal taps or their well and bucket. Vutsidei has another tap in the kitchen in an enameled sink, which sets him off from the other villagers.

Vutsidei's wife, a sturdy woman, wears a dress of thick black wool, embroidered in gold and red at the neck. On her feet are rubber sandals, still fashioned in the old Turkish style with turned-up points. The dress is cut jumper style, and under it she wears a handwoven white blouse with red embroidery in tiny patterns on the cuffs. Her braided dark-blond hair hangs to her waist, but most of it is covered by a black babushka, which she adjusts and readjusts while talking to strangers. Over the jumper is an apron of homespun, earth-colored wool—browns, deep reds, greens, like the fields that are beginning to show through the February snows.

The unheated entrance hall has a strip of white oilcloth along its floor to keep the mud off, and shoes are exchanged for slippers where it ends. The interior of the house is also fresh white, with the lime green on the doors and windowframes, and the only decoration in the kitchen is a bright oilcloth, patterned in peasant designs, behind the range, and a small cluster of icons. Spice jars with mysterious labels are being put to use for Vutsidei's supper. It is a tomato and onion dish, with paprikas and soup stock from a brown earthenware pot on the range. The squat, blackened stove could also fit into a rural museum, but it is very much in use, warming the kitchen and heating half a dozen containers, enamel and earthenware. Next to the stove is an iron bed, filling one end of the kitchen, and at the other end a blue painted chest for linens and food. Vutsidei's wife makes frequent trips to the chest, keeping out of the way of a year-old baby on the floor. She is their granddaughter, being cared for while the mother works. All three of Vutsidei's sons still live in the village and work on the collective farm. It was simpler for them than for their father.

Vutsidei himself has been in the forest all day, cutting wood for the state timber enterprise, his regular winter job. He often walks the 9-mile round trip to work, but on this particular day there was a ride home in a truck. In the setting of Govedarci, it is easy to imagine the woodcutters working with primitive axes, but Vutsidei's crew has a chain saw. When he comes into the house from the truck, however, he has already left behind almost every trace of the twentieth century.

He is tall and erect, with a deeply tanned face in midwinter from his many seasons in the outdoors, and from the mountain sun, which is already beginning to feel hot at noon, although the air temperatures are still below freezing. He has graying hair with much black in it, a broad, high forehead and wide-set eyes above prominent, almost jutting, cheekbones, and even teeth with gaps that show they are still his own, something rare in the Balkans at sixty-two. He wears a flannel shirt buttoned to the top button, but all but covered by a garment of rusty brown wool, embroidered on cuffs and edges with Turkish-looking designs, dark brown whorls, and forming, with the jodhpur-style pants, a single trouser and top unit. The knees have been patched and repatched, but the outfit looks to have many more years left in it. He had been wearing a sheepskin flapped cap which left a white mark on his forehead where the tan stopped. A denim jacket goes over the costume, and when it is colder a sheepskin vest is added, and often a rough wool shepherd's cloak, thick and oily and about the color of the sheep.

His shoes are moccasins of thick leather, pointed like Venetian gondolas, made of one piece with the point and the top seam stitched together with copper wire. They are bound across his feet with heavy rawhide laces. Vutsidei has been out in deep snow all day in the woods, but his feet are dry in his woolen stockings. His one concession to modernity is to use clear plastic bags as a sort of spats, replacing the usual homespun, to keep the snow from coming in over the tops.

Vutsidei takes his seat next to the stove. Slivova is produced, and the story of a generation spent fighting to stay out of the collective farm begins. He speaks in bursts of rapid Bulgarian, with the Shoppi dialect so thick that the Sofia university student who serves as interpreter sometimes has to ask him to slow down or repeat phrases. He frowns when he recalls some of his history, but there are frequent grins and untranslatable local jokes.

"In 1946," he says, "the collectivization drives began in the village. I didn't want to join. The collective is all right for poor people; if they have nothing to give up they have a lot to gain. I built this house myself in 1932. I had twenty-four decares of land." (A decare is 1,000 square meters, or a plot about the size of the average suburban lot in the United States.)

"They said it would be a better life, but I couldn't see why. So I told them I wouldn't sign up. Then the trouble began. They would come by the house and shout through the windows. When they were drunk it was worse. They would try to beat me. But they were afraid—they know how strong I am.

"These people were mostly officials of the area, but some were peasants already in the cooperative. When the threats didn't work, they said they would take me to court. But I knew they wouldn't, because they were afraid of me, and besides, they kept saying that it was our own choice to make to get in the cooperative, that it was voluntary, and that it was better for us, we would see."

He laughed as he said this, and his wife interrupted. "He is like wood. It would have been better to join at that time, I told him. He could not stand against the whole village. We were not rich, we could not fight forever. He had to find extra work in other districts, down near Sofia, where nobody knew him. We had our three sons to feed. It was a hard time."

After Khristoforov's novel appeared in 1958, it was ever harder. The book had to be written to get past the censors, and it thus depicted Vutsidei's refusal to join the collective as a mistake, the result of outmoded ways of thinking. But somehow Vutsidei emerged nevertheless as its hero. The regime had approved the book, or it never would have been published. But it was difficult for the Party officials in Samokov to have to keep reporting to Sofia that the celebrated holdout in Govedarci was still holding out. The pressure was increased.

"They would come up and shout at me: 'You are wrecking the collective. You are an enemy of the Socialist order.' This was not true, and they knew it. I didn't want to join, that was all. I liked it better working for myself. It is bad for a rich man to join, just as it is good for a poor man. But I was neither rich nor poor.

"They got worse with their threats, but that did no good. Finally they charged me with stealing some wood. I had the papers to prove the wood was mine, that I had bought it. But they did not accept them. They were arresting me for not being in the collective—yet they couldn't say so, because the collective was supposed to be voluntary. They sentenced me to eight months in prison.

"When I got to the prison, the director himself came to see me. He said, 'What a foolish man you are, to go to jail instead of joining the cooperative.' He said nothing at all about the wood. I told him I was sentenced for stealing wood, not for trying to keep my land. I told him I would stay in jail for eight months, eight years, or eighty years, but I would never join the cooperative.

"The director then threatened me. 'I'll send you to work in the forests, cutting wood all day in the cold and snow,' he said to me. 'See how you like that.' I said this was what I had done all my life, what I'd be doing if they hadn't arrested me, and was no threat at all. That's how it turned out. It was work in a different forest with different people, some of them good and some of them bad. It was really no change for me. And for working, they let me out in six months instead of eight."

Vutsidei's experience was repeated all over Bulgaria in the nineteen years it took to complete collectivization. The process was similar in the other countries of the Bloc, although the Bulgarians were always the first and the most severe. The resistance of the private peasants was broken in a series of advances and retreats. Excesses alternated with concessions; in some years hundreds of new collectives would be formed, and in others none. Sometimes the decision to be tough or conciliatory was dictated by local needs, but more frequently, especially after 1948, the reason was the necessity of staying in line with the Soviet Union.

Bulgaria's Communists first permitted peasants to decide themselves whether they would join the collectives. Marx's idea of "armies of peasant laborers," expressed in the *Communist Manifesto,* was discarded, and instead the models were the *zadruga,* the traditional Balkan family commune, and the cooperatives of the Bulgarian land reformers of the nineteenth and twentieth centuries. In both, some land was farmed in common, and individual peasants could draw on its earnings to free themselves from the village usurers. The redistribution policies of Alexander Stamboliisky, the region's first Agrarian Party premier, had given Bulgaria the most equitable land structure in Eastern Europe by World War II— fewer than 6 percent of the nation's farms were larger than 85 acres.

But these small farms disappeared rapidly in the forced collectivization campaigns that followed the early postwar years of voluntary participation. By 1958, Bulgaria became the first Soviet Bloc nation to proclaim full collectivization; by 1963, it could report 99.3 percent of the arable land in collectives.

VUTSIDEI AND KHRISTOFOROV

That same year, Vutsidei was released from prison and returned to Govedarci to resume farming his private 24 decares, his share of the nation's last uncollectivized .7 percent, and Khristoforov, his chronicler, was having trouble with the authorities that seemed to him to grow directly out of the popularity of *Vutsidei.*

At that time, he had known Vutsidei for fifteen years, and regulated their social relations on the basis of an agreement to be enemies in public and friends in private. They would not speak on the streets of Govedarci, since Vutsidei was not supposed to approve of his characterization in the book, and Khristoforov was in no position to be associating with an enemy of the socialist order. But in private, in the author's little cottage on the edge of the woods, or in Vutsidei's house, many glasses of slivova were exchanged.

One encounter between the two men in that period illustrates how each was coping with the authorities. Khristoforov, unable to get any more of his original writings past the censors, was restricted to translating English literature into Bulgarian. But even in this area there were political perils. A translation he did of James Joyce's *Dubliners* was accepted, set into type, and then locked in the censor's files. Khristoforov turned to safer authors; a contract to translate Dickens's *Bleak House* was the result.

Khristoforov was going over the proofs in the cottage one day with two young writers from Sofia when Vutsidei approached. The peasant had come out of the forest and had a small tree over his shoulder. He had cut it down on state land, an offense that could have got him a month in jail. When he saw the strangers, he set the tree down, and instead of the rough and open language that he usually used with Khristoforov, exhibited the kind of circumspection with which he dealt with officials, strangers, or townspeople.

The visitors, of course, were well acquainted with Vutsidei's story, but they did not let him know this. They asked him what he thought about collectivization. As Khristoforov later recalled, his answer was a model of Shoppi evasiveness: "Well," he replied, "they're overcoming the problems. True, the sheep all miscarried last year because the collective members didn't take care of them before birth. Yes, the hay crop ought to be good this year, even though it was left in the fields too long and got soggy in the past two years. Now, we're going to have a good corn crop, but the tractors and cultivators have been broken down for weeks, and the weeds are ahead of the corn right now. But these are problems that will be overcome, we're sure of that."

If the collective idea is such a good one, the visitors asked, then surely you are a member? "I am steeling myself and preparing myself to attain the moral qualities that a member needs," Vutsidei replied, with a slight smile that reflected his pride in his grasp of the official terminology. "But I have not yet attained them."

Khristoforov is known in Govedarci as the Professor because of his prewar job. When he first arrived in the village in 1947, he must have seemed like a visitor from the moon. The son of one of Bulgaria's wealthiest families, he grew up in Plovdiv, the nation's second city, in surroundings of conspicuous Balkan luxury. Khristoforov did not like to reminisce about the period, but friends from those days talk with nostalgia about the family's private film theater and literary and artistic salon. There was also the means to give Khristoforov an excellent education—first, at the American Robert University in Istanbul, and then at the London School of Economics. Khristoforov was proud of his fluent English and his schooling; he once carefully removed from his shelves John Maynard Keynes's *A Treatise on Money* and remarked: "This is the Beveridge prize, for the best foreign scholar at the LSE. The year afterward, they gave it to Jack Kennedy." In the thirties he was Bulgaria's youngest professor of economics, and managed the difficult task of teaching Keynesian thinking under a variety of dictatorships, military, monarchial, and fascist, until the Communist takeover in 1944.

The postwar years were a time of unprecedented savagery in the settling of political accounts. In none of the Eastern European countries was the takeover the joyous act of liberation that it is now described as being, but Bulgaria, as in collectivization, managed somehow to outdo the rest. One reason was the debt the Reds owed the Whites from 1923, when the Communists attempted an uprising after the assassination of Stamboliisky, and the Tsankov military regime massacred them, in numbers estimated from 10,000 to 30,000. Another reason was the need of the Bulgarian Communists to prove their manhood to the Russians after five years of relative quiescence during the war, when their government was allied to the Nazis. Their comparative lack of guerrilla fervor was particularly noticeable in contrast to the record of their neighbor Slavs who had rallied behind Tito.

More than 2,000 death sentences were handed down in the first postwar years by the "people's courts" formed to serve justice on the bourgeoisie, and an equal number of life or long imprisonment sentences. Khristoforov was not surprised to find himself among the arrested; he knew he was as guilty as anyone of class crime. But he was not prepared for what followed. Because he had been in London, he was accused of heading a Western intelligence apparatus. He was interrogated, by his own record, 210 days during his investigative arrest. The questioning could be conducted day or night, and often both. He was confronted with the confessions of men who said they were his assistants and agents and who described in minute detail how he had sold out his fatherland for Western pay. "In the cells, it was impossible to kill yourself," he said once in recalling his nine months in prison. "They even took the buttons off your clothing, your belt, your shoelaces. Hitting your head against the concrete walls produced, at best, unconsciousness."

Even under the people's court rules, not much could be made of the Khristoforov espionage case, and the sentence was to an indeterminate time in a concentration camp, which seemed to him like paradise after the interrogation cells. By 1947, he was out, and looking for work. His first job was as a bricklayer's helper. But after a few days, he was fired, since it was a provocation against People's Bulgaria to have a university professor doing such work. It was useless to argue that he could get no other. He took in typing at home, until that, too, became a provocation. Then, one morning in 1947, he said goodbye to his wife, got on an overcrowded country bus outside Sofia's railway station, and rode it to the end of the line, to Govedarci.

"The Keynesian economist survived in a Communist society only by returning to the methods of laissez-faire," he once said. He knew no one in the village, and could not understand much of what the villagers said. But he did have a little money left. His first task was shelter, and with the aid of the villagers, he built the cottage, far enough from the rest of the town to be isolated, close enough to be able to buy his few needs. He lived mostly off the land, from the goats, sheep, and chickens he kept, with all the usual blunders of the townsman. His water came from a stream near the cottage, his heat from a stove and wood he cut himself. The villagers were sometimes helpful and sometimes cruel. Vutsidei was on the scene from the start, with advice of all kinds and some voluntary labor at times. But once, after a drunken festival, other villagers tortured and killed Khristoforov's dog, the stray he had adopted and treasured as his only companion. All villagers were to be paid back eventually in the pages of *Vutsidei* for their help or their cruelty. ("He made money off the book," Vutsidei's wife complained, "but *we* are made fun of in the book, and lied about. He should have given us the money.")

Although Khristoforov was considered such a political risk that his wife was not permitted to join him for some years, he did, to his surprise, remain a member of the Writers' Union, which he had joined after publication of his 1945 *London Sketches*. He was even more surprised when the Union approached him with contracts for translating Dreiser, Dickens, and other writers whose critical works about Western society were in demand. Later, his own carefully nonpolitical tales of the Rila Mountains were accepted. *Vutsidei* started out as another such tale. But he found himself writing not about animals and nature, but his neighbors, their strengths, their weaknesses, and above all their reaction to the cataclysmic changes Communism and collectivization brought to the patterns of centuries of living.

Vutsidei helped write *Vutsidei,* Khristoforov said, dropping by for a drink and tales of his latest battle with the authorities. The literary thaw after the Soviet Twentieth Party Congress also helped. But the main impetus for the book was Khristoforov's own experience as an individual in the hands of the state, and his need to express the feelings of other individuals thus mistreated. Other Bulgarian writers, he said, either ducked the issue or wrote glowing socialist realistic praise of the Communist transformation.

"Kamen Kalchev, one of our greatest writers, inserted fifty pages into one of his novels to tell how one village dropped its work on its own harvest to go twenty miles to help another village get the crop in. All this was supposed to show the success of the collective spirit on the countryside. But it was simply not true.

"Penyu Penev, a true revolutionary, a Party member since 1918, the Mayakovsky of Bulgaria, was as bad. He wrote of a scene in my own village where a young activist from the town comes into the tavern, buys brandies for the old peasants there, and within an hour, through the righteousness of his cause and the magnetism of Communism, has them marching down to the village Party secretary's office and signing collectivization agreements.

"To think that a nineteen-year-old bureaucrat could persuade these peasants to give up their land, which they had jealously guarded for centuries! Or that these people, with their bitter experience in making a living, with the instinct of survival ground into them, would neglect their own work to help strangers and rivals! The books were laughed at. They were not read."

When *Vutsidei* was finished, Khristoforov was summoned to Sofia by the

Party actif of the Writers' Union for the obligatory writer-censor conference. The Party secretary passed him a slip of paper. "Brilliant," it said.
"But negative." In the manuscript were dozens of underlined passages, entire pages of dialogue. All were references to the political side of
collectivization. "Take them out," the Party secretary said. "Put something
of animals in these places. You write well of animals. Give us some more
of the feeling of nature in the Rila."

Khristoforov, disheartened, went back to the village, carrying the underlined manuscript and the Party guidelines. To comply with all the demands for changes would have cut the heart out of the book. To leave it
unchanged would have kept it from publication. Khristoforov was faced
with the decision that every writer must make under totalitarian rule: how
much to compromise to get his work before the public but how much to
refuse in order to preserve his own honor and dignity—and to have the
book worth reading. He decided that the way out would be the fullest use
of his intelligence and writing skills in outwitting the censors. He would
take out the offending passages, he said, and put in the sketches of animal
and rural life. But he would also bear down with every stylistic and
intellectual resource that he had to get across the plight of Vutsidei and
every other individual in Bulgaria who found himself at the mercy of the
state, the victim of the new order that was supposed to benefit him.

But all this had to be between the lines. From the start, Vutsidei was
shown as being in the wrong, a stubborn old man out of step with the new
style of history that was being written on the Bulgarian countryside. Here
was a man, Khristoforov's readers would discover, who was so stubborn
that being put naked in a cell while being interrogated did not cause him to
see the way of good sense. Here was a peasant so recalcitrant that he
would escape into the snow, with the guards unable to hit him with their
rifles and afraid to chase him. As the tale progresses, Vutsidei makes his
way to Sofia, checks into a hospital, and demands to have his appendix
removed. He doesn't need the operation, of course, and when it is healed,
he also does not need to get out of bed too early and rip out the stitches,
causing another two weeks in bed and out of controversy in Govedarci.
When he returns, the dust has settled, his farm is still his, and the
authorities are reluctant to pick on a sick man.

All this was written in such a way as to show to what foolish lengths
Vutsidei would go to avoid cooperating with his neighbors. It satisfied the
censors, and so did the ending of the book, which shows everyone in the
village in the collective except Vutsidei, who is depicted as a lonely and
bitter old man. But the Bulgarians who bought up the initial printing of
3,000, the second of 8,000, and the third of 16,000 saw the moral otherwise. Vutsidei had somehow managed to defeat the system. He was the
hero, not the agitators, the organizers, or the peasants who had given in
to their pressure. He had done something against the overwhelming power
of State and Party that the readers wished they could do themselves. And

so had Khristoforov. *"Vutsidei,"* he said, "is written in praise of old-fashioned individualism. My friends said they could see me behind Vutsidei on every page of the book. They were right."

THE OLD WAYS

Khristoforov agreed that whether Communists, Agrarians, or Socialists had taken power in Bulgaria in 1944, some kind of more efficient farming would have been introduced, the dwarf holdings would have been consolidated, and the underemployed rural proletariat resettled in the towns, with industrialization to provide them jobs. The difference would have been the lack of compulsion.

If the element of compulsion had been removed, Khristoforov felt, there would have been no real argument against what happened on the Bulgarian countryside after 1944. Even under the terms under which it did take place, it did much good; above all, it brought about the emancipation of the Bulgarian peasant woman.

"I can remember walking through my village and seeing women getting beaten with sticks by their husbands," he said. "Often they lost their hearing or had their teeth knocked out; it was especially severe when the husband was drunk. When his cow died, the peasant wept a little, but when his wife died he wept a lot—not because he loved her, but because she was more valuable as a work animal.

"The father was the absolute despotic head of the group of people he lived with, and that meant his sons, even if they were forty or fifty. They could not marry without his permission, and often it was he who selected their brides—for their working abilities, nothing else. It was the custom to marry off a boy a few days before he left for his two years' military service, so that the girl could take his place in the family work force. Sometimes the girl would be much older, as much as twenty-five years older in some cases, because *her* father tried to hang on to his free labor as long as he could.

"Once, when I went into the village to get bread, I saw one of our most intelligent young peasants beating his wife in public with a stick. Afterward I met him again and told him what a shame it was, that it was not modern, and all the rest. We walked under the window of his cottage and continued talking. He said nothing. But suddenly his wife leaned out of the window and said: 'Shame on you. Mind your own business. How can the other women of the village know that I have a good husband, one who cares about whether his house is clean and his children well brought up, unless he beats me? Do you think I want them to think he's a weak man, a man who doesn't care?' "

But most of the beatings were genuine, not contrived as a means of maintaining the family image. It was a serious social problem, but it has all but disappeared since the collectivization of the countryside. Collectivization did more than take away the individual property holdings. It broke up the feudal labor relationships that gave most of the rights to the patriarch, the few residual ones to the other husbands and fathers, and none at all to the women. Now the working unit is the brigade, and 70 percent of its members, on the average collective, are women. They are responsible to one another, not their husbands, for completion of their work and the amount of pay they earn. (The dominance of the male has not been removed, however. It is still present, although not asserted as openly. The Party secretaries and collective farm chairmen, the entire chain of command from brigade leader to the top Party echelons, in fact, are men in more than nine out of ten cases. Once, while visiting a collective farm, as he saw the women bending over in the fields in the heat of an August afternoon and the male brigade leader under a tree watching them, Vutsidei remarked: "The women of Bulgaria are building Socialism. And the men of Bulgaria are guarding it.")

Under the new conditions, however, if a woman shows up for work unable to keep up with her brigade because her husband has beaten her, or if she cannot come to the farm at all, this is brought up in the weekly meeting of criticism and complaints. If the husband continues the beating, he will be called in for a talk by the Party secretary. He probably will not be punished, but there are hundreds of ways in which favors can be withheld: if he needs permission to add a room to his house, or fell a tree, or wants a better-paying job driving a tractor, the Party official can cut him down with a shrug of the shoulders, and continue to do so as long as the wife beater refuses to become progressive.

THE NEW WAYS

The Kazemete Cooperative Farm, an hour's drive from Sofia on the broad, fertile valley between the Balkan range and the Rila, is known throughout the area as a showplace of emancipated women and well-organized labor. The energetic Party chairman, Vlasto Dluki, a man of peasant stock in his fifties, brought out his handwritten payroll records to prove that the collective workers were making up to $150 a month, nearly double the usual farm pay. "Organization," Dluki said, "and incentives." And then, after the ritual refreshments, cooperatively distilled slivova and coffee, he led the way through the red and yellow iron gates of the collective, past pictures of Lenin and Todor Zhivkov, the bald Bulgarian Party chief, past banners promising to work more in honor of various anniversaries and Party congresses, past carefully tended shrubs and flower beds, to the bright blue and green farm buildings, built, like the peasants' houses, of cooperatively made brick and stucco. The organization was impressive: women in denim smocks and babushkas scurried around the cow barns, feeding the cows with fodder formulated for high milk yields. A West German milking machine efficiently filled the cans, and other women entered the daily totals in record books. Their own pay depends in large part on what the collective earns; the more milk produced, the more they get. They are helped by a staff of experts, including a veterinarian to supervise breeding and select the best dairy stock, and agronomists to prepare the fodder formulas.

The private plots and houses of the farm workers cluster outside the gates. Dluki surveys the scene with pride. "Before September," he says, with the usual reference to the days before the Communist takeover in 1944, "there were few houses here, and certainly no one had his own, not to mention TV antennas on the roofs." The village does have a good antenna crop, and the houses, blue and green like the barns, are neat and new. They can be built with the help of friends and the use of cheap materials from the farm for the equivalent of $2,000. Stolen material often brings the price down even lower, but the Kazemete farm seemed too tightly organized for much of that. The organization failed later on the farm tour, however, when an old peasant found a chance to contradict the Party secretary when no one else was listening. "Of course there were few houses here before September," he said. "The main village is down the road. These houses were built after collectivization, when people had to move here. And September didn't bring us wealth. This district was rich, is rich now, will be rich. It is the soil."

It seems true that the Kazemete farm's success is only partly due to the efficiency of its workers and leadership. It is, after all, close enough to Bulgaria's largest market to have no trouble selling all the dairy products it can produce, and it has some of the best land in the country to raise fodder.

But the farm also illustrates how after decades of experimentation and reorganizations, Bulgaria seems to have found a way of combining collective work and incentives in a way that was never possible before.

It was the lack of incentives that kept the peasants out of the collectives as long as they could manage it; once in, they produced as little as possible for themselves on their private plots. In the early years of collectivization, production stagnated. By 1951, Bulgarian farms were producing no more than they were in 1938, and in some crops, such as rye and potatoes, less. In the five-year plan from 1948 to 1953, production rose above the 1948 level only in two years. All through the fifties and early sixties, agriculture limped along with a rate of growth of 2.5 to 3 percent a year, and in many years, agricultural Bulgaria had to import wheat from the West.

But the private plots showed astounding productive power. With less than 10 percent of the farmland in Bulgaria, they produce nearly 30 percent of the meat, a quarter of the potatoes, half the plums, 41 percent of the eggs, and 22 percent of the corn. They are restricted by law to half an acre or an acre and a quarter, depending on the kind of farming country. The animal population is also restricted, to one cow or buffalo, seven pigs, five sheep, and until recently, there was a deliberate regime policy of neglect of the fertilizer and equipment needs of the little holdings. Nevertheless, the plots grew in importance. In 1960 they provided 30 percent of peasant income; a decade later, it was 44 percent.

For decades, the government conducted intermittent warfare on the private plots, since it was obvious that too much of the collective peasant's energy, time, and skills went into the cultivation of his backyard patch. They were attacked as remnants of capitalism on the countryside and threatened with liquidation. There were some cases of private plots' being disbanded, then re-formed again when collective production did not respond to the medicine. A more common tactic was to move a peasant from a productive plot of land to one less favored, turning his old plot over to the collective, and thus depriving him of the enriched soil, vineyards, and other improvements.

Peasants' uncertainty would increase each time one of the series of sweeping reforms was introduced. There was consolidation of collectives into larger units (and one attempt, during the Chinese-style Great Leap Forward of 1958, to form a single huge commune of all the farms in an entire county). This would be followed by disbanding and redistribution; often the private plots suffered. It was not until 1967 that the authorities hit on the idea of making the work on the collective more attractive instead of trying to punish work on the private plots.

The new Model Cooperative Farm Statute adopted that year contains, for the first time, provisions for a real system of rewards for efficiency and initiative. The experience of the Kazemete Farm shows that it works; that peasants there work harder because they earn more, and that as a result production rises and their earnings increase even more.

The statute got rid of the old Soviet-style labor day system, which contained no incentive, and substitutes a plan of payment on the basis of "participation in work." Abuses are possible, of course, but there is a provision for farmworkers to help set the norms through membership meetings and the secret election of the managers.

Families or individuals are also permitted to stake out a plot of collective land to work on their own responsibility. Fifty percent of the yield above the plan is theirs to keep. Peasants have been granted the same social security benefits as townsmen. There is even a rough form of unemployment insurance for the event of a bad harvest.

The statute is supposed to pave the way for a "higher stage" of collectivization, the agro-industrial complex. The industrial age on the farm, officials in Sofia call it. Collective farms are grouped around an industry—orchards serving a cannery is the simplest example—and the methods of the factory are to be used in the fields.

The plan evokes pictures of confident men in white coats pushing buttons to open irrigation sluices or sprinkle fertilizer from the sky. But Bulgaria's peasants, and the nation's economy, have been done great damage in the past by such schemes. The larger the unit, the less likely that individual interests will be paid attention to. The result could be another drop in morale and productivity.

The agricultural planners are particularly hazy on the issue of the private plots. The statute says it is possible for them to be returned to the collective holdings at some future date. This caused a barrage of questions by anxious private plot owners, which were answered with official assurances, but there was always some kind of qualification, such as "not in the near future." Private estimates by Sofia officials give the private plots another fifteen years, or perhaps twenty, the period of the current long-range plan for the economy.

If the incentive system on the collectives works, and peasants are kept happy with bonuses and pensions, then they may be willing to give up 'heir little farmyards, or at least reduce their importance to that of supplier of immediate family needs. The key is persuasion, as opposed to coercion, and it is the same problem the regime has faced since 1944, through all the drives and campaigns. Bulgaria's agricultural problem could not be solved because the Communists did not try to solve it as a problem; they tried to win it as a battle. But recent years have brought indications of more reason.

VUTSIDEI'S TRIUMPH

Such, at least, seems to be the case with Vutsidei. Coercion was a notable failure with him. For a generation, he resisted the man with the writ and the man with the gun. But in 1970, as he describes it, "I went down to their office and signed their paper." After twenty-four years of struggle, Vutsidei joined the collective.

His reasoning is hard to draw out. He shrugs his shoulders, glances at his wife. There is no hint of defeat in his attitude, however; indeed, there is the feeling that it was a final and triumphant act in his long process of outwitting the bureaucracy. It is only after more slivova and certain deductions, mathematical and otherwise, that the reasons begin to emerge.

When his three sons were young, they could help with the family's 24 decares. They started as he did as a boy, tending sheep, and as teenagers could do a full share of work. But they grew up and wanted to marry and build their own houses in the village. They were no longer going to be available as farm labor, and what is more, they wanted their own land.

The second reason seemed to be the Party's surrender to Vutsidei's stubbornness. "He would never join as long as they tried to force him to, no matter what they did," his wife said. "But in the past few years, they have stayed away. They gave up on this peasant. He was too hard. After that, he got the idea that he was his own master, that he could join the collective if he wanted to, that he no longer had to give in to anyone."

There was also the attraction of the new statute, with its pension and sick leave benefits. Vutsidei began his struggle against collectivization as a thirty-eight-year-old. By the time the statute went into effect, he was a grandfather of almost sixty and, although vigorous, was thinking of how much longer he could work and how he could support himself without some kind of pension. As it turned out, Vutsidei receives more than the regular monthly payment of $10 because of his contribution of land, but he will not say how much more; only that he draws that amount and lets the rest pile up. In any case, it is enough for his needs.

It is only when Vutsidei concludes his account of joining the collective that the final reason comes out. "It caused quite a stir in the office," he said, "when I went down and signed. I gave them their ten decares, and I agreed to work for them, and they agreed to put me on the partial pension list until I am older, and then I will draw the whole thing."

Ten decares? But there were 24. Vutsidei does not explain the discrepancy. What happened to the rest can only be conjectured. Vutsidei is allowed to keep three, his private plot with the slivova-producing tree, the vegetable garden, the chickenyard, and a little grazing space for the calf. This is standard. It is likely that he shaved a few square meters here and there from the parcel handed over to the collective, for a total of four decares. Each of his sons then received his three decares from the family land, with some extra scraps to total ten. That added up to 14 for Vutsidei's family, 10 for the collective. It is possible that Vutsidei's surrender had enough propaganda value for the bureaucracy that it chose to ignore the fact that the collective was getting only two-fifths of the land and that the family retained three-fifths. But such stretchable boundaries are a frequent occurrence when peasants stake out their private plots from the common land.

What is important is that Vutsidei made the collective system work. When he was young and had the help, he remained a private farmer. When he got old, he contributed some of his land and labor in exchange for being taken care of. He acted for his own selfish reasons, without the good of the community in mind, not to mention the needs of Bulgarian Socialism. But this selfishness, for better or worse, is the basis of true cooperation. Those cooperating contribute because they hope to benefit. For a generation, the Bulgarian regime suspended these rules, created artificial togetherness, and suffered the consequences in stagnating production and recurring farm crises of one kind or another. Since the introduction of the liberalized rules, there has been a marked increase in production—26 percent in the last five-year plan, which ran from 1966 to 1970 and thus included four years of the new system of incentives. Good weather and a more practical central investment policy that permitted better fertilization had a part in the increase, and it must also be noted that production still fell short of the plan by 4 percent for the period. But the incentives must be given a large share of the credit. Exactly how much statistically will emerge from the next few years of agricultural production, when the reorganization is completed and the incentive system shaken down. An 8 to 9 percent annual increase is projected. As with all previous plans since the war, there is no objective reason why it cannot be fulfilled.

KHRISTOFOROV'S DEATH

Vutsidei now works for the collective in the fields between the village and the forest, planting, weeding and digging potatoes, and growing fodder and wheat. His work often takes him to the fields near the Professor's house, but the cottage is empty. Khristoforov died in the summer of 1970 at the age of fifty-eight. There is no real connection between his death and Vutsidei's entering the collective that same summer, except that both events marked the end of careers of remarkable individualism, and that both were brought on to a great extent by a regime that has no place for individualists in its society.

Khristoforov was a tall, beefy man with great appetites—two packs of pungent Bulgarian cigarettes a day, most of a bottle of Pliska brandy. Once in the Writers' Club he ordered another dinner after finishing his first one, and both were heavy Balkan fare with generous portions of potatoes and gravy. He read books at the same rate, and wrote and talked past what should have been his limits of physical endurance. He said he was making up for what he had missed in his years of imprisonment, concentration camp, and banishment in the Rila, but there seemed to be a deeper reason.

Imprisoned for a crime he had never committed, singled out for persecution because of who he was, not what he had done, barred from ever teaching again, having his literary ideas distorted and censored by Party hacks incapable of writing a clear memorandum: all this had an effect on him that even his powers of description could not convey to those who had not experienced it. He still felt hunted, years after the persecution had stopped, and he had even been given permission to make a trip to England again. He was certain that conversations were being overheard, that he was being followed on walks with me through Sofia.

"Don't write about what I have told you," he would admonish me, after detailing the latest purges in the Writers' Union or forthcoming changes in Party policy. "If I am ever taken in for interrogation again, it would be my death. I know I would not last more than a few days. And they know it, too. I have told them." The stories, of course, were never written, and Khristoforov died peacefully of an apparent heart attack while spending a summer week in the cottage in Govedarci. His friends in Sofia are not sure, but they suspect that his morning brandies and late evenings of talk were a last defense of the individual against the collective, that it was his own choice to ruin his body so that he could deny the state the possibility of claiming his soul.

Neither Vutsidei's courage nor Khristoforov's insight in describing his struggle stopped collectivization in Bulgaria. But both the novel and the peasant contributed, in their ways, toward making the system more humane. Vutsidei, the peasant, surely was not considered as an individual when Party and Ministry of Agriculture were drawing up the 1967 reforms in the collectives, but the sum of all the peasant resistance all over the nation was an important factor in the decision finally to establish real incentives. *Vutsidei,* the book, may have had a more direct role. It was reported to have been required reading for the Politburo when it first came out, and its bright green dustjacket, with cow, sheep, and peasant sketches, is a familiar sight in bookstore windows, as the third edition, prepared by Khristoforov just before his death, sells out.

The message of the book and of the peasants is a complex one, not easy to sum up. We are aware, it says, that we live in the twentieth century, when the little individual farm and a man's own labor are not enough to cover the needs of a growing, modern economy; we know that some kind of modernization and cooperation are necessary and good. But if what is proposed is so beneficial, this should be apparent of itself, or at least apparent after competent people have explained the benefits to us. Then participation would be voluntary, with commensurate results. The message is a call for returning to what was good in the past: the banding together for greater efficiency and marketing and purchasing power, but not what was bad: the dwarf farms and marginal existences. And finally, it says that the key to the whole complex issue is contained in the phraseology so prevalent in the constitution and the other documents that rule Bulgarians' lives—democracy, voluntarism, control from below—but which, except for the most recent trends expressed in the Cooperative Statute, has remained without meaning.

VIII

IN SOVIET EUROPE

A profile of Soviet Europe is difficult to draw. Statistics are often un-available, incomplete, or deliberately misleading, and officials often repeat entire policy statements and answer questions as though they had been coached by drama teachers. The situation is never quite as bad as that described by Jan Myrdal in his *Report from a Chinese Village,* in which he quotes a young Maoist bureaucrat as having said: "We have here in our part never had any difficulty, never committed a mistake, never made a fault and we have no problems today." But it sometimes approaches this level, as when a visit to the sleek new East German Foreign Ministry building, which took all day to arrange, results in consultations with three spokesmen, each higher than the other, with the final result the reading of a passage from that day's party paper, *Neues Deutschland,* which the correspondent had had in his coat pocket since 6 A.M.

Yet the attempt to describe life in the Bloc, its personal, religious, eco-nomic, and political problems, must be made, not only as a means of understanding the present condition of the 100 million Soviet Europeans, but as a help in charting possible courses for their future.

Because of the difficulty of obtaining trustworthy official information, this profile is by no means a complete, systematic survey, but neither is it a mere retelling of the liberal amounts of rumor and gossip that supple-ment the official means of communication in the Bloc. In addition to the protectors of official secrets, there are also many government and Party people of an openness and frankness that would seem refreshing in Washington.

Another source of information of great importance is Soviet Europe's journalists. Reporters covering Western capitals do not need other jour-nalists for their information, since there is usually direct access to the official source. Such is not the case in dictatorships, whether of the proletariat or bemedaled generals. But these systems have their compensations, not foreseen by the planners, for outsiders who seek information. The journalists in Communist countries are among the best-informed people in the country. All those in key posts are Party members; often they are members of the Central Committee or even the Politburo, and are considered to have political futures: Communist leaders from Marx and Lenin to Janos Kadar have had earlier careers in journalism.

These Communist journalists are given regular Party and government briefings on inside information of a quality that Western correspondents seldom are privy to even in their own government's offices. This is done because of conditions that do not exist in the relationship between most Western governments and the press: the journalists are considered another arm of the regime, with the special tasks of persuading their readers and viewers to accept and support Party policies. In addition, despite their broad knowledge of government secrets and the background to the decisions, personnel shuffles, and plans, they are in no position to reveal them, because what goes into the newspapers and is broadcast is subject to several levels of control, with the censor the final filter.

With all this information they cannot disclose, the journalists of Soviet Europe turn naturally to their Western counterparts. Any such relationship must be built up carefully and slowly. Its absolute essential is the protection of the source. But once it is established, it provides great insight into some of the inner workings of Soviet Europe.

This profile is thus composed in part of material gleaned from the official releases and statistics and Party press, and in part from a long series of highly unofficial contacts, in a medieval wine cellar in Bratislava, on a darkened Prague street under the curfew of the first days of the Soviet occupation, in a greasy village tavern in Bulgaria, where peasants sit in their overcoats under brilliant fluorescent lights and contemplate the dirty white tablecloths, in a gypsy camp in Hungary, in a "People's Own" tavern near the Wall in East Berlin, in a monastery in Romania, where nuns announce the break of day by marching around the courtyard, beating boards with mallets. Information was supplied by crisp and businesslike foreign office types in the capitals, with suits and American accents picked up on previous tours of duty in the West, from unshaven provincial Party officials in country towns, toasting the future success of farm collectivization in America with plum brandy made in the local still, and from anxious members of the congregation of the Warsaw Synagogue, in their shabby house of worship on a muddy back alley lined with bomb ruins and junkyards.

Refreshments were an important part of the surveying process: the little cups of coffee, with the muddy grounds mixed in, the legacy of the Turks; the wines that date from the Romans; the Crimean champagne that marks a real occasion—although, with East European drinking habits, that could be eight in the morning, and finally, the ever present vodka and brandy.

If all these conversations reveal anything in general, it is the East European's intense preoccupation with his or her condition, political, economic, and cultural. This preoccupation is apparent in every encounter, whether it is with official spokesmen, shopgirls, or taxi drivers with rumors to pass on. It is the number one topic of conversation in Eastern Europe, not only with Western visitors, although that inspires surges of it, but with each other. It is, in short, the level of political consciousness that any democracy would cry for, but cannot get, and that any dictatorship says, on paper, that it wants, but is frightened to death to have. Because this political consciousness is directed not at fulfilling the plan or excusing the shortcomings of daily life or marveling at the vapid literature about socialist construction, but just the opposite: attacking, criticizing, carping, complaining.

It takes on some wondrous forms, including uncritical acceptance of everything Western, complete condemnation of so many things that are good in the Communist system, from free health care to subsidized mass transportation. But there is an excuse for these failings. Most of the critics can't leave the country to see the West for themselves.

To describe Eastern European society must be to describe injustices, in the political, economic, and cultural areas, in family life, and in schools. No amount of regime apology can erase these facts; it is because of the conditions in Eastern Europe that the barbed wire and watchtowers exist, as do the restrictions on teachers, artists, students, scientists, journalists, and writers, that men and women are put in jail only for advocating rights guaranteed in their own constitution, that even leading politicians are afraid to make statements as critical as thousands made daily and routinely in the West's parliaments and city councils. But it would be wrong to insist that the entire scene is one of injustice and wrong. Much is right in Eastern Europe, as indeed it would have to be if 100 million people are to be kept fed, housed, working, and creating. The right as well as the wrong appear in this profile.

THE RIGHT

Most of what is right in Soviet Europe can be summarized in a few words, words that might be a slogan for Westerners weary of their consumption-directed society: more doctors, fewer refrigerators; more college students, fewer cars. There is also a quality harder to define: the spirit of mutual help that the disadvantaged show, sometimes to the extent that it becomes an advantage.

Material presented the Joint Economic Committee of the U.S. Congress in 1967 provides direct and startling evidence of Eastern and Western priorities. In the early fifties,* the West Germans had 21 refrigerators per thousand inhabitants, the Czechs and Slovaks 8, and the Poles a statistical one-third of a refrigerator. About ten years later,† the Germans had 167, the Czechs 91, the Poles 32. There was thus some progress, but East continued to lag behind West.

In the number of doctors, however, East caught up with and passed West, a remarkable achievement for a number of reasons, the difficulty of educating a doctor compared to the ease of making refrigerators being only one of them, and the great difference in national wealth the main one. In 1956, Czechoslovakia and West Germany were nearly even, with 14 and 13.6 physicians per 10,000 inhabitants; Poland was far behind with 6.8. By 1966, Czechoslovakia had gone far into the lead, with 21.2 to West Germany's 14.5, and Poland was catching up rapidly with 13.

Automobile production and ownership also increased rapidly in Soviet Europe in the sixties, and the indications everywhere are for a further surge. One of Poland's answers to the 1970–1971 worker unrest was to build a third automobile factory. Czechoslovakia and East Germany, with about 13 percent of the population of the Soviet Union between them, produce nearly as many cars as the Russians, about a quarter-million a year. But compared to the West, Eastern Europe's automobile ownership figures are in the Henry Ford era: in 1967, 48 per thousand in East Germany, 36 in Czechoslovakia, 10 in Poland, compared to 230 in France and 419 in the United States. The Soviet Union, it should be noted, is even further behind with 5, which puts it ahead of Romania, with 3, but no one else.

Prices, adjusted to industrial wages, help explain the gap: where the American worker must work six months to pay for his Ford and the West German five for his Volkswagen, the Czech or Slovak must pay 28 months' wages for his Skoda, the Pole 31 for his little Syrena, the East German 11 for his Trabant, and the Russian 40 for his Moskvich.

These car owners might reflect, however, that their wages and savings are not going for doctors and dentist bills or schools. Free medical care and education through the university are taken for granted in Soviet Europe. In both cases, there is not enough to go around, but a further comparison with Western figures gives an indication of the priority the East is giving education.

Soviet Europe's effort shows up most remarkably at the college level. In 1950, Bulgaria had 381 students per 100,000 citizens. By 1964, it had the highest ratio in Europe, 1,260. Other Bloc nations also do better than most Western European governments in sending young people to college; France, for example, has only 940 students per 100,000. But both sides of Europe are well behind the United States, where the ratio is about 2,000.

Education and medical care head the list of the benefits the regimes pro-

---

* The figures are for 1951 for West Germany and 1953 for the Eastern countries.
† West Germany, 1962; Eastern countries, 1965.

vide. Family allowances, day care, dollar opera tickets, throwaway prices for the Party press, bargain books, controls that keep basic foods at 1950s prices and haircuts at a dime, and, finally, full employment make up the rest of the list.

It is a welfare state system that owes something to many currents of social thought: the paternalistic plans set up by Bismarck in Germany, the progressive ideas of the Czech left of the thirties, Lenin and Stalin's social blueprints, a little Hungarian and Balkan populism. Its defects are many, as is clear from this book. East Europeans who come West share the experience of initial shock over the prices being replaced with satisfaction over the quality of the services.

If the rights of Soviet Europe's system are debatable among its citizens, the wrongs are not, and their list of them, whether the basic economic complaints like shortages and subsistence-level income or the larger issues of dissent and the right to travel, is long. But, as Marx taught, in every situation of exploitation there is a silver lining, that of increased class consciousness and the will to organize against abuses. What Marx saw in the nineteenth-century capitalist society is equally true under twentieth-century state socialism. The difference is that the exploited are not permitted any formal organization, like Marx's International Workingmen's Association, to improve conditions.

Nevertheless, they organize, and they work and cooperate, not to defeat the system, because they consider that a hopeless endeavor, but to make it work for them. Like people confined to a prison or army barracks, they do not waste time trying to scale the wall, or pacing before it, but they do connive to get an extra ration, or get a few places ahead in the line. Since resources are limited, often someone must suffer if others are to benefit. They hope it can be the guardians of the system; if it cannot, it must be other citizens, those lacking in organization or guile. Their efforts are thus a mixture of helping each other and victimizing each other, but the former seems to predominate, and the result generally seems to be a kindness and sense of the need to cooperate that is far less prevalent in Western societies.

One example that must stand for many is that of a Czech priest who had served ten years in prison in the fifties. "After 1952," he said, "the Party men themselves were suddenly thrown in among us. The reaction wasn't pretty. Here were our persecutors, now among the persecuted. They got it from both sides, I am afraid. Their Communist jailers treated them worse than they did us. And the old prisoners turned on them. A prominent Communist had his jaw broken, teeth knocked out. Finally several of us said it was enough. We, victims of Communism, rallied to help the Communists. On one occasion I hid a new arrival from vigilantes. At last our intercession helped, and most of the prisoners, bourgeoisie, priests, Party men, accepted the fact that we were all in the same boat."

This spirit of joining forces against adversity keeps recurring in any examination of the society of Soviet Europe. Its purpose is survival, and the need for it is great. It is, however, a quality too often missing from Western societies and one they could use. Thus, in a peculiar, reverse way, the regimes of Soviet Europe should be given credit for it, just as they deserve credit for their other achievements. How much the six regimes do to provoke self-reliance is apparent from an examination of Soviet Europe's society in detail.

THE ECONOMY

The economies of the countries of the Soviet Bloc are of the command type, the origins of which can be traced to Lenin's and Trotsky's War Communism and to Stalin's industrialization drive of the thirties. "Work, discipline, and order will save the Soviet Republic," Trotsky said on assuming command as commissar for war in 1918, and the order has stood over the years, with the economy mobilized ever since then to face the recurrent crises on a wartime basis. Command economy means central planning, orders flowing from the center, generals to issue them, and majors and lieutenants and privates to carry them out.

The command economic policy has achieved much in the Bloc; it industrialized backward Russia in time for World War II, and after the war it put Russia ahead in the space race for a time. It converted Soviet Europe's agrarian economies into industrial, and it made it possible for Romania, the least developed, to double its gross national product between 1955 and 1967.

The growth and the pace of industrialization was spectacular because it was extensive—there was constant building of new plants, hiring of new, largely unskilled, labor. The figures looked good, but the products did not, and the efficiency indices were even worse. In Poland, for example, each unit of labor produces two and one-half units of gross national product. In Japan, the Labor–GNP ratio is one to six; in Italy, one to five.

Nevertheless, in the Bloc today, reform has taken very small steps indeed. Of the three different patterns of reform, the first kind is really none at all: keep central control, but do away with overcentralization. The trouble with it is that no one can define overcentralization, and those with the power in the capitals are unwilling to give it up. The next step is to decentralize but to maintain the elements of the command economy—in other words, to make several centers to pass down the orders instead of one. East Germany and Czechoslovakia have tried it with regional and industrial groupings. But it does nothing to correct the basic flaws; indeed, it adds to them by tangling the lines of command.

The final stage has been to break with the whole long tradition of central direction, and to let the market regulate what the bureaucrats had been regulating. Hungary has taken the furthest—and about the only—steps toward this, but its reforms cannot be completed as long as there is no concomitant political liberalization, and as long as it must worry about going too much further than the Soviet Union.

As large an economic question as reform is that of Soviet exploitation. Is the Bloc an asset or a liability to Moscow? Often Soviet officials claim the latter. But Western analyses of Communist economic statistics show a clear pattern of exploitation at least up to the Khrushchev era, and much evidence of disadvantageous economic relationships after that.

There is also the testimony of the Bloc's own economists, foreign trade officials, and political leaders. Most of the time, of course, they praise the economic arrangements that tie the Bloc together. But occasionally there are breaks in this solid front and unexpected frankness.

The first such break was in 1948, when Yugoslavia was expelled from the Cominform and Tito and other leaders began to tell the truth about the terms of their alliance with the Russians. Vladimir Dedijer, in his book *Tito*, recounted that the Soviet arrangements for the joint exploitation of Yugoslav oil "contained conditions far more difficult than the Soviet Union had proposed for a semi-feudal country such as Persia." The Yugoslavs found they were paying twice as much as the Soviets to ship their own goods on their own ships. Dedijer said Stalin finally recognized that such Soviet exploitation was not good for an ally such as Yugoslavia, but maintained that "such companies are suitable for satellite countries." Stalin's successor Leonid Brezhnev apparently feels the same way; since 1960, when large-scale sales of Soviet coal, crude, and fuel oil to Yugoslavia resumed, prices have been as much as a third lower than those paid by the Bloc countries, which are unable to shop around. In 1967, for example, the Yugoslavs were paying 10.80 rubles a ton for crude oil and the Hungarians 15.27.

In 1969 the Czechoslovak Party daily *Rude Pravo* felt it necessary to reply to the charges of Soviet exploitation in fuel imports. Its answers were hardly reassuring: it was true, the paper said, that Czechoslovakia was paying 24 percent more for Soviet oil than it could have paid in the Middle East, and that the Soviet oil had a higher sulfur content. But it juggled freight costs to prove that the price was only 30¢ more a ton for the inferior Soviet oil. Why buy it, then? Because of the oft-cited "reproduction value" of the dollar and ruble. It takes nearly twice as many exports to earn a dollar than it does a ruble, the paper said, and thus the soft-currency deal for oil from Russia was actually nearly half-price. This seemed to be another way of saying that the exchange rate of the ruble was not realistic, and it ignored completely the fact that the Russians shipped their oil farther and sold it for less to the Yugoslavs. Dr. Evgen Loebl, director of the Slovak State Bank, disclosed in 1968 how the Soviets systematically cut off Czechoslovakia's trade ties with the West, placing politics above the nation's economic welfare. One by one, profitable automobile, glassware, machinery, and china markets in Western Europe and the United States were abandoned. Czechoslovakia's trade with the East in 1947, the year before the Communist coup, was 14 percent of its total; by 1953, it was 78.5 percent. Those who objected were imprisoned or executed; Loebl, now an exile in the United States, was one of the imprisoned. Soviet economic policy, he wrote, meant the power to "decide what was right for Czechoslovakia and what was wrong . . . and the power to arrest and execute people who had formulated and realized a different economic conception."

There have been three stages in the Soviet economic exploitation of Eastern Europe. The first two, which overlapped, were reparations and the turning around of trade, through either political pressure or formation of joint companies. The third was the integration efforts of Comecon, still current. Each was scrapped or modified when it was discovered that it was not working.

The reparations program and the joint companies were designed to right wrongs inflicted on the Soviet Union by Nazi Germany and its allies. Reparations lasted ten years in the major target country, East Germany. In two waves, Soviet forces dismantled factories and shipped them off to the East on the single-track rail lines that were left after every double track line had surrendered its second set of rails. Railroad cars, locomotives, machinery, livestock, lumber, and of course prisoner labor, from the unskilled to the scientists and engineers, went eastward or stayed there. Estimates of the total cost vary widely. West Germany's ministry for all-German affairs put it at about $20 billion. A study prepared for the U.S. Congress Joint Economic Committee in 1970 said the cost was well over $10 billion at 1955 prices.

Romania and Hungary were ordered to pay $300 million each in prewar dollars to the Soviet Union and its allies; Bulgaria had a $75 million reparations commitment to Yugoslavia and Greece. The American economist John Michael Montias estimates in his book *Economic Development in Communist Rumania,* however, that the total cost to Romania was more like $3 billion.

Nicolas Spulber, in his *The Economics of Communist Eastern Europe,* said that Hungary's reparations deliveries to Russia accounted for 71 percent of its total exports in 1946. In East Germany, the 1970 congressional study said, "uncompensated deliveries averaged 20 percent of gross industrial production. Much of the cost was absorbed by the East German population, but the regime also had to hold down investment." It found that the effects of this underinvestment were still being felt in the East German economy in the seventies.

The next stage, the joint companies, was intended to make more efficient use of confiscated German property and East European material and manpower. The West German ministry estimates that subsidizing, equipping, and finally buying back their joint companies cost the East Germans about $2 billion. The companies were a continuing drain on the

East European economies. They paid no taxes, were guaranteed profits, and had exclusive use of the countries' best rail and port facilities.

The joint companies, the reparations deliveries, and political pressure had the long-term effect of reorienting the trade of Soviet Europe from West to East. None of the six nations except East Germany did more than 1 percent of its business with the Soviet Union in 1938. Ten years later, the percentages were as high as Bulgaria's 58 percent and Romania's 51 percent.

Comecon, the third stage of the economic relationship, has elements both of exploitation and of the purpose announced in its title, the Council for Mutual Economic Assistance. The mutual help has been extensive, although the multinational arrangements are far behind those of the Common Market. The main links are the Investment Bank, the Friendship pipeline and international electricity grid, the freight car pool, and the industrial organizations. Cooperation in the future is directed toward joint production of petrochemicals through the use of Soviet raw materials, the pipeline, and Eastern European chemical plants. There is to be emphasis on containerization and computer technology, in which Comecon lags badly behind the West, and rationalization of agriculture, an attempt to smooth out the chronic peaks and valleys in food production in the Bloc. None of this sounds like exploitation, although details of costs and prices are secret.

It is also difficult, in analyzing Comecon's progress reports, to determine what part direct Soviet aid to the other members has played. When the Russians provide technical documentation, as, according to a Polish report, they have done in 75,000 cases, is it to aid an allied nation's technology, or is it to use that nation's factories for processing Soviet raw materials into finished goods for the Soviet market? Bloc statistics make no distinction. Soviet aid of all kinds, according to a 1962 report to Congress, amounted, per capita, to $78 for East Germany, $73 for Bulgaria, $38 for Hungary, $33 for Poland, and $10 for Romania. Against this must be entered the aid, willing or unwilling, these nations have given the Soviets. In East Germany, for example, if the lower figure of $10 billion in reparations used by the 1970 congressional report is divided by the 17 million population, it works out to $592 per capita.

Any balance sheet of Soviet Europe's postwar economics must also take into account the long-range effect of Soviet policies in the area. And here, the balance is all on the negative side. Dismantling, reparations, the joint companies, the ambitious Comecon integration plans, have all come and gone, but the command structure set up in those early years remains. Its effect has been to depress living standards, hamper efficiency, and inhibit reforms. As long as the Soviet Union keeps its command economy, its bureaucratic planning, and its network of party and police controls to enforce them, it will be difficult for Eastern Europe to do otherwise, and some form of economic exploitation of the people, from without or within, will continue.

Soviet officials do not dispute this, although of course they use other terms to describe what has happened in the six nations in the past generation. The view from Moscow, as might be expected, is that there has been a steady stream of blueprints, gifts, loans, and experts, and that this has gone a long way toward pushing Bloc development, often at the expense of domestic needs in the U.S.S.R., and often unfairly. "Unless you have experienced the war and what it did to our country, you cannot possibly understand this," one Soviet official in Czechoslovakia said. "The Czechs survived the war intact. We, their allies, suffered. Why should they have a higher living standard than we? And the Germans?"

THE WORKERS

The workers respond to the shortcomings of the command economy with the kind of passive resistance that only rarely flares into strikes or rioting. Worker attitudes in Soviet Europe vary from country to country and factory to factory, but there is a common denominator that can best be explained by comparison to the mixture of cunning, obsequiousness, knavery, thievery, petty empire building, goldbricking, buckpassing, and timeserving displayed by an intelligent young man to cope with the military, whether the U.S. army or that of the good soldier Schweik.

"When they're not working, which is much of the time," an annoyed Polish official said on one factory tour in the provinces east of Warsaw, "they're measuring things here to steal, to take to their farms, to see if there's any possible use for them." In Slovakia, a doctor who had fought the authorities for years to get permission to build a clinic in a mountain village pointed with pride to the building, completed three years behind schedule at double the original cost. Then he pointed to a neat row of new houses at the edge of the village. "There's the rest of the material, and there's the extra building time," he said. "They simply took the bricks home with them. I complained to the authorities, but it was useless. They're all Party members, and I'm not."

It should be no surprise if members of the working class help themselves to state property they are constantly being told they own. If the means of production are in the workers' hands, if the factories belong to them, then it seems illogical that they should be told to work harder than they did under the capitalists. And although there is little real worker or union voice in production targets, working conditions, and pay, there are countless private arrangements to make life more bearable. In one Romanian factory, for example, the time clock that the workers must punch remains set at 6:58 A.M. until 9 every morning, so that no one will be late and have to forfeit pay. "We want to be fair," a functionary said. "Some workers have troubles at home, some have transportation delays." On

Budapest's industrial Csepel Island, a young Communist engineer complained: "The Hungarian worker considers the factory his club. Too many of our workers use the plant to catch up on football results and gossip from the papers, to get cheap subsidized meals, and do as little work as possible."

The regime, and management, counters with endless campaigns of "socialist emulation," and paid and unpaid overtime to make plan targets. The day after the plan is fulfilled, everyone collapses, and a new deficit soon builds up. No one has ever reckoned the man-hours it takes to paint the banners that drape over factory entrances, or the placards next to the time clocks that list the targets and the contributions that each worker must make in honor of some forthcoming friendship week. These bursts of effort, however, are more than compensated for by the idleness in between them. One Romanian time and motion study showed that a work process that was supposed to take 20 seconds took an average 220 seconds. Throughout the Bloc, the offices, shipping rooms, and work areas of the state-owned enterprises often look more like short-order restaurants. There is elaborate coffee- and tea-making equipment, little stoves for heating soup. Beer is sent out for and kept cold in the sinks, or brought in foaming in mugs. Diplomats who wait in the magnificent entrance hall to the Czernin Palace, the Czechoslovak foreign ministry, can watch the beer runners come through with their mugs, filled at the baroque Loretto restaurant across the square, for the bureaucrats inside. The worker club is also a good place to entertain friends. Former employees, women who have brought in their new babies, messengers and deliverymen—all can stop the work of a store or office for half an hour.

A last important factor in worker attitudes is the thought that after he is through with his present job, there is a second one he must perform if he is to make ends meet. A Polish newspaper cited the case of a man whose work, if he had really performed it, would have totaled nineteen hours a day. He had a regular job, a consultant job for which he was paid a lump sum, a half-time job, and a quarter-time job. Those who have second jobs, a Budapest newspaper reported, are the envy of their friends: "What clever fellows these colleagues are! 'They are in on a good racket,' and 'live like fighting cocks.' And they talked about their job in terms of the cabaret joke: 'We work slowly, just as we get paid slowly!' "

THEN AND NOW

All this may be true, the defenders of the Bloc economic systems concede, but we have a level of prosperity here undreamed of by our fathers, and we are free from the recurrent crises and unemployment problems of the capitalist world. It is hard to argue with a Polish party veteran, an organizer in the southern mountain region since the thirties, and a survivor of both prewar jail terms and wartime partisan fighting, who compares conditions then and now: "No one starves in this district any-more. That may seem a simple fact, something that needs no discussion. But before the war, there were many peasant families that starved. We've eliminated that." Or a Hungarian government official: "A third of our nation—like yours, in Franklin Roosevelt's term—was not only ill-clothed, ill-housed, and ill-fed, but reduced to actual beggary. You won't see beg-gars anymore."

If middle-aged Americans have sharp Depression memories, those of East Europeans are far worse. They went from chronic poverty into de-pression into war, with the street fighting and political murders of their various conflicting extremist factions as an added burden Americans es-caped. Thus the regime economists can point with great pride to the before-and-after effect and, without having to accept responsibility for the before, take full credit for the after.

They are right when they say much has been accomplished, but some of the accomplishments fall short of the claims when they are more closely scrutinized. The one great achievement of full employment is an example. The first exception to the claim is the prevalence of youth unem-ployment. But this is dismissed as parasitism, the fault of the young peo-ple, not the system, and in some countries it is combated with sentences to labor camps, which solves several problems at once.

The other exception is the massive underemployment, called by one Hungarian economist "unemployment inside the gates." Even in rela-tively efficient Hungary, officials estimate privately that there is no work for 10 to 12 percent of those employed. Western diplomats in some of the other countries place the figure as high as 25 percent, which means four men and women are doing the work three could do. But does it matter whether the regimes are paying their unemployment compensation in the form of lower, but better-distributed, wages to all?

To some, it does. The ambitious, whether they are the young managers who want the economy to function at a higher rate of efficiency or the academicians who object to the penalty of grayness of life, wonder if it is better to avoid the peaks and valleys of Western economic life in order to keep things on a plateau, but a very low plateau. Unemployment inside the gates is costly. It is paid for by everyone, those who want to con-tribute more and be rewarded, as well as those who benefit from it. All pay for inefficiency, the standing in line, the constant worrying about money, the low living standards. Is it worth it? Those who live crowded into inadequate flats don't think so. Those who plan for them, and live elsewhere, say it is.

Another question is the credit. The Communist regimes have accom-plished a great deal. But would it have been accomplished anyway, under another kind of government? There has been a general rise in living stan-dards since the war in East and West, for much the same reasons. East Germany, like West, had to build up its shattered industry, provide new housing, create new industries: electronics, petrochemical, data processing. Sometimes the Western living standards spill over to help the East, such as the millions of vacation trips in the past ten years, or the export orders. No one will ever be able to chart how much of the Bloc's prosperity is as dependent on the rest of the world as its poverty was. But there is every reason to maintain that other regimes would have reached the same goals with less human cost.

EVERYDAY LIFE

It would be wrong to describe daily life in Eastern Europe in uniform shades of gray, because there is much that is colorful and gay, some of it despite the system, some of it because of it. It is possible, for example, for ordinary wage earners to sit in the best cafés of Bucharest and drink a twenty-cent cup of coffee without worry about domineering waiters or cover charges. And it is sometimes necessary for a family to spend huge sums of zlotys or leva on a dinner with flowing wine and gypsy violinists, because there is simply nothing else to do with the money—it seems impossible to save it for a car or an apartment, if that is the family's objective, since the waiting lists are so long and costs so high. Travel is limited by visas; clothing by shortages. East Europeans thus cannot save for many things Westerners take for granted.

"For me to own a car," a Czech office worker once mused, "is theoretically possible, but it would require such a drastic change in my way of life, with my wife and me working, saving every heller, putting off having children, that I won't think of it." But a car, as a Polish doctor explained, is more than status, more than wish fulfillment: "A car is a tool in the shortage economy. With a car parked somewhere in Warsaw, if you see something scarce in a store, you can buy it and tuck it in the car—boots, a light bulb, other scarce items. You can also get in and rush across town when you hear things are available." This imbalance of supply and demand extends to services. In Sofia, an editor there observed, it is wise to stay away from the restaurants on the first three days of the month, because that is when everyone has been paid, and is spending the money on food, since there's nothing else to buy.

Why don't they complain? Consumerism is still in the dark ages in Communist Europe. There are selected letters to the editor to point out outrageous abuses, and a few meek journalistic investigations. Many concern problems that Americans first became familiar with in the winter of 1973–1974. Gasoline shortages are a common complaint. The replies are usually couched in terms of temporary difficulties, the need to iron out supply holdups, personnel shortages, and the like. They avoid, as do most official reactions to the complaints about daily life, the three major forces at work in the shortage economy. It is possible to spot them in any queue in Soviet Europe.

The first is that many of the people standing in line or parked in their cars are not unhappy to be there. They are on the company time, and they would just as soon be there as adding up figures or digging ditches. In a Czech gas station where I once waited for two hours, there was ample time to discuss the situation with the others waiting. One truck was from a nearby collective farm, and the time spent in line was considered pure recreation for its three-man crew. Another truck had a large machine in the back, and the extra wait meant a stopover in Brno that night rather than a drive all the way to Bratislava. One man said he was going to be late to work, but that the long wait would be accepted as an excuse. Just as many others were there on their own time, and were angry but powerless.

The second thing this or any other line discloses is that there is a two-class system, with a complete set of private facilities for those on top and another, inferior, set of accommodations for the public.

There were no high- or even middle-level Party or government officials in the line, because they have their own gas pumps back at the ministry or district headquarters, or if they don't, they have underlings they can send out to stand in line. The same system governs dining out. The little man faces a dreary choice of restaurants, but the bigger man has his club: engineers', writers', journalists', actors'. They serve the best food in Eastern Europe, in the best atmosphere, and the subsidies for these members of the working intelligentsia are generous. The Actors' Club in Warsaw has warm paneled wood, excellent service, and meat even during the shortages. A few doors down the street, in the public buffet, there is standing in line for a plastic-topped table and lukewarm soup. In Sofia, the writers' club serves fifty-cent lunches, and anyone remotely connected with publishing, including wives and teenage children, comes there at noon. Often they discuss new books on the building of socialism over their elitist meals.

The final reason that there will continue to be lines is that no one except Hungary's reformers, to a limited degree, can figure out how to change the shortage economy without changing the system.

WOMEN

In Eastern Europe, babushka-clad women in orange protective clothing wield shovels along the roadsides, sweep up and hose down the capitals early in the mornings, and unload trucks and drive tractors. They also work as doctors and dentists, teachers and lawyers. The Bloc nations' constitutions guarantee them equality, and in most cases, laws provide for child care facilities so that women cannot be kept from jobs or professions. There are also generous provisions for postpregnancy leave, and job guarantees. Women serve in the cabinets of some of the countries, and the opinions of the Women's Front organizations are always listened to in Party councils.

There are more working women in Eastern Europe than in any other part of the developed world, and, it is safe to say, more said about women's rights and equality. But despite the guarantees and the undoubted advances over the prewar period, when many of the East European societies were emerging from feudalism, it would be wrong indeed to look on the East European women as the liberated equals of their men.

They are disadvantaged in every way that the male citizens of the Bloc are, and more. If standing in line is a problem, it is the women who do most of it. If making do on small wages, figuring out meals with shortages of everything from meat to lemons and coffee, trying to rear children in crowded, inadequate nurseries and day care centers, and putting up with housing of the same kind are the lot of the East European, then the share of the women is far greater. It is plain that many of them do have a chance to become professionals, where the chance never existed before. But even in the best-developed educational system, East Germany's, where women constitute 54 percent of the population, and almost half the work force, they account for less than a third of the university students.

The main injustice that East Europe's women have to put up with is not being prevented from going out and getting jobs, but being forced to go out and do so. They work because they have to to make ends meet. With complete regime control of the economy, it is a simple matter to double the labor force by paying the male workers so little that their income must be supplemented by their wives. It is possible that this was not the original intention of Communist wage scales, but it is certainly the way it has worked out in practice.

How many working women are there in Eastern Europe? The United Nations Economic Survey for Europe examined the question in 1969, and found that Bulgaria led not only the Bloc but all of Europe with 81.5 percent of women in the twenty-to-fifty-four age group working. Seven of the ten places went to Eastern Europe and the Soviet Union.

The report noted that part of the reason for the great number of working women was the importance of agriculture in Eastern Europe. But there were other reasons. It noted that even in the industrial countries of East Germany and Czechoslovakia, two-thirds of married women work outside the home. Why is this so? *Pravda,* the Slovak Communist party daily, reported after the U.N. survey came out that "young mothers return to work, almost exclusively because of financial reasons, after their maternity time. Their children go to a nursery. The difficulties connected with this, however, are so great that every woman thinks twice before having more children, or even the first. The household equipment, the running around, the frantic hunts mornings and evenings, all this is not exactly designed for good family relations. . . . In this, we haven't even touched the basic evil: the effect of the separation of the child from the mother in the first years of life."

The Communist Party Executive Committee of Budapest commissioned a study of the condition of working women in the capital, where 85 percent of women of working age have jobs, and found much to criticize. Only 23 percent of the women were trained for skilled work, and nothing was being done to make up for past failings in this sector—only one girl out of four or five was entering training courses, and many were dropping out: "This is also due to the circumstance that enterprises seek mainly semiskilled female workers." Although women's wages have increased faster than men's since 1960, "in identical fields of work, the wages of women are on the average 10–15 percent lower," and often the women are better qualified.

The report then took up "the so-called second shift," the woman's job in taking care of the household. (Little mention is ever made in East European publications of a male role in this.)

"The servicing sector calls for immediate attention. Those who have bitter experience of this daily do not require details. It is precisely in the vicinity of factories working two or three shifts that there are the fewest shops. Daily shopping, therefore, takes much time and causes much annoyance."

Women routinely take the situation into their own hands, or their doctors', and decide that if they have to work, they at least will have few or no children. The sum of these decisions is reflected in declining birth rates. Between 1950 and 1965, the natural increase of the population of Eastern Europe, including the Soviet Union, was 1.4 percent compared to 1 percent for Western Europe. For the period 1965–1980, a .9 percent natural increase is projected by the U.N. for both parts of Europe. This may be good news to zero population growth advocates, but it is not welcomed by the regimes, and in 1967 Romania took a series of draconic measures to remedy the situation. It banned abortions and contraceptives and imposed a tax of up to $300—two months' pay—for couples wishing to divorce. The order soon crowded the maternity wards (there were reports of two women to a bed) and sent the birth rate surging to 27.1 per thousand inhabitants, nearly double 1966's low point of 14.3.

More socially advanced methods are being tried in Czechoslovakia and Hungary. There is no restriction there on abortions, but women who do have children are given a long maternity leave, with continuing child support about equal to half-pay. If there is more than one child, the subsidy doubles, and lasts as long as the child is being taken care of by its mother and is not yet in school.

YOUTH

When these children grow up, what kind of citizens do they become? The authorities in Eastern Europe have had a full generation to see. "We have worried through the years about the lack of the mother ingredient," a Polish woman doctor said of the day nursery system of rearing children.

"It cannot be defined. And no one is sure what behavior its lack has caused, because there are so many other new influences on the young."

If any critical findings have been uncovered, they have not been publicized, since so much is built into the system of working mothers and cared-for children that it would be risky to question it. Everything from national and personal economic need to Marx's treatise on the reactionary role of the family is on the side of impersonally raising the children.

In lieu of any scientific study, two personal observations can be offered. One is the general one that young people in the Bloc, whether reared in day care centers or homes, seem to be like young people everywhere, except that they have an enthusiasm for everything from learning to patriotism that would make large sections of the fashionably blasé Western youth cringe. American or French university students can drop out and live like proletarians because the choice is not a real one; they and their nation are rich enough and flexible enough so that they can enter the system any time they want. The East European student has struggled to get into an overcrowded university, has perhaps had to face a quota system because of family background, and knows what a real proletarian existence is. This is why an example cited by a visiting American professor of English at the University of Cluj, Romania, is by no means unusual: one of his peasant students had memorized a full page of the English dictionary every day, seven days a week, until he knew enough English to be admitted to the class.

In addition to these general observations, one case in particular illustrates one aspect of what the impersonal upbringing can do to children. Let the person affected, a Prague woman, tell the story: "Before the border was closed in 1969, I wanted to leave. But my sister is arthritic and needs someone to help her. I had taken care of her for years, so now I turned to her children, married, with good-sized flats. They were amazed that I would suggest such a thing. They love their mother very much, but the idea of care is one they simply did not seem to grasp. Without any rancor, they explained to me quite patiently that from the time they were born, they were sent somewhere to be cared for while their mother worked. They went to a nursery, then to an all-day school. They went to pioneer camp in the summer. In their university summers, they worked on harvest brigades. The state, not their parents, had cared for them as they grew up, and they saw no reason why they should care for their parent when the state could do so." The woman remained in Czechoslovakia, and the children visit and love their mother as much as they ever did.

Soviet Europe's youth, in scores of conversations, stress two main themes: their inability to change things around them, from university quotas to the inhumanity of the police and bureaucracy, and their inability to travel. The first is not surprising, and is shared by the youth in the West, although the latter can do much more about it.

What Soviet European young people want to change, first of all, since it is closest to them, are school conditions. The discriminatory admission policies of the immediate postwar period are mostly over. Until the early sixties, children of bourgeois or former bourgeois background were denied admission to universities, or put on lists below those of worker and peasant background.

This led to situations like one described by a Warsaw taxi driver. He had been a machinist, was pure proletarian. But his Uncle in America (a fine phrase heard often in Poland) had sent him enough hard currency to finance a Warszawa cab, and he became an owner-driver. At just about that time, his son applied for college admission, but was turned down on the grounds that his father was a capitalist.

There is no longer an absolute ban on bourgeois students in Poland, but a system of points. The pointies, as they are called in rough translation, are the sons and daughters of workers and peasants who get an extra five points on their university entrance examinations, where a good score is 24. The idea is that the points make up for the deficiencies that society imposed on them. Students and professors have mixed feelings about the system. They tend to approve it in principle but say it lowers the level of classes and keeps better-qualified students out.

Despite recent progress, more students are on the outside than on the inside. In Romania, there are about 60,000 graduates of academic high schools every year, and only about 20,000 places in the universities. In Hungary, one professor estimated that there are ten qualified students for every vacancy. Once the students are in, their studies are subject to the vagaries of the plan. An East German history department head complained that twenty-five of his thirty graduate students were suddenly cut off from funds and told to become engineers, because there was a need for them and not for historians.

What they are forced to learn is another problem. An entire thesis could be written by any student about the time and effort taken up by the study of Marxism-Leninism. There is not much official comment on the theme, but a Budapest publication disclosed that third-term medical students there had to pass a Marxism-Leninism examination that required the study of a thousand pages of text, compared to the 1,300 pages required for their medical examinations. Equal emphasis was placed on both. "In high school, I found the study of Marxism-Leninism stupid," a Czech teacher said. "But my father had been a shopkeeper, and I saw it as my way into university. I, one of the few bourgeoisie in my school, became the star pupil in Marxism-Leninism. It got me a higher education. I suppose it is ironic that it gave me a middle-class life, because otherwise I would have been a worker."

Restrictions on other areas of life are shared alike by youth and adults, but the young people have been singled out for some special attention. Their dress and haircuts are subject to alternate waves of scrutiny and neglect by police and officials. There are times when police seize and clip bearded or hairy youths in downtown Bucharest, or slash Western-looking jeans and miniskirts. There are times when they leave them alone. The other nations also have periodic campaigns, but the trend is to tolerance of much more bizarre outfits than would have been dreamed possible a few years ago.

But there is absolutely no tolerance at all in the field of politics. Students have frightened East Europe's officialdom at least since the 1848 revolutions. The ferment of the sixties reached Soviet Europe's youth, but was quickly bottled up. Themes at meetings are carefully selected and controlled; expulsion and arrest are the frequent penalties for overstepping the limits.

Hungary and East Germany have introduced "youth bills of rights" which turn out to be more like lists of don'ts than do's. Hungary's bill announces its aim is to "assist youth in fitting themselves into life and society, set down the rights and obligations of youth, and deal with youth's role in work." Those dissatisfied with the lack of revolutionary fire in everyday life in Hungary are warned by officials that there can be no "revolution within the revolution" and that the real way to continue the revolution is to do a good day's work. "Communism is the final alternative of humankind," one student group was told, "and the fight to make it attractive for further millions is as much a revolutionary deed as in other places, other conditions, is the armed fight in the jungle or on the barricades." But let the students take to the barricades at home and the consequences are swift and sure.

Much is left to the discretion of the police. Romania's antiparasite law makes it a crime to "go against the obligation to earn one's living" and leaves it up to the arresting policeman to judge the case and pass sentence. Labor camp terms of up to six months can be the result. Expulsion from school is a constant threat and a means of enforcing conformity. "We're quiet," a Hungarian university student said. "We have to be, or we'll lose our places in the school." Camps and expulsion, it should be noted, are only for minor manifestations of youthful dissent. The real political crimes, such as passing out handbills or trying to form political groups, are punished with prison terms.

Western influence is perceived as as great a danger as student activism. Young people are told in dozens of ways that behind the wealth and glitter of the West lurks a sick society, and despite what they read in *Newsweek* or *L'Express* or hear from tourists, they are much better off at home. But how do they know? They cannot travel to the West, with rare exceptions, and travel is what they want to do. American youths who have only to strap on their backpacks and leave cannot understand the frustrations of a sealed society. But the citizens of Soviet Europe experience it all their lives.

"I feel like a criminal when I go to apply for a passport," a Hungarian medical student said. A passport is not something that an East European keeps in a drawer until needed. It must be issued by the police, and along with it the all-important exit visas which determine where the traveler can go. "They screen you and your record," she continued. "I always feel I have done something when I am rejected. I haven't, of course; there are no marks against me at all, otherwise I wouldn't even apply to go to the West, but they make you feel like there are."

The travel experiences of an East German engineering student and a young Bulgarian government trainee will have to stand for many other such tales. They illustrate different aspects of the same point: that free travel is a privilege that most other people in the world seem to have, and that its denial is particularly painful ónce a little is permitted.

The East German: "We were all in Budapest. We met at a youth hotel, where you can stay cheaply. The group included a Canadian, a West German, two Poles, a Hungarian, and a Bulgarian. We had long talks about every topic, and we roamed the streets, afraid of nothing and no one. I began to feel more like a man than I ever have. It wasn't the West, but it was free, and we all felt that way. Then it was time to go, and then it hit me. The Westerners could go anywhere. My passport was good only to go back home. I suddenly felt like less of a man."

The Bulgarian: "We got permission to go to Yugoslavia, my friend and I. In our compartment was a young, primitive peasant. He was going to Vienna to work. He had an address of a friend on an envelope, but we couldn't read it, and neither could he. We were certain he wouldn't be able to survive. He couldn't even give us a coherent account of his past life.

"His clothes were terrible and he was filthy. We were well dressed, we spoke both his language and ours, we have good educations, we are intellectuals. Yet his passport let him go to Vienna and ours did not."

Eastern Europe's youth are frustrated because of their inability to change the system or even the faces of those running it. One of the illegal leaflets distributed for a short time in Hungary proclaimed that "our enemy is a small group of people who decide almost everything that happens in the state." A young government employee in Bratislava expressed her frustrations in similar language. A recent sociology graduate, it was her hope to go immediately to work to improve housing conditions in the old slum sections along the Danube. But after a year, she felt she had done nothing but take an unwilling part in the petty power struggles of her office.

"There are so many people in office, high and low, who will never give it up," she said. "It seems to be both an East European and a Communist trait. Our political leaders usually die in office. But at that level and at mine, they are doing nothing for their country, only themselves, and if it is a question of their career or the good of the country, they decide on those narrow grounds and we all suffer. We young people have ideals and want to change things. But it is impossible to have any position of influence, because they never let go, and they work full time to make sure they stay in power. We cannot wait that long."

THE INTELLECTUALS

Eastern Europe's intellectuals play a role with many layers of responsibility. They must remain creative and innovative, despite the restrictions and censorship of the regime, and must also put up with the general kind of restrictions affecting every other citizen. And those in the creative arts and in the universities have the added task of trying to put it all in place, to work out the ever recurring questions of how much, if any, dictatorship is necessary to achieve the goals of the new society, whether police can get the nation closer to Communism by cutting hair and bugging playwrights' apartments, whether incentives lead to elitism and betray the ideals of socialism or whether the system would collapse without them.

A constant debate on these themes goes on in the Party press and academic journals, and in the universities and institutes, although much less so in the classrooms and seminars. Sometimes the regime listens to the intellectuals; most of the time it is at odds with them, censoring, wheedling, bribing, persuading. There have been two brief periods when the intellectuals thought they were in charge, in post-October Poland in 1956 and pre-August Czechoslovakia in 1968. But neither period lasted long, and in retrospect, even the activist intellectuals involved say that they overestimated their influence, and certainly their ability to bring about permanent change.

Regime meets intellectual at the marketplace, no matter how both sides would like to disguise the arrangement.

The Party card is everything, and the Party controls it. The intellectuals in Czechoslovakia who have been refused even factory laboring jobs (on the grounds that they would subvert their fellow workers) know this. One of the dismissed journalists in Prague put it this way: "You don't need to put me in prison—all you need to do is take away my Party membership. I'm finished, then, except for menial jobs. But as long as I have the Party card, no matter what happens to my political career, I can be taken care of. I can disappear into the government somewhere, or I can be sent abroad." Unfortunately for most of the liberals, the usual mild treatment of the intellectuals—a few years in a job a couple of notches down—was not enough. They lost it all—Party card, job, often freedom.

"I'll just wait it out," a Czech academician said shortly after the invasion. "Five or six years of quiet, of interest in cars instead of politics, in writing, even if for the drawer, instead of political activism." But the choice was not to be his. He was one of those arrested and sentenced to prison in the trials of 1972.

Those creative artists who are not in trouble with Party or government are in constant trouble with themselves over the problem of censorship, covert or overt. "We can write to be read between the lines, of course; every Polish writer has done that since the times of the Partition," a Warsaw novelist said. "And we can hope that things will get better. But so many times they get worse."

The conversation then turned, as it does inevitably, to the third area of intellectual concern in Eastern Europe, that of goals, individual and societal, the gap between aspirations and accomplishments, and perhaps the most important, what those aspirations should be.

The Polish writer had vacationed in Hungary, and he talked more of the supermarkets and gas stations there than he did the literary scene. It is as natural for East European writers to be concerned about the lack of expressways and Coca-Cola in their country (Poland has since acquired both) as it is for American writers to be concerned about the surfeit in theirs. The writer is also a wage earner, a buyer of coal and payer of bribes, and an owner of a jealously guarded little car, buried most of the year under a canvas cover with the license number stenciled on it, and as fondly washed, polished, and caressed as that of any other citizen of the country.

In all their lives, however, something is lacking. They are materialists, much more so than the Americans they denounce in the essays they write to keep the Party happy, but their material is so poor. With many notable and brave exceptions, they sell out a thousand times over, attending Party meetings, signing petitions, denouncing Alexander Solzhenitsyn, and then they get as a reward a Skoda that won't start and leaks water.

"It was no problem to give up material things when we couldn't get them anyway, and to talk about the building of socialism," the writer concluded. "But now the Polish national pastime is the pursuit of the available."

THE NEW CLASS

The writers, the intellectuals, and the graduates of the growing number of engineering and management faculties make up Soviet Europe's New Class. It is not the same group that Milovan Djilas attacked in the fifties in Yugoslavia; his target was the leaders he thought had betrayed the revolution, replacing dedication with consumption. Soviet Europe's New Class does not lead, and many of its members know nothing of revolution.

It is made up of the vast white-collar group that is responsible for and behind the scenes of the triumphs of blue-collar socialism. Party leaders and workers get credit for these achievements, but both know that the working of the economy and ultimately the government depend on the efforts of the New Class.

The Communists tried to eliminate this class in the forties and early fifties with jail terms and death sentences. But roughly at the end of the first decade of Soviet Europe, the regimes made two surprising discoveries: first, they needed the brain power that the white-collar people had provided, and thus, as the prisons were emptied and the bans relaxed, some of the old bourgeoisie began to reappear in their old offices.

The second discovery was more shattering than the first. It was that an entire new generation of bourgeoisie was in the process of formation from the young Turks put in offices and important jobs to replace the old. As their work for the Party in the building of Socialism was crowned with success, praise, and bonuses, they began to acquire the material goods that that also provided, but also began to acquire some of the cautiousness and reserve that the possession of material goods, and the hope of getting more, seems to create. Typical of the class is a Czech engineer, a Party member since his days in the Communist youth at the end of the war, one of the leaders in the Red Guard-like collectivization campaign on the farms in the forties, when young people went around with searchlights and loudspeakers to force farmers to "voluntarily" join.

And today? Today he will discuss, with his wife, the merits of acquiring wall-to-wall carpeting like they have seen in a West German magazine. He is no more willing than the next man, in East or West, to risk Party card or job, and he cherishes above all the pearl-gray Polski Fiat that represents much of the family savings. The true test for this man came during the disturbances that followed the Soviet occupation, in which he played a truly risky and honorable role in helping organize the underground Party Congress. But on one day when demonstrators were gathering, police found his car parked near Prague's Central Telegraph office, and impounded it, fearing it was filled with explosives. He was incredulous, and horrified, and frightened—not that he was suspected of such an act, which he would have been completely capable of, but that anyone would think that he would sacrifice his *car* for his political beliefs.

The existence of the New Class in the six workers' states means that a constant class struggle is going on under the placid surface of those societies. Soviet Europe's sociologists have identified and studied the conflict, but few of their findings have been made public, because the authorities do not want to destroy the illusion of harmony. Their studies show the working class constantly losing ground in this struggle, and winning individual battles only by joining the enemy, by promotion or through the next generation.

The real test of whose influence is the greatest is in the number of workers trying to live the bourgeois style of life. Statistics everywhere support this finding of the sociologists—increased sales of cars and appliances, the proliferation of summer places in the Tatra mountains and along the Danube, the gradual change from bicycle to motorcycle, with a sprinkling of cars, in factory parking lots.

The conquests of the New Class cause concern among officials. On the one hand the system must promise that Communism brings bounty, but on the other the possession of bounty tends to blunt the class struggle and revolutionary fervor. This disparity between ideals and reality would be bad enough were it not that the whole catalog of things that the East European is striving for, wall to wall and chrome and the leisurely weekend, are as distinctly Western as if the Made in Germany or USA were stamped on them, and as such the rejection of everything that the Communists have been preaching about for a generation.

The regimes are in a dilemma. They must agree to a steadily rising and widening level of prosperity; otherwise their rule will seem unsuccessful and their five-year plans frauds. But this brings bourgeois thinking and ways of life. It used to be easy, right after the war, to stamp out the bourgeoisie with "administrative methods," but that action could be justified by charges of subversion and diversion, links with the old regime, perhaps with the occupation, espionage. Besides, there were cadres of eager young people and recent converts to Communism willing and ready to take over the flats and jobs thus made vacant. But now the bourgeoisie is the backbone of the economy and regime, and since its leading representatives are either Party members or completely clean of any political charges (part of its wisdom) they cannot be arrested or evicted. Even if they could, there would be only more bourgeoisie to take their place.

THE NEW CLASS AND POLITICS

The New Class is a danger because it wants political power to match its economic gains. With the growth of education and affluence, the realization has come that being instructed in politics like children is increasingly out of place. This feeling has been intensified by the economic reforms: the managerial privileges extended in Hungary and the greater or lesser degrees of decentralization in the other countries. It is only natural that greater economic decisionmaking power brings the wish to have greater political decisionmaking power. It is hard to dissect from an individual political being what goes into this wish: is it higher standards of living and education, which permit more time for reading and thinking, or is it the need to preserve or enhance living standards threatened by the poor planning of the regime, or is it the gap between the great leeway granted individuals in production and sales as compared to their small role in selection and control in politics? It is probably a combination of all three.

"I can spend a morning working on advanced industrial design," an engineer in Sofia said. "And then in the afternoon, I must go to a plant rally to give my approval to a set of slogans in honor of some Party or foreign cause. It is supposed to be democracy, but when we see that the other enterprises around here have suggested and unanimously adopted appeals of identical wording, you know the truth. Not that it's anything new. But we are beginning to tire of it."

There are some encouraging signs: the parliamentary commissions in

Poland and Hungary, where there is genuinely open debate and where some real legislative work can be accomplished; the multiple candidacies in the Hungarian elections; the growing number of non-Party people in key posts, although generally a Party card is still a shortcut to promotion and success.

These minor improvements point the way to major ones in politics and other areas of life. It is a conclusion that seems inevitable, but it must be unsettling to those in power in Soviet Europe.

It is that the hope for real improvement in political, economic, and cultural conditions lies in abandoning, either tacitly or openly, the basic premises of Communism as it has come to be known since the time of Stalin.

Less Communism. It means scrapping Trotsky's command economy and mixing such capitalist ideas as the market, profits, even the stock exchange, in with the plan.

Less Communism for the family means privately financed cooperative housing, wage differentials, less need for women to work, an abandonment of compulsory Marxism-Leninism and the parasitism laws for the young, permission to travel.

Less Communism in politics means putting the Party in a truly competitive position, matching economic decentralization with political, moving the work of the parliamentary commissions out of the closet, and giving individuals and citizens' groups real rights of advice and consent.

But Soviet Europe's rulers cannot permit this. Domestically, they could somehow rationalize it, because it must be remembered that Party membership and doctrines are like membership and belief in the ideals of Christianity for most Westerners. It is often necessary to belong for business or social reasons, but few Westerners bother much about the details of living a Christ-like life. That isn't part of the game, any more than the rules carried out by the average East European Party member are.

It could be worked out—domestically. But the six nations of Soviet Europe cannot make their own domestic rules. They must be constantly concerned with external factors that influence the course of their development, and of these, by far the most important are the attitude, plans, and fears of the Soviet Union.

IX

THE SOVIETS AND EASTERN EUROPE

The balance of power in Soviet Europe in the years immediately after World War II could best be described as a seesaw with all the weight on one end. The weight was that of the Soviet Union, and its control was complete. Soviet advisers sat in the government ministries and in the departments of the Party central committees, Soviet secret police officials had unlimited power, including that of purging the leading members of the national parties. Every area of life in the Bloc, from the way pictures were painted and books written to the acceptance or rejection of the Marshall Plan, was subject to Moscow's wishes. The weight was so overwhelming in the immediate postwar years that few could imagine the other end of the seesaw ever descending.

The balance of power in later years, however, could be depicted as the seesaw's gradually gaining a little weight at the upper end to counterbalance Moscow's influence. Sometimes these new weights turned out to be only temporary; sometimes they remained. Nikita Khrushchev's policy of giving more autonomy to the Bloc had only a temporary role, as did the Czechoslovak reforms. The gains of the uprisings in Poland and Hungary turned out to be of less weight than originally thought, but they did remain. Other elements that changed the balance were Tito's successful defiance of the Russians, the ideological warfare between Moscow and Peking, and the rising influence of the West in the area. At certain times and in certain countries, in fact, the balance was actually tipped away from Moscow for short periods, but it always came back, even though the angle was never again as steep as it was in the beginning. In the long run, the presence of Soviet troops, the control possibilities inherent in the Communist party structure, and, above all, the determination of the Soviet Union to risk everything—invasion, public opinion, image, occupation—in order to remain the dominant power in the area outweighed all the rest.

The Soviet plan for Eastern Europe at war's end was to make the area a faithful reproduction of what had been achieved in the Soviet Union, and since Stalinism had just won a long and difficult war, collectivized a continent, and industrialized a backward nation, those rules and operating methods were mandatory for the new People's Democracies. But exact duplication of Soviet experience proved impossible. Russia was still a nation of peasants: the countries it was trying to remake in its image were far more advanced. Only in the 1970 census did the Soviet Union "tip" from predominantly agricultural to industrial. In 1945, when this nation of muzhiks tried to impose its economic pattern on the countries it had won in the war, those countries resisted.

The Soviet reply was to consider these objections proof of anti-Soviet policies. Moscow decided that the area could not be trusted merely to remain neutral; the risk of its joining the West was too great. It had, therefore, to be forcibly wedded to the East, as the outer section of a two-part buffer zone. The first section was created by outright annexations at the start of the war: conquests in Finland and the Baltic republics, the dividing up of Poland with the Nazis and the eventual swallowing up of its eastern territories, the extension of the Ukraine into what had been the Ruthenian area of Czechoslovakia, and the formation of the Moldavian S.S.R. out of Romanian territory.

Next came the postwar creation, by conquest and coup, of the outer ring of friendly states, Soviet Europe. The six states were supposed to be both friendly to the U.S.S.R. on their border and hostile to the Western states on the other side. The Soviet Union wanted to end forever the kind of pinprick hostility that the Eastern European governments had shown against the young Soviet state.

But overshadowing all these considerations, then and now, was the fear of Germany, a fear that persists despite the drastic action of incorporating a part of Germany into the cordon sanitaire. The Germans were defeated in the war, and their country was divided, but in Soviet eyes, the problem remained.

The German problem became more complicated in the mid-sixties, when West Germany introduced its new Ostpolitik. Eastern Europe's dual policy of friendship to Russia and implacable hostility to Germany had to change. Moscow reacted first with suspicion, but then gradually came to accept the need of Eastern Europe to get along with its powerful Western neighbor. And once the Germans had signed treaties with the Soviet Union itself for trade and technological help, it no longer made sense to object if the Bloc did. There were, and there will be, conflicts, as in the case of Romania, because often a nation must choose between the Soviet Union and the West in determining whether to accept certain industrial processes or aid. It is up to skilled negotiators of Soviet Europe to convince the Russians that rejecting Soviet machine tools in favor of German ones does not constitute a hostile political act, although it would seem that a sum of such acts would eventually do so.

This is so because the six-nation buffer is more than a geographical concept. Russia needs allies. It uses neutrals when it can, of course, but quite naturally prefers those nations whose loyalty can be enforced.

The advantages of the growth of the Socialist world system, as it is referred to in the material coming out of Moscow, cannot be overestimated. In 1945 there were only two Socialist countries, by Soviet definition, the U.S.S.R. and Outer Mongolia, and the main one had just narrowly escaped annihilation. But as the Red army ground forward, forming governments in its wake, the numbers increased rapidly, and by 1948, after the Prague coup, there were eight new Communist countries in Europe. The world total has not increased by very much since: North Vietnam and North Korea were already parts of the system; China, with its enormous population and potential, was soon to follow; and only Cuba has been added. Eight countries switching sides—most of them from fascism—was a great shift in the balance of power in Europe.

The advantage can be seen in United Nations votes, or in press and propaganda campaigns orchestrated from Moscow, or in the international peace movement. There are frequently ten voices, ten columns of signatures on Soviet-sponsored petitions. The aura of international, broad-based support is largely a false one, but it is there. To someone in the Third World, having six or seven European nations shipping arms or technicians or supporting a Soviet policy initiative is far more impressive than would be a single action of the Soviets. The fact that little independent diplomatic activity has been carried on in the chancelleries of the six nations since the war is frequently forgotten in such circumstances.

It might seem logical to Westerners that the Soviet Union, with more than twice the population of the six nations and many times the might, would expect to call the shots when area interests were at stake. It does not seem logical to many people in those six nations, who point not only to their theoretical ability to outvote the Russians in the United Nations but a long history of cultural differences dating back centuries and having nothing to do with Communism. Each of the nations of Soviet Europe harbors feelings of cultural superiority to each of the others. They cannot all be right, and it is not only perilous but useless for an outsider to attempt to decide whether Polish or German rule in Wroclaw/Breslau represents progress or decline. Poles and East Germans are likely to agree, however, on their feeling of cultural superiority to the Russians. It comes out in conversations with strangers, in serious discussion with intellectuals, and in many published works, although only between the lines. Justified or not, the feeling is a fact of life in Soviet Europe.

The real dividing line in Europe, the argument goes, is not the Iron Curtain but the high-water mark of the Renaissance. The revival of learning and the spirit of free inquiry reached Poland and Czechoslovakia, but not Russia and Bulgaria. It reached Hungary, but not Romania. Thus it is no coincidence that the four East European countries that have had revolutions of one form or another since the war—Poland, East Germany, Czechoslovakia, and Hungary—lie in the Renaissance area, and three of them, in addition, were strongly influenced by the Reformation.

Where the Renaissance did not reach, in Romania, Bulgaria, and Russia itself, there have been no such challenges to authority. The reason for this is that the Renaissance left Europe divided into Latin- and Byzantine-influenced cultures. The Latin was a skeptical culture; the Byzantine patriarchal. Stalinism, in its original form or later adaptations, was ideally suited to the patriarchal way of thinking. Imre Nagy and Alexander Dubcek thought alike, although one was Hungarian and the other Slavic. They were both the skeptical men of the Renaissance.

Bulgaria is at once the most patriarchal of the cultures of Eastern Europe and the nation where the Russians are held in the highest esteem. In Bulgarian peasant society, the father maintains control over the family well into the adulthood of his children. The Lenin cult of contemporary Soviet society and the Stalin cult of old both fit into this system. Romania is more complex. It belongs to the Latin world through its language, but its Orthodox religion places it in the Byzantine sphere of influence. Yugoslavia, too, is split, with the Renaissance influence stopping at the borders of Orthodox Serbia, and with Roman Catholic Croatia and Slovenia the avant-garde of the nation in both economic progress and political dissent.

The patriarchal society tends to be suspicious of new ideas and contact with outsiders; the Renaissance open to outside influences. History shows that the Russians have imported foreign experts for certain specific tasks, whether it is the building of St. Petersburg or Togliattigrad, the Fiat factory city, in preference to opening their borders. One expects this suspicion in contacts with the West, but it is surprising to find that movement across the borders with Eastern Europe is just as restricted. The Iron Curtain, as foreign residents of Moscow discover, does not begin east of Vienna but east of Warsaw. It is almost impossible for a Soviet citizen to get permission to travel to the West unless he or she is a member of a group, and here the West means Poland as well as France.

Is this picture of backward Russia true in the era of space travel any more than it was when the Russians of the nineteenth century, under the rule of a medieval czarist system, were producing novels and music of great impact and modernity? With or without benefit of historical knowledge, East Europeans do seem to feel superior to the Russians. And Russians, as individuals and rulers, seem in turn to feel inferior. The imperious Red army officers' wives who descend on the shops in East Berlin or in Mlada Boleslav, a Czech garrison city for the occupation, are only showing their inferiority complex, according to an admittedly biased Czech psychologist who has watched them.

But there are ways of measuring a feeling of political inferiority. The most obvious one is the thousands of miles of barbed wire and concrete and the tens of thousands of border guards needed to keep Soviet Europe's citizens from leaving the place. The restrictive terms of the alliance are another. If French leaders smart under NATO, they simply walk out. Soviet Europe does not have this option. Satisfying the Russians takes precedence, for Soviet Europe's leaders, over the needs of their people or the goals of their nations. The fact that Moscow demands this obeisance is the direct result of its lack of confidence in the system it acclaims so loudly. If Communism has so much in its favor, it would seem that the Soviet Union would have been content to bring in the Red army at war's end, establish a Communist system, and then let it function in the six states, confident that relations would remain fraternal and friendly without the need for interference.

But instead it has watched over them with dozens of divisions of troops and further armies or spies and advisers, including whole staffs of language specialists whose job it is to ferret out any newspaper article that might be derogatory. "Why is it that the most powerful nation in Europe trembles when a few lonely demonstrators try to pass out leaflets on Red Square?" the late Austrian Marxist philosopher Ernst Fischer asked in despair.

This lack of confidence in the ideas that are supposed to form the basis for the mighty Soviet state is demonstrated not only by the barbed wire put up to restrain the average citizen, but by the vast structure of restriction and control put up for the leaders of the six countries, all of whom, of course, are dedicated Communists, many with long records of sacrifice and prison for these ideas. Why is it necessary? Lack of confidence breeds lack of trust. The leaders of the Czechoslovak reform movement had not had more than a few months of freedom of action before the Soviets began to accuse them, lower ranks and Jews first, of being first the unknowing and then the willing accomplices of the Imperialists. The process is repeated in other Bloc countries every time a leader or a thinker comes up with a heretical new idea.

Most of the time, the ideas are repressed before they get that far. The Bloc's leaders must deal with frequent visitors from Moscow to consult and advise at all levels of government. The Soviet Embassy in each capital serves as a similar conduit of advice in one direction and information in the other. Leaders and officials of all levels shuttle to Moscow, and the Soviet leadership spends a great deal of time on visits. The most important form of meeting is the summit, which has the special capability of producing a general line to which all parties are pressured into agreeing, and then must follow under the rules of democratic centralism. These summits and visits become intensified when a Party leadership post in any of the countries is due for change because of death or such outrageous incompetence that the mistakes can no longer be covered up.

These reasons, incidentally, are the only acceptable ones for rotation in the top posts of Soviet Europe.

Individual states must conform to a certain expected pattern of activity and policy. It was first codified by the Soviet theoretician Mikhail Suslov in 1956, a year of some trauma for such systematizers. Suslov said that to qualify as Socialist, each nation must have Communist one-party rule, cooperation between workers and peasants, economic planning and socialist ownership of the means of production, and vigilant police control. What he meant was that members of the Bloc had no choice other than to qualify. These points were extended into nine at the 1957 summit meeting, the last at which the Chinese accepted the Soviet lead. The new ones were dictatorship of the proletariat, socialist revolution in ideology and culture, national equality, and most importantly, proletarian internationalism—that is, the recognition that what is good for the Soviet Union is always good for the individual nations, but not necessarily the reverse.

In addition to the controls designed for the leaders, there is a second set designed to keep the populace in line. They are not pure Stalinism. The methods of the fifties, to use a phrase that is familiar, did not work, and a search has been on ever since to find new methods. East Europe has made some progress in the past decade.

The trials that followed Czechoslovakia's and Poland's upheavals could hardly be described as models of jurisprudence, but most of the charges were provable overt acts, such as the dissemination of illegal leaflets, rather than what the defendant had thought or advocated, and they were a whole era away from the purge trials of the fifties. It is apparent that a milder form of police terror is being used, relying on little injustices, such as the apartment superintendent as informer (a hangover from the Hapsburg days), loyalty declarations required for passports, and Party and job sanctions. The trials have been infrequent and exemplary, for the Russians, and for home consumption, as a warning.

RECENTRALIZATION

It seems clear that the cloud of 1968 and Czechoslovakia will influence Soviet Bloc relations for many years to come, just as the 1956 events in Poland and Hungary set the whole tone for the next dozen years. The Prague Spring so badly shook the Soviet Union that an entirely new Soviet policy toward Eastern Europe was ushered in in the wake of the tanks, the proclamation of the Brezhnev Doctrine being only its beginning.

East Europeans call it recentralization. It is based on the apparent belief in Moscow that the leaders of Soviet Europe cannot be relied upon any more than the populace. The cautious experiments that permitted them freer reign in the late fifties and sixties did not work. The Bloc leaders could not cope with the conflicting demands and pressures in their societies. They needed popularity, but as soon as they began to court it by relaxing the leading role of the Party, they were forced to tighten up again with police powers, because dissent and opposition flowed up too fast. They wanted creativity from their artists and writers, but as soon as they gave them more rein they began dragging out Stalinist skeletons.

But if the countermeasures they took were too strong, that was bad, too. They had to stop short of being so tough that they paralyzed the economy by reducing worker morale or putting the innovators in politics and economics behind bars. Yet there must be a certain level of control, because as soon as it is lifted, the press and the public, like actors in a movie film that has been stopped, will resume their questioning of their economic misery, their criticism of the Soviet Union, and their wishes that their nations might be permitted to become neutral in the cold war.

The only answer seemed to be to return to the old system. Recentralization meant an end to the loosening process begun by Khrushchev. He tore down part of the empire in two stages in 1956, the first in his secret speech, when he destroyed the myth of Stalin's infallibility, and the second in his concessions to national autonomy in Soviet Europe.

Khrushchev himself began the process of rebuilding soon afterward when he tried to centralize the Bloc economies through his Comecon integration plan of 1962. But at the same time, he continued to grant domestic political leeway to those leaders, like Hungary's Janos Kadar, bold enough or desperate enough to accept it. Since then, recentralization has proceeded in every other area of interstate relations in the Bloc: in the military, where only the resistance of Romania to an integrated command has kept it from being complete; in ideology, where there have been persistent suggestions from the ultraloyal in Prague and East Berlin to revive the body of the Comintern or Cominform, to achieve "a unified interpretation of Marxism-Leninism," or, as the East German Politburo member Alfred Kurella put it, "permanent organs for the objective settlement of serious theoretical differences of opinion." These are not isolated ideas from the field; they are actively encouraged by Moscow, despite its failure to revive unity through summit meetings. In a 1972 commentary, the leading Soviet journalist Vyacheslav Chernyshev spoke favorably of "what the comrades in the German Democratic Republic call the ideological integration of the socialist countries."

Besides the economic recentralization of Khrushchev and his successors, parried with greater or lesser success by the Romanians, the movement extends into scientific, cultural, and academic life as well. Since 1968, there has been a steady stream of exchanges between Soviet and Bloc historians, scientists, and professors, with the aim, according to East Europeans who have had to attend, of coordinating research and writing. It has been made clear to them that the relatively liberal attitudes toward differing interpretations of history or more frankness in sociological studies that were beginning to develop in the sixties will no longer be tolerated. Coordination of research, they have been given to understand, means coordination of findings. This goes much further than the previous strictures about what could *not* be written and discussed, and which were effective enough so that Soviet Europe still awaits its first honest history book.

Why does the Soviet Union consider this *gleichschaltung* necessary? The subject is a difficult one to discuss with Soviet officials, since their first reaction is to deny that such a movement is under way. But the following explanation, a synthesis of the opinions of two officials whose special areas are Eastern Europe and foreign affairs, not only admits the existence of recentralization attempts, but seeks to justify them.

The new policy, or the reversion to the old, is necessary because Czechoslovakia showed the Soviet Union how much it had overestimated the attractiveness and the depths of the roots of Communism in Soviet Europe. There has been no abandoning of the Soviet faith that ultimately the doctrine will take hold, but the timetable for its eventual acceptance has been set back. In 1945 the Soviets were convinced that their job could be done in a generation, which meant that by the seventies, there should have been stable regimes in Soviet Europe, without the need for the obnoxious and embarrassing presence of troops, and with trusted and faithful local leaders able to control their own people.

At the end of the war, the thinking went, all that was needed was to install the Dimitrovs, Ulbrichts, and Gottwalds in the capitals of Soviet Europe, in effect transferring them from their wartime jobs in the shadow governments to the real seats of power. The reason the Soviet Republic in Hungary failed after the first war, the Russians had always thought, was the overwhelming power of the forces of reaction, not any inherent defects. This time, the Red army was going to be around to make sure that no White terror was possible.

With this protective shield, it was thought to be enough to purge and rebuild the government, press, universities, and businesses and factories in the new image. If the first purges did not work, then the Parties themselves should be purged. In all of this, however, the resistance of the people was underestimated, and the capacity of the schools and places of work to reeducate them greatly overrated. Their apparent ingrained reluctance to accept the new way of life was reinforced by the spectacular failures of the first years, when everything seemed to be going badly for Communism. First there was the severe war damage to repair in most of the countries, and usually there was the added burden of reparations and joint companies. With everything poured into heavy industry, the shortages were so bad that wartime supplies in some countries seemed bountiful by contrast. But the high officials, with their Soviet-supplied food and luxury goods, lived like the old aristocracy or the interwar dictators, in fenced and guarded villas, sweeping past the public in their

ZIS or ZIM limousines, the Soviet models named for Stalin and Molotov. Disaster piled on disaster: the anti-Semitic campaigns of the last years of Stalin, the brutal tactics and the resistance in the collectivization drives, the fawning speeches of praise of everything Soviet, and the monuments put up to Russian soldiers and leaders by people who, in most cases, feared and hated them.

Thus the new life that was brought to Soviet Europe was a bitter one indeed, and when Stalin died and hopes for liberalization were increased, a common revolutionary effect took place instead, and the citizens of the Bloc speeded things up by revolt.

After twenty years of influences ranging from the presence of an army to the raising of a whole generation of schoolchildren, more than half the population, to cherish the Soviet Union, nothing that Moscow could do seemed to work toward the desired goal: loyalty without the need for watchmen. But much of what it did seemed to have exactly the opposite effect.

The only answer, then, seemed to be the reimposition of tighter controls. Limited sovereignty, the doctrine of a higher duty to the Socialist Commonwealth than to national interests, the idea that if the Bloc falls we all fall—these were propagated with great energy. Some of the propaganda seems childish in the extreme, as when everyone was forced to retract the condemnations of the Soviet invasion. But these rather foolish manifestations should not be used to write off the campaign and the policy as ill-considered. It has all the force of the Soviet state and Party behind it. Will it be powerful enough to prevail against the many currents pushing Europe in the opposite direction of big-power domination? The answer depends on many factors, some in the Soviet Union, some in the Bloc, and some in the outside world.

THE AMERICANS

Despite the growing number of little Renaults made in Bulgaria or Romania, or of British and French diplomatic initiatives, or of Austrian or Swedish trade initiatives, the West, to Soviet Europe, means the United States and West Germany. Both have a long history of links to the area, and records that are both good and bad.

Soviet Europe's relations with the United States have risen and fallen with the political conditions in the world outside. The peaks have always been more pronounced than the valleys, however, and the Uncle in America is probably responsible. He sends the hard-currency coupons so that his relatives can buy Western consumer goods in the special state shops, or even bricks and mortar on the shortage-plagued market to build their houses. Sometimes he appears in person, squeezing his enormous Ford through the narrow streets of the family village and showering largess on relatives and friends. This process of discovery works two ways. Countless second-generation Poles and Hungarians find out through their visits that they are not only American ethnics, but part of a culture centuries old. They discover, to their delight, that the language of their neighborhoods in America is still alive in contemporary literature and drama.

The arrival of the Uncle is celebrated by feasting and the drinking of the local spirit. Villagers come from miles away to fondle the Ford or feel the texture of the latest American polyester knit suits. But there is more to the relationship than material envy and pride. The United States' help to Eastern Europe on the nation-to-nation level, limited as it has been in the postwar years because of the cold war, is known and appreciated. Every Czech and Slovak knows that their 1918 Declaration of Independence was proclaimed in Washington, and that the federated state idea was approved in Pittsburgh. A variety of East Europeans, from Lev Trotsky to the parents of Gomulka and Dubcek, found asylum or jobs in the United States. Most important is the realization throughout the area that Woodrow Wilson's principles of self-determination were responsible for the rebirth of their nations as independent states after many centuries.

The dominant position of the Soviet Union after the Second World War prevented the United States from encouraging self-determination a second time, although its attempts to secure free elections in the area are remembered with gratitude by many in Soviet Europe.

Now the revival of East-West trade has produced new hope. Cold war considerations kept most American economic aid, including the Marshall Plan, out of the area. But even before the Nixon-Brezhnev détente, both trade and aid from America were in the area. Several U.S. agricultural extension programs are available to the Poles, and American experts on United Nations assignment also contribute to Poland and Romania through the ILO management centers. It is still dangerous for the average Bulgarian to walk into the USIA library in downtown Sofia and borrow a book. A similar situation existed in Romania until President Nixon's trip produced agreement on a Romanian cultural center in New York and an American one in Bucharest. Now borrowing a book, formerly a politically hostile act, is officially welcomed in Romania.

Détente is viewed with mixed feelings. It is much more widely discussed in the Bloc than it is in the United States, and everyone, from farmers to intellectuals, seems to have an opinion about it. The positive aspects, in their view, are its potential for liberalizing politics in the Soviet Union, which in turn would benefit the Bloc. Its negative side, they fear, consists of increased possibilities for more deals dividing up the world. In addition, they worry that American grain and technology might help the present Soviet leadership out of its difficulties and thus postpone, not accelerate, liberal trends.

A final American link to the area is the diplomatic service. American diplomats have had a perilous history in Soviet Europe. In the forties and fifties, dozens of local employees were arrested or forced to work as spies, and many diplomats were expelled on espionage charges. In many countries, diplomatic relations were broken and embassies shut down. In contrast to its record in many other countries, the United States has chosen well-qualified career men to man most of its ambassadorial posts. It has backed them up with staffs of a high level of expertise, for the most part, both in languages and in specialties. At diplomatic cocktail parties in Eastern capitals, it is often the Americans who can be seen speaking Bulgarian or Romanian to their hosts, and the other Westerners who are trying to find out what they were told.

THE GERMANS

The Germans face complications in their relations with Eastern Europe that the United States and other Western candidates for a role in the area do not have to worry about. In remote and recent history, the Germans were rulers in Eastern Europe, and memories of World War II are still sharp. The Germans were eventually at war with every country in the area, and at war's end, every country, whether spontaneously or under Soviet pressure, declared that there would never again be a place for Germany in Eastern Europe. As the millions of German refugees streamed from Königsberg, Breslau, and Teplitz-Schönau, and the names of those places became Kaliningrad, Wroclaw, and Teplice, it seemed as though the tide, and the hatred that impelled it, could never be reversed. The creation of a Soviet-sponsored German state, "the first worker and peasant state in German history," did little to change attitudes.

The Soviet leaders apparently thought that all of Germany might someday be Communist. But when that failed to happen, East Germany served a useful purpose in intra-Bloc relations. Politically, the German Democratic Republic was like an actor who had learned his lines and could be brought on stage to speak in favor of peace, ceding of former German territories, willingness to pay reparations (except to Israel) and participation in exploitative economic arrangements. By contrast, the Bad German actor in Bonn would then be brought out to recite the villain's lines.

In the economy of the Bloc, East Germany served the purpose of introducing a higher level of technology, German technology, without the political embarrassment of having to go to Krupp or Mannesmann during the cold war years. The Russians could say to the Czechs or Bulgarians to go ahead and import their German machine tools, as Eastern Europe had done for years, but make sure they come from our Germans, not theirs.

This Eastern image of good and bad German states was reinforced by a single-issue propaganda campaign that pointed out to the recent victims of the Nazis that the Germans were rearming, joining NATO, and refusing to give up their claims to their Eastern territories. It was not difficult for Eastern Europe to accept this picture of a militarist Germany. Few of its citizens ever got outside the country to Bonn to see that military uniforms there were a great deal rarer than in their own capitals. As was perhaps natural, they paid far too much attention to the cold war rhetoric of Konrad Adenauer and his Christian Democrats, who were piously vowing to reacquire Middle Germany (meaning the GDR) as well as Eastern Germany (meaning parts of Poland and the Soviet Union), and naming autobahn picnic grounds and new suburban streets after the lost cities of the East. More alarming were the rallies of the Pomeranians and Silesians, who seemed at times ready to start marching eastward, and the growth of neo-Nazi feeling in the mid-sixties.

There was one important divergence of view between the official line and the opinion of the people of Soviet Europe, however. Their fear and distrust of the Germans did not stop at the zonal border. They feared and distrusted East and West Germans alike. They remembered the war. And their own resistance to reeducation made them skeptical that much had been accomplished in that direction in East Germany. Every village hall and high school in Poland, it seems, has its exhibit on the occupation, so that the new generations know the history and can read for themselves the original handbills ordering the roundups of hostages and their executions. If this is not enough, there are regular visits to the concentration camps. The East Germans, in fact, advertise their concentration camps in their international railway timetables. The rusting barbed wire and the remains of the gas chambers in Auschwitz and Terezin, the exhibits of thousands of pairs of eyeglasses, a roomful of empty suitcases, the toys of the children who died in the camp: all are more powerful than any words.

Until 1966, the Soviet-German-Soviet Europe triangle of relationships seemed to be one of those permanent arrangements of foreign policy that not only do not change but for which no possibility of change can be foreseen. As long as West German politicians wanted to be reelected, or so they believed, their platform had to be reunification of Germany, and that meant an end to East Germany as well as great territorial losses for Poland, and these were conditions the Soviet Union could never be expected to accept. And as long as the first two sides of the triangle remained in these positions, Soviet Europe, even its member nations without the remotest interest in the territorial questions, could have nothing to do with the Bonn militarists.

But in 1966, when Willy Brandt and the Social Democrats joined the Bonn government, the relationships that had seemed so permanent began to become very fluid.

Romania was the logical starting point for the Germans, and soon a long, low embassy building flying the red, yellow, and blue flag appeared on the banks of the Rhine at Cologne, downriver from Bonn. The limousines, official ones from the capital and unofficial ones from the Ruhr, began their calls, and cultural agreements, technical aid programs, and business deals resulted. Romania's indebtedness to West Germany rose to a billion marks, but West Germany's to Romania was even greater. The

Germans were back in Eastern Europe for the first time since the Wehrmacht retreat of 1945. Brandt's Ostpolitik had meshed with Ceausescu's open-door foreign and trade policy: the right men, the right policies, the right time.

By 1970, dangerous Germany had become desirable Germany for the Soviet Union, and fears of counterrevolution were subordinated to desires for Mannesmann gas pipes and a Mercedes truck plant. The Russians also sought a political price: they wanted to set the seal on the division of Europe, and have Germany, the main victim of the Red army victory of 1945, accept its losses as permanent. In a series of negotiations in Warsaw and Moscow, the Germans agreed to nonaggression treaties that make as permanent as anything can be in international relations the "temporary Polish and Russian administration" of 40,000 square miles of former German territory.

Brandt had his own reasons for agreeing to give up the Eastern territories. Germany gained from trade with Russia, as Russia did from Germany. Germany has always looked on the vast interior of Russia as an immense market for German consumer goods, a construction site for German engineers, and an investment area where joint companies might be set up to combine German machinery and technical knowledge with Russian labor and market needs.

But idealism also motivated Brandt. No one who witnessed his sudden, impulsive falling to his knees that gray November day in 1970 at the Warsaw Ghetto monument can doubt the depths of his feelings about the wrongs inflicted by Nazi Germany on Eastern Europe. Brandt felt that guaranteeing Poland's postwar borders, no matter how painful it might be for the Germans who would never be able to return to their old homes in the East, was essential if Germany were ever to face and come to terms with Hitler's aggression. His view of the war and its consequences was shaped from his own personal experience as a wartime exile in Norway.

East Germany was more difficult than Poland for the West Germans in their search for détente. Brandt could not say so in public, but in 1970 he decided that recognition of the East German state was inevitable, and that reunification on the Adenauer terms was impossible to attain for as long a time as anyone could foresee. The negotiations that followed did not bring direct diplomatic relations, just as Henry Kissinger's talks with Peking produced "liaison offices," not embassies. But in both cases, the effect was the same; the links were established, political realities recognized.

There are dangers as well as benefits for East Germany in the new arrangements. The main one is the fact that, in the seventies, the other Germans will be back in Eastern Europe, but not in Wehrmacht or SS uniforms. They will be the engineers, the traders, the tourists, and the old folks seeing the old farmstead, able to cluck about how things have gone to hell under Communism, and then, however, to return to Düsseldorf with promises never to yearn again for the lost East. When this happens, the capable men and women in the East German information offices will yearn as well for the comfortable old days when a revanchist was a revanchist.

CHINA

When, at the end of the convulsions of the great cultural revolution, China decided to restore its international contacts, it began to pay more attention to Soviet Europe than it had at any time since the dispute with Moscow began. It sent ambassadors to all the Bloc capitals, patched up and increased trade relations, and began to dispatch and receive delegations at all levels.

Special attention went to Romania and Yugoslavia. Whenever the Soviet Union increased its pressure on Romania, China would come to its aid. During Ceausescu's visit to Peking in 1971, Chou En-lai said in a speech that "medium and small countries in the world are uniting to oppose the hegemony of the 'superpowers' . . . and this has become an irresistible revolutionary line." As if its $244 million loan to Romania, negotiated in 1970, were not enough, China announced that its trade with Romania had increased by 187 percent in the 1966–1970 period, and that trade in 1970 alone went up by a third.

China, of course, sees Soviet Europe as an important weapon in its struggle against the Soviet Union. It needs allies in the world Communist system, and it is less careful than it used to be in choosing them. Eastern Europe sees China in a different light. Its main concern is what China can do to help it solve its Russian problem. There are many ways.

The Soviet preoccupation with China ranks first. How to deal with the Chinese occupies much more thought and energy in the Soviet Union than, for example, American policymakers devote to either the Soviets or the Chinese. American soldiers have not fought Chinese or Russians, but the latter two have fought each other. Washington is on a course of détente with both Moscow and Peking, but the latter two are on a course of enmity. Soviet officials have admitted that their problem is a long-range one. Nothing in their long relations with the Chinese, and nothing in the intrinsic nature of Communism, equips the Russians to predict what the Chinese are going to do or how to cope with it. Marxism-Leninism is of little value as guidance when dealing with a new kind of socialist society so recently created from feudalism. It makes the Russians' problems with Soviet Europe, a lukewarm kind of socialist society not yet separated from bourgeois democracy, seem mild indeed.

China also affects the Soviet economy and, by extension, that of Soviet Europe. This effect is viewed with much less equanimity than the political influences, because it means that the military lobby in the Soviet Union, already strong, becomes even stronger. The border fighting so threw off the

Soviet budget projections that the 1970 Five-Year Plan was delayed, and this in turn delayed those of Soviet Europe.

In foreign relations, China's rivalry for better relations with the United States makes it more difficult for Moscow. The United States is in the position Soviet Europe would like to be in. It can consider an offer, political or economic, from one of the Communist powers, and then check it out against the other's offer.

For all these reasons, China figures large in East European hopes for relaxation on the international scene in general and in its own area in particular. No one talks very seriously about Chinese military help, despite the Soviet bridgehead charges and the hopes of some of the Romanians. Its economic aid is welcomed, where that is possible, but no one thinks it would ever reach the level at which it might replace Soviet help.

China's real value is symbolic. Since the split between Peking and Moscow, there has been more than one version of Communist truth, more than one accepted body of doctrine. Yugoslavia proved in 1948 that a nation and Party could be out from under Moscow's control and still do very well in ideological innovation, political arrangements, and the economy—better, in many ways, than its former mentor. The Chinese example is far more important. The rights and wrongs of the Sino-Soviet dispute do not matter to the people of Soviet Europe. What does is the fact that leaders and theoreticians of equally sound background, equally thorough dedication, can disagree on the right road to socialism. This is as stirring a theme as the "Internationale" in the corridors of government in the Bloc, because it concerns an issue central to all of them: the separate, individual road to socialism, not a Chinese one, not a Soviet one, but a national one. That is the real contribution of China to Soviet Europe, whether or not aid arrives or border conflicts flare again.

The United States, Germany, and China: all are influences, but they are limited when compared to the influence the Soviet Union exerts on its empire. Bridge building from the United States involves a shaky span of 4,000 miles. The ability of German tourists and machine tools to improve conditions is limited. China is even farther away. But all these influences do add some weight to the other side of the seesaw. When they are combined with others inside the Soviet Union and Soviet Europe that seem likely to develop in the next decade, the chances for a better balance improve greatly. These internal influences can be gathered together in two general headings: nationalism, which means going backward in history, and modernization, going forward.

NATIONALISM

To the dissidents in Soviet Europe, the burden of Communist rule is bad enough for the 130 million Great Russians, but it is only a single burden.

Hungarians and Poles bear a double burden. They must put up with the system, and put up with foreign rule.

No nation wants to be ruled by another. The fighting in Northern Ireland and Africa, the demonstrations and attacks of the separatists in Canada, Belgium, Scotland, Wales, Croatia, Puerto Rico, Okinawa, in the American Indian reservations: the list is added to regularly. All of the trends toward international thinking, all of the trading blocs and customs unions, are counterpoised by trends toward intensified nationalism. And yet, in this era, the Soviet Union has made no concession whatever to nationalism, and indeed has proceeded in exactly the opposite direction. As old empires crumble and new nations swell the rolls of the United Nations, the Soviet Union continues to practice colonialism.

But just as the situation in Mozambique is different from that in Ulster, so Soviet Europe's nationalist aspirations have their unique qualities. They result from historical and political circumstances not wholly duplicated in any other part of the world.

Soviet Europe's history has been a long and often sorrowful chronicle of attempts to achieve national identity and independence. In all of the nations except East Germany, there were periods of foreign domination of a length that would seem to kill the hardiest seeds of nationalism. But mother tongues, institutions, literature, religions, and culture somehow survived. In all these dismembered and dominated nations, there was also a glorious period of national revival, in the nineteenth century, or after Versailles. Other European nations like Finland and Belgium share this history of late independence. But in none of them was the independence that had been yearned for so long to be of such short duration. Slovaks lived for a millennium under the Hungarians and enjoyed only two decades of nationhood before Hitler marched in. Three years after the defeat of the Nazis, it was the turn of the Communists. The pattern was the same throughout the area.

The second special circumstance is the twist that history and current politics give to the natural resentment against foreign rule in Soviet Europe. The ethnic hates and ideas of Slavic or Magyar inferiority or superiority that made Eastern Europe a playground for assassins and bombers between the wars have not subsided. No argument about the number of Russian books published, or symphonies written, or scientific discoveries made, can convince the dissatisfied in Soviet Europe of the inherent equality of peoples. But the Soviet Union does not try to convince them, beyond the standard propaganda about internationalism. Indeed, many of its acts exacerbate ethnic hates and rivalries, whether by design or ineptitude. Was it accident or design that caused the Soviet Union to fill the top four posts in Stalinist Hungary with Jews? Were the Soviet leaders ignorant of Hungary's record of anti-Semitism, or was it their intention to have Jews blamed for the inevitable troubles of the early postwar years? Ethnic hates could not have been a major consideration when the invasion of Czechoslovakia was ordered, but one of its effects was to stir up among even normally tolerant Czechs and Slovaks all sorts of talk about primitive Poles and gypsy Hungarians. Why is Hungary, of all the Bloc nations, chosen for the periodic task of putting pressure on Romania? It is surely because of the 1.6 million Hungarian-speaking Romanian citizens, many of whom have never reconciled themselves to Bucharest's rule. But in stirring up these old issues and resentments in the name of the unity of the Bloc, the Soviet strategists instead help its centrifugal tendencies.

Soviet Europe is also different from other areas striving for independence because of the doctrine that is supposed to bind the area to the Soviet Union. The six nations are supposed to be loyal to the one powerful nation because of a system of beliefs that all share. But their leaders consider only about 10 percent of their populations capable of understanding or accepting those beliefs to the extent that they can be admitted to the Party built around them. And even for that minority that does believe, there are so many contradictions between theory and practice that even the strongest faith must be shaken.

One test of the doctrine is its success under the conditions of political competition. Only Czechoslovakia and East Germany had Communist parties of any strength before the Soviet army arrived. Repression by the interwar dictatorships played a large role in the other countries, but even in times of relative political freedom, only a tiny minority, adding up to a few thousand in each country, chose Communism. Does this mean that the doctrine is "foreign" to the area? No more so than it is foreign to Uganda. There is nothing in the blood of the sons of Arpad to cause them to resist Communism, as some of their exile branches contend. The socialist and cooperative movements, in fact, have a long history in the six nations. But the system, as practiced in Russia, was simply not seen as an improvement on what these nations already had. Thus it was not blood, but experience, that made Communism unpopular.

The final circumstance that makes Soviet European nationalism such a potential force is linked intimately with the pattern of modernization in the Bloc.

MODERNIZATION

Most of Eastern Europe was backward and agricultural before World War II. East Germany, the Czech lands, and parts of Poland and Hungary were islands of industrialization in the sea of farms.

In the generation since the war, the area has become not only vastly more industrial but more urban and modern. School enrollments have trebled and quadrupled; literacy and life expectancy rates nearly doubled. The regimes issue statistics to prove this proudly, as they should, because they reflect the achievements of nations and peoples. But the statistics also tell another story. Like the illiteracy rates or the percentage of industrialization, it is a story of change. But this is the change that will take place in the future as a direct result of those that have already been noted and recorded.

The people of Eastern Europe, in short, are not the same people they were when the systems of rule they live under were set up, but the systems have not modernized to keep step with the people. People who are educated, literate, who travel or have contacts with foreigners, and who live in urban environments in slowly increasing standards of comfort do not want to put up with the shortages, the standing in line, and most important of all, the political and cultural restrictions they have been subjected to since 1945. They feel they have come a long way since that time. They have built up their nations and their own personal careers with their own hands and ingenuity, and they do not want a bureaucrat with police powers telling them how to think, how to vote, and how to behave. They look around them to some of the deficiencies of their societies and think that their leaders and officials should have even less of a role in arranging their lives.

But the leaders are afraid to change their 1945 models of rule very much. The powers of the secret police have been curtailed everywhere, and in some nations, travel restrictions are loosening. Shop windows are much fuller and lines much shorter than they were in 1945, of course, but it is a relative thing, and those travelers from Soviet Europe who return from the West wonder why there should be shortages or queues at all. The press in Poland and Hungary is a little more open than it used to be, but not much more open elsewhere. The greatest area of no change has been in Party and government. Despite Hungary's and Poland's progress toward more participation in decisionmaking, the fact remains that any serious or organized opposition to the Communists is against the law, just as much in the seventies as it was in the forties.

But at the same time that the regimes are trying to hold the line against granting more freedom, they are continuing, at top speed, the very policies that nurture the discontent. Industrialization, urbanization, education: people are being trained to run computers, to contribute production ideas, to comment on the humanism of Karl Marx. But they are also learning to think for themselves. And their thoughts are dangerous. "If you think what I *said* was dangerous," the East German heretic Robert Havemann told his Party inquisitors, "you ought to have heard what I *thought*."

The modernization of Soviet Europe has the same effect as the process in other parts of the world in intensifying feelings of national identity. The drabness and uniformity of life in the industrial society, even for the relatively successful, those who manage to acquire look-alike flats and look-alike little cars, seem to hasten and deepen this quest for roots. These new urban societies are collections of the uprooted, the peasant removed from his village and put down amid rows of huge machines in a huge industrial complex, sent to cheer his leaders at huge squares, and then put in huge and impersonal blocks of apartments, to be entertained by the mass program served up by the government television or the mass soccer games at cheap prices in the local People's Stadium. At such times, it is natural that the Slovak worker living in the Czech capital of Prague feels more Slovak than he did in his home village, and that when he thinks about the way the Soviet Union directs his life and his nation, feels more Czechoslovak than he would under other circumstances.

THE PERMANENT CRISIS

The Czechoslovak worker shares with the Pole and the Hungarian recent memories of better times, when it seemed for a while that his life and his nation were going to be directed by people he had chosen himself. He can remember the halcyon days when workers felt like working, when shop clerks smiled, when people were not afraid to speak their minds, when production figures were going up, and when officials told the truth. But now, particularly in Czechoslovakia, he is constantly told that these were bad times, that the nation had fallen under control of evil counter-revolutionaries, and that it was finally saved by the foreign troops he sees playing soccer and lounging around the gates of the barracks on the edges of his nation's cities. All this creates a considerable gap between the official account of things and reality as he perceives it. There are other gaps: between theory and practice of Marxism, between promises and their fulfillment.

These gaps are what make Communist nations so difficult to govern. Every government tries from time to time to push its own version of events, to assure its constituency that things are going to get better. But no system is based as much as the Communist is on such recurring promises that the new life is just around the corner. Things do improve, of course, but never enough, and sometimes they get worse. Then a new set of slogans is introduced. The worsening is not the fault of those in charge, but of the weather, if there are food shortages, or of the Imperialists, if there are political difficulties, or perhaps of the Jews, or of the needs of the Soviet Union and a "higher level of foreign trade considerations than the mere economic" if there are complaints about low export prices.

Often it seems that this balance of promises and excuses can be maintained indefinitely. Then suddenly the whole thing explodes, as it did in Poland in 1970. There seems to be every likelihood that the explosions will be more and more frequent in the years ahead. The reason is that the system that has been imposed on Soviet Europe, despite its undoubted strengths and attractions, does not serve the needs of the people in the long run. When it reaches the point of deterioration where that fact is apparent to all, all that is needed to touch off the trouble is a particularly outrageous decision on the order of pre-Christmas price increases or the raising of workers' norms. The results then are extremely difficult to control. In the future, control may be impossible.

POLAND

But there are alternatives to this chaos. Poland showed one way in the 1970–1971 crisis on the Baltic; reformers in Yugoslavia and Czechoslovakia have tried other ways.

The Polish events demonstrated the gains that can be made by reverting, at least temporarily, to democracy in times of crisis. The causes of the rioting that killed forty-five persons are drearily familiar to those who live in Soviet Europe: the price increases and the official priorities that put shipyard expansion ahead of housing needs for the workers. These are examples of the kind of political activity practiced under the glass bell in Soviet Europe. There is no opposition, and thus these decisions are automatically correct. No attention has to be paid to pressure groups or protests, unless they are from the Soviet Union. But just as the central planners who direct the economies are hampered by their lack of market intelligence, and cannot get it without freeing the market from controls, so are the political planners of the Bloc hampered by not knowing what people think, and they cannot find out unless they free them from controls on expression. But a major crisis shatters the glass bell, and leaves them no choice. The forces that it was excluding from the political process start to work again.

The only time the system begins to behave in any kind of democratic way, the way it was intended to by Marx and to an extent by Lenin, is thus in time of emergency, when the backs of the leaders are almost literally against the wall. This was true in the early days of Soviet power. It was true in Imre Nagy's brief period of rule in 1956, and true again in the first days of the occupation of Czechoslovakia, and once again in Poland in the winter of 1970–1971.

These crises breathe life into the tired promises of socialist democracy, worker participation, power to the people. The workers have to step in and run things because their strikes, demonstrations, or warfare has paralyzed the old regime. At the same time, the workers are able to run things because the regime is too weak to resist their newly discovered power.

In Gdansk, trade union officials who had been captives of management for years were swept out of office within hours, and angry men from the rank and file were put in their place by open elections. In this one action, the unions' role as transmission belt of Party and government policy to the workers was destroyed. The old officials were fired because they had not been doing their jobs. Wages were too low, prices too high; workers had no shower or changing facilities; those on dangerous jobs lacked safeguards and protective clothing. In the next few days, the system suddenly began to work. Office walls were knocked out to make lunch rooms. Safety problems were remedied. The prices were lowered and the wages raised.

Thoughtful officials in Soviet Europe's ministries and many writers, journalists, and university people think that as long as the system remains as rigid as it is, these explosions are bound to recur. They stress that there will not be another fourteen years between them, as there was between Poznan and Gdansk, and that the Soviet Union itself will not be spared.

The Polish workers have pointed the way. Twice they have managed to change their government by going out into the streets. That has never happened anywhere else in Soviet Europe. But now the knowledge is there, and the workers and intellectuals in all the other countries know that if things get desperate enough, and if they are willing to pay a high enough price, then change can indeed be worked from below. Some of them think that not only can the system be changed by determined action, but that it *must* be changed in this way, because there is no other way to get rid of undesirable governments in the Bloc.

Since Gdansk, the people of Soviet Europe also realize that many of the changes wrought under crisis conditions are only temporary. The frankness of the press in those winter days did not last. Officials listened to worker representatives only as long as they thought the threat of strikes was a real one. The first days of working democracy have never returned. The middle levels of the Party and state apparat have seen to that, and most of these men have kept their jobs. "There is no real opposition to them," a Pole who once occupied such a post before going higher said. "They sit behind desks with telephones and they are all-powerful. There is no way to remove them; unless they are angels they won't regulate themselves. I'm very lucky I got out of that stratum, because I am sure that I would have been as corrupted as they are."

If these middle men block reform, then the chances are even greater that resentment and frustration will build up again, there will be another outburst, people will get killed, things will get better, and then the whole cycle will begin again. Why not break the circle with wholesale personnel changes and a bold program of innovation? The official answered: "The Russians. As long as there is no democracy in their country, they can't permit it here. We Poles can't do what their own Ukrainians, just across our border, are forbidden to do. As long as Dubcek's ideas cause them chills, then the progress permitted anywhere will be only very limited, and there will be no change in the structure. The outbursts and the concessions are measured in every country by the number of dead. The Hungarians bled the most and benefited the most. Not enough Poles died in Gdansk for it to have made enough impact. There was not the national sense of horror that would either produce far-reaching reforms on the Hungarian pattern or rule out further uprisings. But it is in the nature of political tempos that the outbursts will become more and more frequent."

But is it necessary that to achieve the modest standards of political freedom and economic well-being that many nations take for granted, Soviet Europe must pay periodically with violence and death? There are many voices, inside and outside the Party councils, that say it is not. They have put forth a variety of alternatives, and two working models. One is Yugoslavia's, a working model with problems, and the other Czechoslovakia's, a model that developed so many troubles that it never really got a chance to work.

YUGOSLAVIA

When Yugoslavia was expelled from the Cominform in 1948, the event was seen as a disaster by all but a few in the leadership, and the first years of isolation and Soviet economic blockade were difficult indeed, as officials admitted at the time and recall with satisfaction today. It was not the threat of an invading army, but economic collapse that would have made the invasion unnecessary, that faced Tito then. Part of the feeling of satisfaction now comes from the fact that Yugoslavia's expulsion gave it unexpected freedom to experiment in politics and economics, without the dead weight of Soviet dogma. Within a short time, Western aid and the opening of trade with the Third World gave Yugoslavia another advantage: diversity of markets and investment.

With all these disadvantages that turned into advantages, Titoism has very naturally attracted the planners of Soviet Europe. It is not a distant model like the United States or West Germany. No one is going to refashion Hungary in America's image, but one can reasonably expect to borrow from the Yugoslavs on Hungary's border. Yugoslavia's federal structure, for all its problems, is often seen as a solution for the Bloc, if it is ever permitted to decentralize. Yugoslavia has as many different republics as Soviet Europe has nations, and there is a parallel difference in levels of development.

But the main model is internal. Yugoslavia seems the ideal compromise between free enterprise and socialist industry, central and local control, alliance to Russia and independence. It is the possible, and politics in the Bloc is the practice of the possible. East Europeans in the Bloc are aware of Yugoslavia's problems: the economic peaks and valleys, the serious crisis in the republics that has fragmented national political life, the unemployment, the question of leadership after Tito, the threats of subversion by the Soviet-backed Yugoslav conservatives, the crackdowns on the intellectuals and minority leaders. Many of them have similar problems, with few of the advantages the Yugoslavs enjoy. They are convinced they could accept the good and reject the bad.

The good, in their view, begins with the openness of political life, which despite the purges and restrictions of 1972 still is far freer than anything in the Bloc. The main differences are the relative freedom permitted the press, the acceptance of a role for pressure groups ranging from unions that can strike to philosophers who are revising Lenin, and the adversary role played by the competing republics.

Yugoslavia's commitment to decentralization and self-management, even though incompletely fulfilled, is tremendously attractive to East Europeans fighting Soviet recentralization. As early as 1952, the Yugoslav Communists faced the problem that Soviet Europe's theoreticians cannot yet solve. They decided that the Party cannot exercise a commanding role, but must become an educational force and ideological inspiration. A faint echo of this position is discernible in Hungary's Party program, most modern of the Bloc, but it stresses that Communists must control as well as inspire. Viewed from the West, Yugoslavia may seem a land beset by problems, without a particularly efficient economy or high standard of living. Viewed from the East, it is a country with many, many advantages that Soviet Europe's nations do not share.

The other model before the reformers of Soviet Europe was still in the experimental stage when its designers were forced to abandon it, but its influence is as great as Yugoslavia's on their thinking.

CZECHOSLOVAKIA

The Prague Spring without its mistakes. That is the goal of the student rap sessions and the private conversations of social scientists, wherever the liberals in Soviet Europe get to talking about what should and might be. In this quest, their thoughts are directed more to what would have happened in Czechoslovakia had the Russians not invaded than what did happen in the eight months of Dubcek. After the delirious Spring, what would have followed? The Soviet Union did not give the world time enough to see; Czechoslovakia's leaders were still trying to work it out themselves when they were dragged away to imprisonment. But fortunately for those trying to use the Czechoslovak experience in the future, the Prague leadership and theoreticians had prepared their plans. What they left was not a hypothetical account of what might have happened, but the main document for the Communist Party Congress of September 1968—the Congress the invasion was designed to stop.

This Fourteenth Party Congress met instead in secret emergency session on the day after the invasion, August 22, and gave its overwhelming support to Dubcek and the other arrested liberals. But its most important work was to present the document prepared for the regular Congress. Had events gone according to plan, the document, written by the leading thinkers of the reform movement, would have been the basis for Dubcek's keynote speech.

The document made it plain that the reforms accomplished in Dubcek's eight months were only a beginning, the start of a three-year transition period that would last until 1971. The period was to be one of gradual change, not the abrupt destruction of the old system. The three-year plan included political rights for all citizens, truly representative democracy, the existence of more than one party, division and control of political power, and legal guarantees of civil rights. The National Front was to be the framework for political activity. All the nation's pressure groups, and here the English term was used, would be permitted to act within it. But one condition was stressed for this action: there would be a system of guaranteeing that the Communist Party would never be outvoted. Even this most liberal of Communist Party Congresses had to concede this safety measure, whether for the benefit of the Russians or the domestic Communists. With this one exception, however, there was to be complete legality and freedom for all parties. Censorship would not return; nor would the political police. There would be independence for the courts, reorganization of the security apparatus, and workers' councils.

So great was the concern that the Party, despite its new popularity, would be outvoted, that a plan to have independents belong to the National Front was rejected.

It examined the problem with unusual frankness: "The basic question is whether the new political system in the CSSR can be a so-called open political system in the sense of a free play of political forces. For the transition period, until the new constitution, this is clearly out of the question. Without the anchor of the monopoly position of the National Front, a power-political conflict, which would be directed against the leadership of the Communist Party, cannot be ruled out (and indeed, such a conflict would be quite probable)."

The experiences of 1969 and 1970 were going to be used to evaluate these controls. If they worked, they would be continued for ten to fifteen years. It depended on how the Party fared in the National Front under the new conditions. (Under the old ones, the Front had been completely under Party rule.) It was also thought that a constitutional court might be established to rule on the formation or dissolution of parties. But it was clear that even with these safeguards, Party theoreticians were worried. Their dilemma was how to combine a degree of freedom that was supposed to surpass that enjoyed in the West, but still keep the voters from turning them out of office.

"It is impermissible to conceptualize the National Front as an *open* organization," they decided in their draft. "The National Front, therefore, must have the possibility of excluding organizations, including political parties, if they operate against the political sense of the institution."

They recognized the benefit of multiple candidates for legislative and local council posts, but were again worried by the very real possibility that the Party would be voted out. Even if other parties could be controlled within the Front, there was the risk that enough independent candidates would put themselves up for election to defeat the Communists and their Front allies. The way this was to be dealt with was to permit anyone to run for office if he or she could get the required number of petition signatures. But each individual candidacy was to be decided on from the point of view of the "current political situation." Otherwise, there was the risk that "the institution of the independent candidate might be taken advantage of, organized from forces outside the National Front."

The speech Dubcek never got to deliver leaves an impression of a real resolve to break with the past, but at the same time it reflects the timidity and hesitation of the Prague reformers. Like all professional politicians, they knew their constituency well, and they knew that on one side was an electorate very likely to vote against the Communist Party if it ever stopped performing miracles, which, in the nature of politics, it would have to eventually. On the other was the Soviet Union, which would not permit the power won against such odds and defended with such sacrifices to be wrested from it by individualists at the ballot box.

Freedom was necessary to give the Party the popularity it had to have if it was to lead with the consent of the governed. But the same freedom gave the governed the right to give their consent to someone else. Whether these opposites ever could have been reconciled is not known. Certainly the conflict between the centrists and the radical progressives in the press and academia would have sharpened, as would the running debates with Moscow and its orthodox allies. The Czechoslovak talent for compromise and accommodation might have produced a solution possible in no other country.

But the world will never know how the struggle would have come out. As if to emphasize the realities of power in Soviet Europe, Red army armored units rolled up outside the meeting place of the emergency Congress on August 22. The protocol, brought to the West by Jiri Pelikan, records the reaction of the chairman: "In front of the gates, that's confirmed, there are Soviet armored personnel carriers. Perhaps we ought to speed up our work a bit."

The Czechoslovak model for the other states of Soviet Europe seeking freedom was thus destroyed. The role of the Soviet Union had turned out again to be of such overwhelming importance that no other considerations counted at all. Yugoslavia's model had been possible only because the Soviet Union had cut Yugoslavia off from its influence. Czechoslovakia's was not possible because a new set of Soviet leaders did not dare to risk losing another nation.

The conclusion is plain. In order for reform to progress very far in Soviet Europe, the Soviet Union has to approve of it, but until there are changes in the Soviet Union, nothing very daring or basic will get approved. That is why Poles and Hungarians and Czechs seize on every scrap of information about unrest in the Ukraine, the latest revelations of the *samizdats,* or trouble on the Chinese border. It is their hope and belief that the sum of these internal problems will lead to the changes in Moscow that will permit changes in their own nations.

"We feel that we are in a waiting room on the Russian State Railway," one of Poland's leading intellectuals said. "We are waiting for something to happen. But there are first, second, and third classes in this waiting room of the Socialist Commonwealth, and we'd like to wait in first class if we can."

In this long wait, it is not only the intellectuals in their clubs and cafés who scan the Party press for hints of change, or swap rumors about tensions and plots in Russia and China. Sober discussions of the paths Soviet Europe's nations should follow are held in factory canteens, in managerial offices, and in the universities and institutes, but most of all in the privacy and security of gatherings of friends at homes. What strikes an outsider is that here are groups of intelligent, informed people as capable of governing themselves as are the Swedes or French or any other people lucky enough to be on the right side of the great power boundaries of modern Europe.

They cannot change the geography, but if conditions are right, they might be able to change the politics. Their basic hope, often repeated, is that the same kind of political crisis that overwhelmed four of the six nations of Soviet Europe since the war will reach the Soviet Union. And they think that when it does, the same reaction will take place: a sudden revival of elementary democracy, a toppling of the bureaucrats and their apparatus of repression, their substitution with men and women and laws chosen by the people and responsive to them.

If all this happens in the Soviet Union, there will be one important difference from the brief periods of crisis democracy that Eastern Europe has known. That is that the other countries will be able to follow the Russian example, just as they must follow it under conditions of dictatorship. And it is possible that a period of sudden freedom in the Soviet Union, even if ended by force, might cause so much political turbulence that Soviet Europe would have time to institutionalize some of its gains.

There is an inevitable feeling of passivity as Soviet Europe waits for changes in Russia, but there are also currents of activism, feelings that Hungary had to pay heavily for the latitude it enjoys, that Czechoslovakia got eight months of freedom by taking risks, and that Poland's more progressive leadership was very costly in terms of lives lost and the threat of intervention. Even so, they hope the changes will not have to be sudden and violent.

Another current in these plans of Soviet Europe's dissidents is a feeling of mission: the Western states of the Soviet empire must show the Russians the way, however egotistical that may seem to the leaders of a great power. But there are both practical and historical arguments in their favor.

It would make sense, they believe, for the Soviet Union to use the six nations as a proving ground for some of the ideas and practices it does not yet dare try at home. There are already considerable differences of degree in what is permitted in Russia and in the Bloc. Poles could read the satirical comments of the late Russian author Mikhail Bulgakov about Soviet society a decade before his books were permitted in the Soviet Union. Their own authors can go considerably further than the Soviet without too much trouble with the censors. There are many other examples of these differences in what is permitted in the Bloc and in the U.S.S.R., ranging from the legislative process to economic reform. But all seem concessions to Soviet Europe rather than any conscious Soviet policy of using the area to try out new ideas. Those who favor the plan in Eastern Europe are convinced that the Russians would be pleasantly surprised at how much liberalization they could permit, first abroad, and then at home. But they do not have many realistic expectations that anything will come of it.

The historical arguments are based on the legacy of the nineteenth-century nationalists, the role of Mickiewicz and Kossuth in fighting for the causes of others as well as their own nations. Today's nationalists also feel they have a real contribution to make. They would like to have the chance to join with their counterparts in the Soviet Union, the embattled dissidents, and help in their struggle to open up society, not only in Russia, and not only in Romania, but throughout the area.

They know it is possible to be friendly to the Soviet Union without being subservient; open to the West without being hostile to the East, in keeping with the area's traditional cultural role and geographical position. They think that reform can be achieved without upheaval, but are prepared for that, too. They think that when change does come, there will be no need to substitute feudalism, fascism, or capitalism for the system being replaced. Their long opportunity to study other systems convinces them that Soviet Europe, when it is finally free to make its own choice, will introduce a kind of rule that incorporates every nation's best features and none of their mistakes. This, too, can be dismissed as naïveté. But after such long experience with dictatorship, it is natural to strive for the ideal.

Upheavals in the Soviet Union, the chain effect needed to reach the six nations, the creation of new political systems: these are events that will take time. But the whole history of the area has been one of gradual groping toward greater freedom, over the centuries, and over the three decades of Communist rule, with the rulers painfully slow in granting it and often retaliating with harsher measures when they had the strength. But gains were made. They were slight by the standards of nations that have always enjoyed freedom, but they were remarkable when the odds against them were considered. Life is freer in Soviet Europe in every sphere, cultural, political, and economic, than it was in the bleak days of a generation ago. The 100 million people who enjoy these slight gains in liberty appreciate them as those never deprived cannot possibly do. But the fact that they can measure past progress, however slow, has another meaning, equally important. It is the basis for their hope for the future.

INDEX

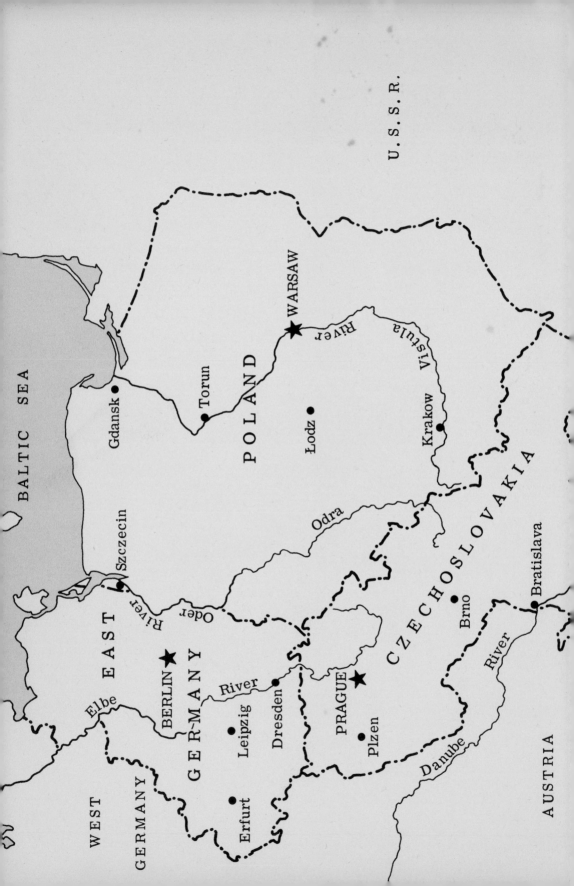